RUPERT WIELOCH

Belfast
TO
Benghazi

Untold challenges of war

RUPERT WIELOCH

Belfast to Benghazi

Untold challenges of war

Waterford City and County
Libraries

MEREO
Cirencester

Mereo Books

1A The Wool Market Dyer Street Cirencester Gloucestershire GL7 2PR
An imprint of Memoirs Publishing www.mereobooks.com

Belfast to Benghazi: 978-1-86151-566-7

First published in Great Britain in 2016
by Mereo Books, an imprint of Memoirs Publishing

The address for Memoirs Publishing Group Limited can be found at
www.memoirspublishing.com

The Memoirs Publishing Group Ltd Reg. No. 7834348

The Memoirs Publishing Group supports both The Forest Stewardship Council®
(FSC®) and the PEFC® leading international forest-certification organisations. Our
books carrying both the FSC label and the PEFC® and are printed on FSC®-certified
paper. FSC® is the only forest-certification scheme supported by the leading
environmental organisations including Greenpeace. Our paper procurement policy
can be found at www.memoirspublishing.com/environment

Typeset in 10/15pt Plantin
by Wiltshire Associates Publisher Services Ltd.
Printed and bound in Great Britain by
Marston Book Services Ltd, Oxfordshire

Dedication

To soldiers who share
To comrades who fall
To veterans who struggle
And families of all.

Human fragility touches all the stories in this book about military operations. Mere sympathy seems to be an inadequate response to the harrowing stories of those suffering from depression, or the after effects of battle shock and trauma. That is why a part of the proceeds of this book are being donated to the veteran's mental health charity, Combat Stress.

The views expressed in this book do not necessarily reflect those of the British Government. The author's conclusions are drawn from open source material listed in the Bibliography on page 291 and academic research at the Universities of Cambridge, Oxford, Reading and King's College London together with strategic institutes in London. The names of some individuals have been changed to protect their identity.

CONTENTS

Part 1 – Death and Glory

Part 2 – No More Just War

About the Author

Rupert Wieloch was born in Yorkshire, but grew up in London. He was taught English at school by Count Nikolai Tolstoy and History at university by Professor Arthur Marwick. He joined the Army as three momentous events shaped the world: an Islamic revolution overthrew the Shah of Iran; President Sadat of Egypt and Prime Minister Begin of Israel signed a Peace Treaty; and just after he was commissioned into the 17th/21st Lancers, the Soviet Union invaded Afghanistan.

During 35 years' service to Queen and Country, he deployed on most of Britain's major operations, ending up as the Senior British Military Commander in Libya in 2011. He now divides his time between a dangerous sport in Switzerland and fundraising for veterans' charities in London.

The six chapters of this book tell the colourful story of Rupert's journey from serving as an itinerant rifle platoon commander in West Belfast at the end of the 1981 hunger strike to his final command in North Africa. These previously untold tales will be of particular interest to students of conflict studies, military history and international affairs.

Acknowledgements

The author would like to express his thanks to the following:

The Rt Hon The Lord King of Bridgwater CH

Admiral of the Fleet The Lord Boyce KG GCB OBE DL

General Sir Michael Rose KCB CBE DSO QGM DL

General Sir John McColl KCB CBE DSO

Brigadier Jolyon Jackson CBE

Sir Dominic Asquith KCMG

Nick Henderson

Taniya Dennison

Peter Barlow

Tim Buxton

Freddie Elwes

Kevin Griffin

Ed Carrell

Johnnie Russell

Peter Troup

John Downing MBE, for Photographs

Sophie Neville, for Artwork

Araminta Blue, for Artwork

Hastings Wieloch, for IT

Soldier Magazine and Crown Copyright, for Photographs

Introduction

If you don't believe squirrels play leapfrog, you shouldn't read this meandering recollection of 35 years of military service. But if you do venture forward, I offer three pleas and mitigations for the ramble.

First, for the language that will distress Dot Wordsworth and decently-dressed students of philology. Thirty years ago, I described a climb to the Dôme du Goûter on Mont Blanc with eight adverbs, four adjectives and a simile, but a subsequent life in a great British institution resulted in a more prosaic outlook and an overabundant use of military acronyms. Although this may drain some of the poetic colour from the canvas, I do hope the valiant reader does not lose sight of the texture and heat of each moment.

Second, if one agrees that the past shapes how we live now, then one can also agree the value of history in making the future better. However, on several recent occasions, I have sensed that Britain's national security policy has been rewritten for partisan reasons and hard-earned lessons have been ignored. Current assumptions about the use of Reserves and the employment of women on the front line spring quickly to mind. Unfortunately for some people, this book is based on facts and as such, they might upset those who wish things were not what they are. Please do not diminish our wonderful armed forces.

Finally, I judge any day when I have learned something new as a good day. A horde of enviable events provides the core of this memoir. Erstwhile contemporaries might wish that I had included other incidents, but I believe these unique tales have shaped the person I am more than any other experiences in my life. In recounting the stories, I have tried to remain faithful to Ralph Waldo Emerson, who said "if only a man knew how to choose among what he calls his experiences that which is really his experience and how to record truth truly".

The first part of the book describes junior command experiences from three operational tours at Regimental Duty. Chapter 1 covers the 1981 winter in Northern Ireland, when I commanded a Rifle Platoon at the end of the hunger strike. This was not the first excitement I experienced in the Army, since I had already deployed to Norway for a three-month winter exercise with NATO's Allied Command Europe Mobile Force in the Arctic Circle. However, my time in Belfast did help me to realise that I was doing something really useful for the nation and the killing of three soldiers in my company by the Provisional IRA in March 1982 was the moment when I lost any residual sympathy for Army amateurism.

The second episode is about the years of practice in the British Army of the Rhine which assured success in the Gulf War. When Saddam Hussein invaded Kuwait in August 1990, I was on my third tour as a squadron leader, commanding 120 soldiers on operations in Cyprus. The sedate internal security setting suddenly increased tempo as we became involved in the frenetic activity at the forward mounting base and I was set the challenge of sending a troop to fight on the front line. By the time my B Squadron 17th/21st Lancers tank troop, commanded by Tim Buxton, led the advance into Kuwait on 27th February

1991, I had returned to England for the Army's command and staff course, so I missed the "Big One", but my troops fought with distinction on the front line and accomplished vital tasks in a classic rear area security role.

The third tale is about Bosnia in 1995. At the end of the winter ceasefire, I planned and executed the largest defensive battle fought by the British Army since the Dhofar campaign. My combat force included British armour, Canadian infantry and a New Zealand artillery tactical air control party. They all performed magnificently throughout the extended battle and this tale provides a distinctive juxtaposition to the United Nations response in Srebrenica two months later.

The second part of this book covers Britain's wars in the 21st Century. Almost every soldier serving in the British Army since 2001 has been touched by Afghanistan. In my case, the connection began in 1973 when I bought a pair of cricket pads and a flowery shirt from Prince Mir Wais and my father closed his office in Kabul after King Mohammed Zahir Shah was deposed.

Twenty-eight years later, I was called to work on Operation Veritas, the United Kingdom's military strategic response to 9/11, which remains the biggest loss of British lives to an act of terrorism. I prepared a bundle of papers for Prime Minister Tony Blair's visit to President Bush one week after the attacks. This work, produced by two separate strategic teams, provided the foundation for the United Kingdom's campaign against international terrorism and was used by the Foreign Secretary in his key statements to the House of Commons in September and October. Notwithstanding what happened subsequently in Helmand, Operation Veritas was just in its cause, consensual from the start and successful in all its objectives, except for bringing Usama bin Laden to justice. It was also remarkable that, no British soldiers were killed by hostile action in Afghanistan before we invaded Iraq.

The fifth story is about Baghdad. In January 2003, a colleague at the permanent joint headquarters invited me to join the Coalition's Phase 4 Post Decisive Action headquarters in Qatar. I had tracked the Iraq strategic intent since Richard Perle's keynote address entitled "Next Stop, Iraq" at the US Foreign Policy Research Institute's dinner on 30th November 2001. However, I was sceptical about the prospects for winning the peace and a year later found myself briefing the Parliamentary Under Secretary of State about my concerns in the Foreign and Commonwealth Office Map Room. However, I was not one of those officers who refused to participate because they didn't agree with the reasons for war, so when an opportunity arose to command the British contingent in the NATO mission, I took it with open arms.

The final account covers a small part of the Arab Spring. Thirty years after deploying to Belfast, I was appointed as the Senior British Military Commander in Libya. Two days later, just before I arrived in Tripoli, Muammar Gaddafi was captured and killed as he attempted to escape from Sirte. Although the maritime and air forces received the plaudits at the end of NATO's Operation Unified Protector, the revolution would not have succeeded without the British Army on the ground marking targets and advising rebel leaders. We also played a vital role in the stabilisation of the country after Gaddafi was overthrown and built strong relationships with the leaders in Benghazi, which unfortunately were lost when we pulled out in April 2012.

When I returned to Northern Ireland during the Peace Process speaking to local decision makers, I discovered that many of them did not realise the British Army was involved in such a wide range of operations outside the Province. It was the same after my reconnaissance to Southern Afghanistan in 2005. The public understood we were in Iraq, but did not appear to know that we were still running a small-scale operation in Mazar e Sharif and that the numbers would increase to 3,765 the following year. They also failed to appreciate that British battalions had deployed to Kosovo and the Ivory Coast that summer and that we were conducting humanitarian support to the Asian tsunami, Hurricane Katrina and the Kashmir earthquake in Pakistan.

I hope this book opens eyes to a few unheralded escapades and adds colour to some historic events.

PART 1

Death and Glory

CHAPTER 1

Belfast 1981 – Operation Banner

This terror, cold, wet-furred, small-clawed, retreated up a pipe for sewage. I stared after him. Then I walked on and crossed the bridge.
Seamus Heaney

Nothing in life quite prepares a man for the first time he hears a machine-gun fired in anger or has to clear up bits of bashed brain scattered over a busy street in Belfast. Even after five months of active military operations, when eyes are widened and senses tuned to the smallest detail, the crack and thump of rapid fire inject a surge of adrenalin that few experiences can match.

I deployed as a Rifle Platoon Commander with 2nd Battalion, Royal Green Jackets, to West Belfast by Hercules aircraft early in November 1981. We landed with such a thump on the Aldergrove runway that the Elsan bucket ditched its contents over the officer sitting next to me. His ever-present smile flickered for a second. "Welcome to Northern Ireland," said his Sergeant.

We were greeted with the murder, by the Provisional IRA, of the Reverend Robert Bradford, Member of Parliament for the neighbouring constituency of South Belfast, while he hosted a political surgery at the Finaghy community centre. The following morning at 0700 hours I led my first foot patrol into the Lower Falls, hoping my soldiers would not sense my anxiety when I issued orders to them. We ran almost the whole way, "hard targeting" for an hour, before returning breathless to our company base, North Howard Street Mill.

The atmosphere was tense in the Mill. Although the Provisional IRA had recently called off their Hunger Strike in Long Kesh, their bombing campaign in London had maintained their pre-eminent position on the six o'clock news. The bombs which killed and maimed civilians and soldiers at Chelsea Barracks, Dulwich and Oxford Street between 10th and 26th October were particularly upsetting because they were all familiar haunts for me. The tit-for-tat sectarian murders in the Province added to the sense of anxiety as we prepared for the tour.

At the Sinn Fein convention just before we deployed, Danny Morrison had prompted a change in direction with his question "will anyone here object if, with a ballot paper in one hand and an Armalite in the other, we take power in Ireland?" When the Party agreed the new strategy, Gerry Adams adopted the political route, but we still considered him to be a senior leader within a brutal terrorist organisation.

During the takeover week, I flew across the area in a Gazelle helicopter and familiarized myself with the vulnerable locations where soldiers had been killed in the past. The Mill overlooked the site of one of the very early deaths, Rifleman David Walker, who was shot by a sniper in Northumberland Street in 1971. The ten years between his death and my deployment had not been kind to the Royal Green Jackets, who received more than their fair share of casualties throughout the Troubles.

Our predecessors, 45 Commando, had also endured a difficult time during their short *roulement* tour. Four months was the normal length for battalions posted to the most hostile areas, but just before our advance party deployed in October, we were informed that our tour had been extended by one month. For young families, this was a difficult pill to swallow and subsequently we had to repatriate one of my soldiers for compassionate reasons. However, as a young single officer, I was relaxed about the change. Little did I know that the extra weeks would mean the difference between life and death for three Riflemen in my company.

The resident battalions spent longer in the Province than those on the front line. They were based in less intimidating locations, such as Palace Barracks in County Down, close to where my first cousin Jenny lived. However they still suffered grievous losses, as did the Ulster Defence Regiment which operated in areas where there was comparatively little terrorist activity, but whose soldiers lived permanently with the risks and threats of violence. In fact, our first month in the Province was characterised by Republican attacks on these brave part-time soldiers.

My first patrol in West Belfast was the culmination of intense preparation at the training centres in Germany and England, known as Tin Cities as they were built of corrugated steel. Manoeuvring a multiple patrol of soldiers around a primary route in an urban setting does not come naturally as it is so easy to become disorientated and distracted. The big idea is to ensure that when there is an incident, any one of the four man sections, or "bricks", can rapidly support the others and cover their movement by taking up protected firing positions.

This technique was developed in response to gun attacks witnessed early in the Troubles and adapted as the threat changed, to counter improvised explosive devices, or IEDs as they were called by our troops. To achieve the perfect balance on patrol takes much practice and a deep understanding of time and space. Before deploying everyone has to distinguish how terrorists operate and recognize the layout of the streets with their barriers, dead ends and vulnerable points. Platoon commanders realize very quickly that they are watched at all times by "dickers" and any mistake or weakness is reported to the local terrorist cell leaders. We knew that the Provisional IRA would patiently watch and wait for weeks to see whether we were setting patterns.

My platoon had a secondary role as Buglers. As a result, they were a really tight group of intelligent soldiers with outstanding self-discipline. My platoon sergeant, the Bugle Major, was a 32-year-old Roman Catholic from County Durham. He had been in the Army for 15 years and this was his ninth deployment to the Province. He was a first class Northern Ireland instructor, so I benefited from his vast experience.

Our training was delivered by high-grade officers and soldiers, who maintained their standards by frequently visiting Northern Ireland to learn about the latest tactical developments and procedures used by the terrorists. In our spare time, we studied the contents of the operational aide memoire issued to troops by Headquarters Northern Ireland. The hardest part of the training was to instil an instinctive knowledge about the use of lethal force, which was governed by a very strict set of rules.

The "Yellow Card", as it was known, was carried by every individual soldier in my platoon. It provided them with an interpretation of the law of self-defence, but there was always a tension between the need for clear simple instructions and the more equivocal, legal imperative to act reasonably. Routinely, we rehearsed compromising situations, which was just as well because during our winter operations, several joy riders crashed through late night vehicle checkpoints, so testing our knowledge and restraint.

My Company Commander, Shane Hearn, was a pipe-smoking, jovial officer with a keen intellect and a great sense of fun. He had broken his neck playing rugby during the season after his brother Danny had suffered the same injury tackling New Zealand centre Ian Macrae at Welford Road. Shane made a full recovery, which was fortunate as he was an outstanding company commander in whom all the platoon commanders had total confidence. He "paired" me with 1 Platoon for the whole tour and on the first morning, he sent us out simultaneously to patrol the western half of our area.

I delivered orders to the platoon an hour in advance of our scheduled departure. Ground – the local area in detail.

Situation – the all-important picture from our Intelligence Officer, covering imminent threats and who else was doing what in our area. Mission and Execution – a general outline and a talk through the route in fine detail and then co-ordinating actions in case we had to open fire or lose communications. Service Support – ammunition, baton guns, identity discs, maps, water, spare batteries for the radios, warning devices for radio-controlled devices, mine tape, medical equipment and search kit. Command and Signal – who would take over if I was killed or wounded and the code words for the planned route. I answered a question about the checkpoints and then we synchronized our watches and moved to the loading bay to charge our self-loading rifles, before leaving the base at the appointed hour.

Our area was divided into four distinct zones. In the north, there was the Loyalist expanse of the Shankill. This bordered the Nationalist Clonard area in the west, scene of some of the worst sectarian violence in the early years of the Troubles. Directly to the south of our base was the Lower Falls, where the government was half way through a programme of urban regeneration, and to the east lay the notorious Divis Flats. At the height of the Troubles, more than ten battalions were deployed in our area, but that was before the Royal Ulster Constabulary, or RUC, took the security lead and the British Army's presence reduced dramatically. My platoon was the largest in the company as I held responsibility for the observation post at the top of the Divis Tower, with a permanent presence of at least four soldiers.

Our military objective was the destruction of the Provisional IRA, or PIRA. This comprised a hard core of about 30 senior leaders and 250 terrorists grouped into

Active Service Units. There was a range of ever-present PIRA threats to consider, including direct fire attacks from snipers and rocket-propelled grenades and indirect attacks on our bases from vehicle-borne mortars. They also used an array of IEDs, which could be hidden in street lamps, under cars or by refuse bins. These could be detonated either by a radio controlled mechanism, or by a timer, or command wire, but the favoured method at the time was a victim-operated booby trap. The terrorists' arms and ammunition were provided from hostile states, including Colonel Gaddafi's regime in Libya, but the biggest foreign contributor to the Troubles in 1981 was the Irish population of the USA, who sent over $250,000 for the hunger strikers through organisations such as NORAID.

In the Divis, we also had to contend with the Irish National Liberation Army. INLA developed out of the rump of the Official IRA. They rose to prominence after assassinating the Rt Hon Airey Neave at the Palace of Westminster in 1979. However, they were poorly equipped and during my tour, they were preoccupied with an internal leadership struggle, appearing more interested in petty crime and illicit drug selling than a paramilitary campaign. As a result, they rarely threatened us during that winter.

Framework operations were designed to reassure the public and deter terrorist activity, whilst improving the intelligence picture. The terrorists promoted the misconception that we were partisan and anti-Catholic. However, religion just wasn't an issue in the British Army at the time. In my platoon, there was a Sikh, a Methodist, a Baptist and an agnostic, as well as seven Roman Catholics and a dozen Church of England soldiers, and we all worked together well as a team. Although I never believed we could solve the historical causes of the Troubles and I was not so naïve that I underestimated the deep-seated animosity between communities on either side of the peace line, I did feel that our diversity could change perceptions, at least in a modest, local way.

The multi-dimensional problems of Northern Ireland made co-ordination of effort even more critical if success was to be achieved by the Government and Security Forces. Our routine operations included foot patrols, vehicle checkpoints and a constant stream of early morning house searches and arrests. We were there to support the RUC in their daily policing role. To my mind, some of the bravest men I ever met were four cross-denomination policemen who came to work in North Howard Street Mill despite the incredible personal risks they faced every day. They also had a great sense of humour, demonstrated early in the tour when one of the constables who I was protecting asked a bemused young soldier with a rifle for a firearms certificate.

A vital part of intelligence gathering was the personnel or "P" checks. Before we deployed to Belfast, we were issued with more than 20 photographs of individuals in the local area. Most of these suspects were aged between 25 and 35 and had been involved since 1969, when the Troubles began. The initial problem was public disorder, rioting and looting. Their involvement subsequently transitioned through the pitched battles of the insurgency phase in the early 1970s to the terrorist strategy agreed at the recent convention.

Back in the Mill, we worked at our recognition training and routinely tested each other on the distinguishing features of the key "players". These included the individuals from Belfast who were convicted in 1985 of planting the bomb in Oxford Street which killed Kenneth Howorth of the Metropolitan Police, just before we deployed. There was always a huge sense of elation when a rifleman recognized one of the PIRA leaders on the streets.

When we patrolled jointly with the RUC, we rarely spoke to the population, as we concentrated on protecting them in their work, but when we patrolled on our own, we had more time to gather information. This might include recording where individuals were hanging out, what they were wearing and whose company they shared. Just as we were trained not to set predictable patterns, we looked for anything out of the ordinary in the landscape and anything that changed from our previous patrols.

One of the best sources of timely information was the evening pub checks. There were more than 20 in our area, ranging from a front room in a terraced house to a purpose-built community centre with live music. We often checked Pound Loney in Cullingtree, Walshes in Clonard and the Laurel Leaf in Ross, but the most checked pub was McDermott's in Spinner Street, close to Dunville Park. The key was not to stay too long and to visit before people became inebriated, so we timed the checks between 8 and 10 o'clock. By speaking respectfully to the locals and sharing a joke, it was possible to pick up all sorts of information, such as the assembly plans for Dunville, where many of the Nationalist marches started.

Snap vehicle checkpoints also provided good opportunities to pick up intelligence. We might conduct up to six checks during a two-hour patrol. We were trained in the basics of searching a car in the main areas: the boot, the interior, the engine compartment, the outside and underneath.

If a driver appeared hesitant, we might conduct a deeper search to look inside the wheel hubs, under the arches behind the radiator grilles, headlamps and any double-skinned area. We were taught to be suspicious of strong smells including aerosol sprays or talcum powder, used to mask the smell of explosives. There were also hiding places in specific models of car, such as the space underneath the fuel tank in the VW Beetle, or underneath the gearbox of the Renault 4, but these searches were undertaken by the expert teams, which brought their specialist equipment designed for complex concealment.

A great emphasis was placed on the judicial process, which meant we had to be meticulous in gathering forensic evidence. We had several skilled teams in the Company and one of these joined us for the lift and search operation on the second day after we had taken over responsibility from the Royal Marines. It was really important to establish ourselves as professional and impartial, so despite the fact that we had completed three exhausting patrols on Day One, we prepared thoroughly for the early start on the following day.

The operation was complicated by the fact that I had elements from 1 platoon under command to provide the outer cordon and from 3 Platoon to conduct the house search. My platoon provided close cover for the arrests, which meant I had to nominate a formal witness and make sure no one escaped from the area. Taking account of the support teams involved in this mission, I was commanding half an infantry company as a second lieutenant – slightly different to my peers, who were lolling about at university.

Occupied house searches were hated by the local population, not only for the invasion of privacy, but also for the damage that had occurred when they were first conducted in the 1970s. We had to treat those living in the house with sensitivity and be as certain as possible that what we did was justifiable. For example, we should not rip out a door frame unless there was reasonable evidence that something was hidden in a wall cavity behind it. We also had to give the occupants an opportunity to claim compensation for any damage. To this end, we carried the search damage report forms issued by the Northern Ireland Housing Executive, which had to be completed in quadruplicate.

Despite telling the drivers of the Humber armoured cars to ensure there was no revving of the engines, the "Pigs", as they were affectionately known, made a lot of noise as we drove out of the base at 0530 hours on a cold, crisp winter's morning. It is easy to be distracted when you are standing around on a street corner, but everyone kept their concentration levels well throughout the operation. Once the word went around that we were conducting a search, several groups of local men and women approached us and tested our temper with fruity verbal abuse. I had to defuse a couple of *contretemps*, but these did not escalate into physical violence.

The search was partially successful, with a small find and one arrest, but more importantly, the co-ordination worked very smoothly. It was a really good feeling when we all safely unloaded our weapons back at the base before sitting down to a hearty cooked breakfast at 8 am.

When we didn't deploy in vehicles, we had to exit the Mill by sprinting through the large corrugated steel gate, in order to avoid offering an easy target to long-range snipers. Our soldiers in the fortified turrets, or Sangers, frequently reported shots from across the Falls Road in Ross Street. There were also many abandoned terraced houses, which offered a "through-shoot" location or booby trap opportunity in the Lower Falls. To avoid patterns, we varied the time and length of the patrols and always made ourselves as hard a target as possible when moving around the streets.

On another long operation in the first week, following a tip-off, one of our search teams found a US Infantry 7.62mm M-14 rifle. Inevitably the RUC received the plaudits and publicity, but it was my platoon that stood on the streets and protected the area for ten hours in the freezing cold.

Sometimes we had a specific warning about a particular weapon transported into our area. In the New Year, our Intelligence Officer started warning us that an M-60 machine gun was being moved around Belfast. As the days passed without finding it, the warnings started to lose their relevance and effect, something that would return to haunt us at the end of the tour.

The weather that winter was bitter. My aunt cancelled her annual Christmas visit from London to the family home in Whitby. I received many letters from friends complaining about the freezing conditions, not realizing that Belfast was far worse than England. Conversely, the bad weather was actually good for us because it reduced terrorist activity and put off the stone throwers and rioters. We preferred snow and ice conditions to the horizontal sheet rain that came off the Black Mountain; either way, it was always a relief to return to the warm kitchen in the Mill.

Bugle Platoon, 2nd Battalion Royal Green Jackets in North Howard Street Mill, autumn 1981. This multi-racial group comprised a Sikh, a Methodist, a Baptist, an Agnostic, as well as seven Roman Catholics and a dozen Church of England soldiers. Religion just wasn't an issue in the British Army at the time.

Christmas Day 1981 on the Divis Tower. The Bugle Major blows his silver bugle. The Company Commander is putting his pistol back in its holster. I cocked my Self Loading Rifle several times during the tour, but never fired in anger.

Mark 2 Humber "Pigs" with their Rolls Royce 4.2 litre petrol engines, lined up in the North Howard Street Mill courtyard. The heavy duty bars attached to the 6.5 tonne vehicle in order to drive through barricades provided inspiration in 2004 for the Bar Armour, which saved countless British Army lives in Iraq.

The Hunger Strike Anniversary Protest March Poster, donated by a pub in the Lower Falls.

The company organized our routine with two days on patrol, followed by two days on guard in the Sangers and at the City Centre security gates. I was also required to be a watch-keeper in the company operations room at night. Despite the inclement weather, I always preferred to be on the streets rather than in the base. There was a professional atmosphere in the operations room, which was run very efficiently by the unflappable Company Second-in-Command, James Bendall, but Northern Ireland was a junior commander's war and nothing can compare to the exhilaration of leading British soldiers on tactical operations.

Sometimes the RUC would conduct a series of house-checks following a reported crime. In these cases, our drill was the same as when we stopped for a vehicle checkpoint or a pub check. We had to remain alert and prevent the static element from becoming isolated or vulnerable. Occasionally in the middle of the night, we would conduct a car trawl, recording all the vehicles in a particular area. Returning to the warmth of North Howard Street, it was a joy to make a runny egg banjo in the kitchen, although sometimes you had to fight off the multitude of cockroaches which scuttled out of the dilapidated walls.

The first major incident took place after a couple of weeks. A gunman was caught in a firing point with a weapon. There were no shots, but we had a chase and rugby tackle by an inspired section commander. We became more alert and three days later had the luckiest Rifleman on the tour. He was struck between the shoulder blades by a high velocity round from a rifle, but thanks to the latest protection, he was not injured seriously. Nobody ever again complained about wearing the heavy body armour, as our morale reached a peak that continued for most of the tour.

Security patrolling continued throughout the festive period, when I had to supervise the distribution of one and a half million pounds to local factory workers. We made a big effort to decorate the Mill for Christmas Day. Early in the morning I took presents and food to my soldiers in the Divis Tower. The Bugle Major accompanied me and played reveille, which received a mixed reception from the residents. We then returned to the Mill and served lunch to the soldiers; inevitably this turned into a mass food fight and made our tireless Company Sergeant Major apoplectic with rage.

That afternoon I led another patrol to the Divis. The entry point into the Flats was always a challenge, because the routes were overlooked from many balconies. The local "misguided" youth often threw stones and bottles at us, but we were never subjected to the washing machines and other large white goods dropped on our predecessors, 45 Commando.

On this occasion, I sent two "bricks" in first and then entered from an adjacent route, close to St Peter's Church. I was caught completely unawares by the reception. The residents were both cheerful and friendly and it took me a moment to consider whether it was not a cover for an attack. I suppose it was similar to Christmas 1914, when British and German troops played football together on the front line; a sign of optimism amongst the daily misery of war.

We had very little time off during the tour of duty and I didn't exchange my uniform for civilian clothes until late December, when I managed to see my cousin for a New Year party in Cultra. Between patrols, we watched *The Blues*

Brothers on video, over and over again. A couple of officers became addicted to our Hyperspace computer game, but I never achieved higher status than Galactic Cook Class 5 and was more interested in reading light-hearted paperbacks, including my favourite, *The Book of Heroic Failures*.

Our main topic of conversation when off-duty was each individual's plans for the end of tour leave in April. Several of us wished to travel to somewhere hot and it was a sign of the bond of friendship that four of us agreed to rent a villa in Crete – if we survived to the end of the tour.

We were also allowed a week for rest and recuperation in the middle of the tour. I used the British Airways shuttle at the end of January to catch up with my friends who were at university in London. Otherwise, my only night out was when the RUC took James Bendall and me to dinner in Bangor and on to a night club in Stormont, which played vacuous songs by Tight Fit and Bucks Fizz. It was odd to talk normally to people and to see how different life was away from the front line. The evening certainly convinced us that the headquarters at Lisburn deserved its "slipper city" nickname.

The most popular task amongst the soldiers was the monthly vehicle patrol to the Adelaide Industrial Estate, where I held the company account with Arthur Guinness. There was never a shortage of volunteers to escort me, but we could not drop our guard, so there was always a close protection team nominated to stand and cover the off-duty soldiers, who were given a liquid tour of the brewery.

Apart from the odd trip to a cash and carry or a gym, we were not allowed to leave our base, other than on a formally-recorded patrol. There was a prefabricated squash court in the Mill, but the walls were in serious danger of collapse when I played, as I resembled a baby rhinoceros chasing the ball around the court. Most soldiers maintained their fitness by running up the stairs to the fourth level of the Mill through the transit accommodation on top floor and down and round again. A few, who were training for Special Forces selection, including Andy McNab, who became famous under that name for his SAS memoir, did this with a weighted rucksack, but the limited facilities were frustrating for those who enjoyed serious physical sport.

I received plenty of mail from family and friends informing me about the transport strikes in England and a flasher in the snow who had raised a laugh with the people standing in a long bus queue on Putney Heath. My godfather, who had served in Malaya with the Seaforth Highlanders, encouraged me not to mix with the locals by providing me with the alternative mental distraction of Russian vocabulary, which I am afraid I rather neglected. My contemporaries who were struggling with university exams provoked some sympathy, but nothing made me yearn to be back in London. In contrast, several close friends in my parent regiment in Germany did appear to have a fantastic time that winter.

Wherever a British Army officer might be posted in the world, he will always receive a mess bill and a demand to write an article for the regimental magazine. In the 17th/21st Lancers, he also received a large monthly equitation bill, whether he owned a horse or not. In my case, I had joined a burgeoning racing syndicate and claimed a foreleg on two 'nags', which were travelling across from Southern Ireland to be trained near Paderborn.

To the credit of the editor of *The White Lancer*, he frequently updated me with entertaining distractions during the six hour "drag stag" in the middle of the night. My regimental friends were spending their time tobogganing in Winterberg, dancing the *pas de deux* in the Christmas skits, defenestrating anyone who talked shop in the Mess and driving after dinner to the Bayadera Club in Amsterdam. Three officers rolled their BMW 3 series cars and tragically one of the newly-commissioned troop leaders killed a girlfriend when he rolled his Morris convertible after a party in England. However, this did not appear to restrict the boisterous lifestyle in Münster.

Back in Belfast, there was a discernible increase in patrol tasks at the start of the marching season in February. Our policy of courtesy and restraint was successful in ensuring the protest marches didn't escalate out of hand, despite one of our soldiers being knocked over by a stolen car at a checkpoint by the Royal Victoria Hospital and then shooting the driver dead. Soon afterwards, two Provisional IRA gunmen shot at a patrol, but missed the soldiers and killed a known criminal who happened to be passing. As the gunmen tried to make their getaway, they ran into the remainder of the multiple, who apprehended them and recovered the weapon.

We heard about a plan to hold a huge march on the first anniversary of the hunger strike on Sunday 28th February. To deal with this, we increased our intelligence gathering and went on a charm offensive in the pubs and clubs. I discovered some of the assembly points and on the day of the march, we flooded the area around Dunville Park with troops and deployed eight platoons either on the ground or in reserve. Fortunately, heavy rain fell and this, together with some shrewd policing decisions, subdued any potential violence and meant the event passed relatively peacefully.

The following day I took my platoon on an afternoon patrol at 4pm. The atmosphere was less confrontational and the discernible tension that had been building up appeared to have been released. During the following weeks, we experienced less verbal abuse and more willingness among the local population to engage in friendly banter. As the advance party of 2nd Battalion Coldstream Guards arrived to start taking over our area, it did seem that the situation was becoming more benign.

After a highly successful tour, during which our battalion found 35 illegal weapons and over 3000 rounds of ammunition, the end was in sight. Our company held an emotional farewell games night with our RUC colleagues. Albert the cockroach, who I had caught in the kitchen, won the race for the Hearn Cup and we were all presented with ties and cap badges and swore friendship forever.

Then on Thursday 25 March, I was back on patrol for the final 48-hour stint. Before dawn, the commander of my paired platoon led a foot patrol into the Clonard and along our southern boundary with B Company. Since I had been on watch keeper duty all night, I did not have to deploy onto the streets until mid-morning, when my first task was to show the Coldstream Guards Intelligence Officer around the Divis Flats.

We left the Mill in a pair of Pigs at the same time as two Land Rovers drove to Battalion Headquarters in Springfield Road to pick up a Royal Air Force liaison officer. Our vehicles dropped us off outside the RUC station in Hastings Street and set off back to North Howard Street. We had just completed our radio checks with company headquarters and I was reminding the patrol of the entry drill into the Divis when suddenly we heard the unmistakable bark of machine gun fire to the west.

I called company headquarters on the radio and James Bendall reported the exact location of the firing. I decided that we couldn't delay for the return of the vehicles which had dropped us off, so I gave rapid orders for a move on foot at best speed. "We have to get to Springfield Road now. Follow Me."

The route took us past the Divis Flats, across some industrial wasteland and down the Falls Road towards Dunville Park. It was just over a mile through the most dangerous part of our area; there was nothing for it but to run all the way. Although I could complete a mile in battle order in less than 5 minutes, I had to pace the group at the speed of our slowest soldier, so I calculated it would take 7 minutes and informed James of our estimated time of arrival.

The standard procedure in a platoon is that the officer should lead and the senior non-commissioned officer should encourage the troops from the rear, which is how we set off that morning. All went well as we reached the Falls Road. After about a mile, I could see the turning into Springfield Road, when suddenly my radio burst into life to inform me we had a man down.

I ran back and found one of my lance corporals collapsed in a door way suffering from an asthma attack. I quickly assessed the situation. We could not leave him there or delay for an ambulance as we were needed desperately at the incident point, so I distributed his rifle, radio and equipment amongst the fitter members of the patrol and we helped him complete the final four hundred yards to the outer point of the cordon, so he could recover whilst his team protected him.

Before the tour, I had discussed his asthma with my company commander, but we decided that he was such an outstanding soldier that we should take him anyway. I never regretted the decision because he had been particularly excellent at motivating and inspiring the younger soldiers who were either frightened or bored in the middle of the tour. All this was in my mind as I positioned the other soldiers around the perimeter of the cordon.

The situation facing us was not good. The Land Rovers which had left the Mill at the same time as our group had picked up the Royal Air Force liaison officer at the Springfield Road RUC Station. Setting off on the return journey, the vehicles turned into Crocus Street, where they were ambushed by a five-man Provisional IRA gun team firing the M-60 machine gun we had been warned about since January and two sniper rifles.

The leading vehicle accelerated out of the killing zone and stopped out of view of the firing point. The section commander, Corporal Lindfield, checked his vehicle and discovered that three were wounded. One Rifleman, the Royal Air Force liaison officer and a Coldstream Guards non-commissioned officer all had gunshot wounds to the head, but the latter was able to look after the others, so he took the unhurt Rifleman back into the killing zone to check the other vehicle.

There he found that one soldier had been killed instantly and another had critical gunshot wounds in the neck, body and head. He gave instructions to his section second-in-command and sprinted down to the firing point, which was a house in Cavendish Street. By this time, the gun team had escaped out of the back door and over the fence into B Company's area in Beechmount.

As I arrived at the incident, the scene was very confusing. There was a lot of blood on the streets. The guards from the Springfield Road RUC Station had deployed and were tending the wounded. We decided to locate the control point inside the Springfield Road RUC Station, but there was vital forensic evidence to gather, so I had to establish a robust cordon to prevent anyone interfering.

I positioned one of my strongest brick commanders, Lance Corporal Tim Marsh, at the firing point. Then I placed the other elements of the platoon at the key points and started dealing with the locals, who were beginning to assemble at the edge of the cordon. Very quickly, the area was invaded by throngs of people, including several journalists and television cameramen.

Dozens of military and RUC were drawn to the scene of the attack as the wounded and dead were evacuated. The forensic investigators pored over every inch of the location before they slowly removed the evidence. Eight hours later we were still in our same positions as I went around the troops encouraging them to remain vigilant and not to lose concentration. Eventually, I received a call to close down the cordon and we were picked up by a couple of vehicles and returned to a very sombre North Howard Street Mill at dusk.

Everyone was exhausted. We had a quick meal, but we knew there would be a major follow-up search operation the next day, so I went upstairs to the Officers' Mess and started making a plan.

Suddenly the telephone rang and the Company Commander was called. The local priest reported there was an IED at the firing point which had not been cleared.

Shane looked at me and asked whether I could deploy again with my troops because 1 Platoon was so devastated. I willingly agreed and picked my best soldiers to drive out once more in the Pigs and set up another cordon in Cavendish Street. At the same time the Ammunition Technical Officer, or ATO, was called and he set about defusing the device.

There is no doubt that the Royal Green Jackets had been extraordinarily lucky that day. ATO found the booby trap in the back yard of the firing point. It was cleverly disguised and covered in ash. It should have been set off by someone moving a stick connected to a pressure pad in the ground. At one stage, there were a dozen people in close proximity and there was enough explosive to kill all of them and anyone else in the kitchen when it detonated.

Shane told me that he had moved the initiator, but had not realised that it was attached by wire underground to an explosive device. If it had exploded when the Commanding Officer and Command Group were there, the incident would have been recorded as one of the worst days of the Troubles for the British Army.

When we returned to the Mill two hours later, I felt proud of my platoon. They had performed fantastically well throughout an emotionally draining day. However, I knew that was not the end of it. During the night, we wrote the search plans for the M-60, which we co-ordinated across the whole of the battalion area. We suspected it had been smuggled out of Belfast, but we had to go through the motions and so the hunt for the machine gun took most of the following morning. In reality, it was a good way to take our mind off the tragic loss of the soldiers, who had become our friends during the previous five months.

The television news and newspapers covered the incident in full. On 26th March, Colin Brady explained on the front page of the *Daily Telegraph* how nine civilians had been injured on the crowded streets by gunshot and shrapnel in the indiscriminate attack. Further on, William Weekes reported the condemnation by the Northern Ireland Secretary, Jim Prior, in the House of Commons and his cautionary advice about loose talk in the Press about the demise of the IRA.

However, there was no time to dwell on this because we flew from Aldergrove on a VC-10 to Germany the next day. Returning to Minden, the battalion held a poignant memorial service for the three Riflemen killed during the tour of duty: Daniel Holland, Nicholas Malakos and Anthony Rapley. My platoon played a passionate *High on the Hill* on their bugles, which was a highly emotional, but fitting, tribute.

Inevitably, my departure was muted due to the shooting incident. Even so, the Bugles, who were destined to become the machine gun platoon, gave me a memorable farewell on the same day that Argentina captured Port Stanley. They were superb soldiers and we formed such strong bonds of camaraderie. I will always be grateful to them for the generous support they gave me during my nine-month attachment.

In the subsequent operational honours list, Corporal Lindfield was awarded the Military Medal for his reaction to enemy fire, courage and professionalism in dealing with the multiple casualties. The Commanding Officer wrote to me after the announcement and informed me that he believed the battalion had done as well as could be expected, given the fact that the Falklands War had dominated the news that summer.

In the meantime, I took my tank troop to Canada, where we had a fantastic time on the Plains of Suffield and I was promoted to command the 17th/21st Lancers Close Reconnaissance Troop in Münster. It was seventeen years before I returned to Northern Ireland to organise the first British Army strategic presentation in Nationalist areas and to brief Sinn Fein politicians about wider Army activities as part of the Peace Process. By then, I had no animosity in my heart for those who had attacked my company in 1982.

CHAPTER 2

B Squadron 1990 – Operation Granby

O world! O life! O time!
Percy Bysshe Shelley

Lieutenant Tim Buxton fixed the B Squadron, 17th/21st Lancers' pennant to the antenna on his Challenger tank and issued instructions to the soldiers in his troop for the night move ahead. After months of waiting, it was hard to believe that they were finally about to cross the border and enter Iraq. He settled into the commander's seat and contemplated how he came to be in the middle of the Arabian Desert preparing to liberate Kuwait on Operation Granby.

★ ★ ★

The British Army teaches its Sandhurst cadets to expect the unexpected by waking them rudely in the middle of the night and ordering them to march five miles in full battledress. Despite this training, we were all surprised at the beginning of August 1990 when Saddam Hussein invaded his southern neighbour, Kuwait. As a result of this foolhardy act, my life in command of B Squadron changed gear. A seemingly sedate internal security operation in Cyprus suddenly increased tempo. Not only did we add the frenetic operations in the forward mounting base, we also had to meet the challenge of forming a tank troop out of my reconnaissance squadron and sending it to fight on the front line as part of 7th Armoured Brigade.

The success of Desert Storm has been attributed to many different aspects. The political support of willing Muslim states was critical, as was the military leadership and the air superiority which the Coalition enjoyed. Another vital factor was what John Keegan described in September 1990 as "battle tactics never tried in real warfare", known as manoeuvre warfare in the British and American armies.

This clumsy military term attempts to encapsulate the strategy of the mobile horde. It is based on the approach of warrior tribes such as the Scythians, Huns and Mogul armies, which transformed the organisation of battle with their clever communications and rapid movements, strung together across huge swathes of open plains. It is underpinned by commanders at every level using their initiative to achieve their objectives. It is easy to talk about, but hard to master.

Despite one of our foremost military writers, Basil Liddell Hart, eloquently describing the concept of the indirect approach, most British officers prefer to be told what to do, rather than using their imagination. After Field Marshal

Bagnall introduced the decentralised command system to 1st British Corps, it took more than eight years of practice for it to reach a level of effectiveness that assured victory in the Gulf.

The foundation of this success was the combined arms combat group, a composite organisation bolted together with slices of infantry battalions, artillery and engineer support and armoured regiments. During the previous decade, I had commanded most of the individual components of the 17th/21st Lancers in its role as a tank regiment in Germany. The highlights included the close reconnaissance troop, a main battle tank squadron and the logistic rear echelons, including our wonderful regimental bandsmen, who became medics and stretcher bearers in the Gulf War.

Soldiering in Germany was always fun and tank manoeuvres were never dull, so despite enjoying my tour with the Royal Green Jackets in West Belfast, I was delighted to rejoin my friends in Münster in April 1982. That summer, the eyes of the world focused on the Task Force in the South Atlantic. Several of my school friends commanded infantry platoons in the Falklands campaign and two were unlucky to be on *Sir Galahad* when it was hit by an Exocet missile and lost soldiers in the fire.

However, I had little time to dwell on the dangers they faced as I took my troop on manoeuvres in Germany and then to Canada for two months. The 1300 square miles of prairie in Alberta surpassed the meagre training areas in Europe. We worked 24 hours each day and night on a series of richly-rewarding exercises, avoiding the pronghorn antelope and mule deer, which provided alternative hazards to the asparagus fields and irrigation ditches which had constrained tactical activity in Lower Saxony.

After two weeks on the prairie, news came through about the Provisional IRA mass murders in London on 20th July. My Regiment had a long standing military relationship with the predecessor regiments of the Royal Green Jackets and loved our horses. We were devastated to hear of the indiscriminate attacks which had killed four soldiers, seven horses and seven bandsmen in Hyde Park and Regent's Park.

The high point of my time in Canada was adventure training in the Rockies. At the end of the tank exercise, I took 23 soldiers to a remote location 90 miles from the nearest town between White Goat and Siffleur Wildernesses. We climbed sheer rock faces, trekked across a glacier and kayaked down the Athabasca River. Of all these extreme activities, it was the river that tested us to breaking point and several hardy men dropped out when the white water became more challenging. Most of my soldiers enjoyed their time in Canada, but one dejected trooper had to return early to Calgary for medical attention after a Cree lady took revenge on his little bighorn.

When I was not on exercise in Europe and Canada, I trailed around Germany in support of our race horses. Surprisingly, our three-year-old, Thunder Wonder, was not only victorious at Bremen, but also won the Aintree Prize over 2,100 metres at the Anglo-German race day in Hanover, much to the delight of his noisy owners. After the race we congregated to collect our winnings. Unfortunately, when the Adjutant handed in his ticket, the tote teller said "nein – you have not filled in zee card correctly". The form was not difficult to complete; our boy was the fifth horse in the fifth race, running at 5 pm, so we just had to punch a hole in all the fives. However, the Adjutant made a mistake on his card and like mutton, we copied his work. There was only one thing to do (after defenestrating the miscreant) and that was to celebrate as if we had won a fortune, so dinner went on long into the night.

In August, the Commanding Officer offered me promotion to lead any of the prestigious troops in headquarters squadron. From what I had seen of command and guided weapons troops, they were excellent alternatives, but the role of recce troop appeared to be the most thrilling. There was nothing I enjoyed more than manoeuvring troops at speed and pinpointing decisive points on the battlefield, so after a short course in England, I took over my new role, acting as the Regiment's eyes and ears on the front line.

The year with recce troop did not disappoint. My troop sergeant taught me to catch fish with the radio antenna and live off the land when working behind enemy lines. The weather at our firing camp was poor, but we came away with a high grade and subsequently had a magnificent time honing our skills against other regiments on the Soltau-Lüneberg extended training area. The spotlight remained on us for the whole year. We were invited to participate in several test exercises, working directly for the Brigade Commander, Brigadier Guthrie, who later became the Chief of Defence Staff. The highlight of that training season was the Netherlands' largest fighting troops exercise since the Second World War, Exercise Atlantic Lion.

It is strange to reflect that armoured training took precedence over operations in the 1980s, but the threat of invasion by the Warsaw Pact was perceived by many senior officers as a more important defence role in the Cold War than internal security duties in Northern Ireland.

Commanding Officers' careers were tested regularly with reports written by teams of technocrats and highly trained inquisitors.

In the event of war, my regiment, as part of NATO's Northern Army Group, was projected to defend a line from Hamburg to Kassel and deter aggression from across the Inner German Border. Our life expectancy in this role was not high, but we didn't care and anyway, I joined the Army for the traditional reasons encapsulated by my regiment's motto, Death or Glory.

The sequence for World War III was planned in minute detail. Four national Corps from Great Britain, Germany, Belgium and Netherlands would move into covering force, main defensive and reserve positions. After the recall of troops from leave and the evacuation of non-combatants, the Queen would sign the order to call out the Territorial Army and we would all deploy to places with distinctive names such as the Hanover Plain, the Minden Gap and the Devil's Punch Bowl.

A whole industry was built on the study of Soviet and Warsaw Pact tactics. Although the main threat was believed to be 3rd Shock Army, we were aware of the potential menace of Spetznatz troops and Fifth Columnists. In peace time, we also had to contend with the Soviet Mission in Germany, or Soxmis as they were known. They provided a real threat of espionage and we were allowed to detain their vehicles if they were seen in a restricted area, or if their officers took a close interest in our training. As with everything in the military, there was a bureaucracy attached to the activity and we had to follow precisely the dos and don'ts of capture laid down in British Forces Germany Form 66, if we didn't wish to incur the diplomatic displeasure of the British Ambassador.

On one large exercise, when our tanks averaged over 200 miles in a week, B Squadron identified a Soxmis team spying on their manoeuvres. A plan was hatched and rapidly put into action. After a careful encirclement and a quick chase, the heroic team from squadron headquarters caught Car 57 and boxed it in with two Land Rovers and a Ferret Scout Car. As the police led the Soviet Air Force Colonel and his officers away, our sergeant major chalked a star on the side of his vehicle as if he was a famous wartime fighter pilot.

For the start of Exercise Atlantic Lion, I was handed the honour of leading the United Kingdom formation through the towns and villages of Holland. We travelled by train to the outskirts of Eindhoven and parked in the long lines of a regimental leaguer in a muddy field. Most large exercises began with a major road move, in order to practise the deployment to prescribed activation positions if NATO went to war. The start of this exercise involved a long route march, crossing the River Maas by pontoon bridge and the Rhine by ferry. There was an early start in the morning, so I issued orders for the road journey and set the guards for their night duties.

All went well in the morning with the first parades of our eight Scorpion and Scimitar light tanks. My regiment prided itself on high vehicle fleet availability and some of the soldiers who had spent ten years as tank drivers knew every track pin, gasket and cable in their vehicle, so it did not surprise me when the troop assembled bright-eyed and bushy-tailed ten minutes before H hour.

I set off at the appointed time and was astonished at the size of the enthusiastic crowds lining the streets. We had prepared for small groups of flag-waving families, but did not expect the large quantities that thronged the roads. I threw handfuls of boiled sweets from our composite rations to the children standing on the pavements and looked behind to see one of my troop vehicles at exactly the right convoy distance. I wondered why the crew were laughing in their seats. What I didn't realise was that they had attached a "just married" sign to the back of my vehicle and were enjoying the reaction of the crowds as we drove past.

We nicknamed this exercise "Route Change". Every time the battle group embarked on a move to intercept the enemy, we were interrupted with new orders half way down the route. Map locations were all encoded, so we had a frantic time unravelling the latest direction whilst driving at best speed, and it was particularly tricky for me leading the convoy as we had to swivel round and rapidly lead off in the new direction. The Dutch were fulsome in their praise for our flexibility and response, but we were not impressed with the planning and anticipation in their headquarters.

It was customary in my regiment after an exhausting exercise to celebrate together. After the Dutch manoeuvres, nine of us travelled to Paris for Le Prix de l'Arc de Triomphe. We booked rooms in the Hotel Madeleine Pasquier, which we shared with a group of girls who had travelled from England with nowhere to stay. The proprietor didn't seem to mind that there were twice as many people staying in his rooms, but since we spent most of our time in the cafés and night clubs of the left bank, it was hard for him to count the numbers. In the end, we watched the Arc from a bloodstock owner's box and were delighted when Walter Swinburn won on All Along, who later became the first filly to win the Eclipse Award for Horse of the Year in America.

After a fantastic year with recce troop, tragedy struck over the Christmas leave period, when one of my crew commanders, Corporal Chris Ling, died in a traffic accident after hitting black ice on the autobahn. Chris was a highly-talented soldier and sportsman, who played in the regimental rugby team which reached the Army semi-finals. I drove to the morgue in a melancholy mood and then organised the repatriation of his body to Pinner in Middlesex. His funeral was very well attended by his pals in the regiment and resulted in a lifelong friendship with his parents. He is still sorely missed by all those who knew him.

★★★

In 1984, I was posted back to B Squadron, where I had previously served as a troop leader. My first task was to organise the gunnery camp at Hohne. We paid our respects at the Belsen concentration camp and began shooting with the improved fire control system. Standards in the first week progressed well, but the biggest surprise came as I reconnoitred the notorious battle run on Range 9 with the squadron leader, Jeremy Groves. We were watching a pair of buzzards rising on a thermal when he put down his binoculars and told me he had decided to retire from the Army. I made a polite comment and then he dropped his bombshell by saying that the Commanding Officer had asked if I would take over the squadron for six months until a replacement was available at the end of the year.

Of course I was thrilled, but my emotions were put into context the next day when a soldier in C Squadron, Corporal Nigel Laycock, shot himself in the head with a general purpose machine gun inside his tank turret. It was really important to exorcise his ghost immediately and my best man, who was the Regimental Gunnery Officer, worked throughout the night to clean the tank completely. Poignantly it was the first tank to fire a round when the ranges opened in the morning. This tragic incident seemed to concentrate everyone's minds and we achieved our best-ever results, but somehow these didn't seem to matter after the corporal's death, which hung over all of us that summer.

After returning to our grey prefabricated military barracks, I had to organise the regimental ball. This was held to honour the award of the San Serafino Order of Purity and Truth 4th Class to Brigadier General Sir Harry Flashman, late of my regiment, and celebrate his colourful campaigns. I invited George MacDonald Fraser, author of the Flashman novels, to attend the evening and he sent a wonderful reply from Scotland, but sadly he could not join our guests, who arrived in a splendid array of period costumes to complement the fabulously-decorated Mess.

Jeremy departed after the party in June, whilst I planned the squadron's commitment to guard a nearby ammunition compound. Operational site guards were useful for instilling battlefield discipline in our troops, as we used live ammunition for these important duties. The British Army's bunkers in Germany had to be guarded securely because they not only stored all our tank rounds, but also the battlefield nuclear warheads.

Prior to the site guard, we ran an infantry exercise on our local training area at Dorbaum, a picturesque rural expanse astride the River Ems. Part of this learning programme was dedicated to the new radio procedure with its novel code system being introduced throughout the British Army. This was useful preparation for the brigade test exercise at Soltau later that month when we practised armoured combat group drills with our friends in the Irish Guards.

The main event during my six months commanding B Squadron was Exercise Lionheart, the autumn manoeuvres involving the reinforcement in Germany by United States forces. As the largest British exercise since the Second World War, this exercise was designed to demonstrate NATO political and military commitment to the defence of Western Europe.

It comprised two parts. The first was a logistics operation to move 57,000 Regular, Reservist and Territorial Army soldiers into the Alliance's central region and the second was Exercise Spearpoint 84, the field training for 1st British Corps. This involved 97,000 troops and 750 main battle tanks, with an enemy represented by 1st (German) Panzer-grenadier Brigade and 1st (United States) Tiger Brigade, flown in from Fort Hood, Texas and 41st (Netherlands) Brigade, part of 1st Netherlands Corps, which we had worked with on Atlantic Lion. Although it was important to demonstrate Alliance unity, national rivalries were high on the agenda, with the two most interesting sub-plots being the equipment of each nation and their tactical abilities.

It was a particularly exciting exercise for armoured vehicle spotters. The Americans brought their new M1-Abrams tanks and M2-Bradley infantry fighting vehicles, whilst the Germans deployed their Leopard 2 and Marders. For the British Army, this was the first opportunity on this scale to show off the new tracked air defence Rapier system and the prototype infantry combat vehicle MCV 80 (later named Warrior). However the star of the show was expected to be the new Challenger tank, crewed by the Royal Hussars. In contrast, my regiment was equipped with the veteran Chieftain, which everyone dismissed as the weakest link due to its poor reputation for reliability.

For the deployment, we loaded our tanks onto a train in the middle of the night in the pouring rain and boarded the antique carriages. Unfortunately, these were designed for only 60 passengers, but we had to pack 80 soldiers with their rucksacks into each. There was neither heating nor water, and the loos overflowed very quickly. Our disgruntled soldiers slept on the luggage racks to avoid the flooded floors. Eighteen hours later they were desperately relieved to spill out onto the sidings, rejoin their tanks and drive to the concentration area, which turned out to be a wet, boggy beech wood, where the tanks settled at obtuse angles on the side of a hill.

In 1984, British tanks had no night visibility devices, so we were dependent on the close reconnaissance and guided weapons troops to inform us about enemy movement in front of the battle group. Our primary concern was concealment from above, because we did not expect to have air superiority. Radio silence was another vital part of our camouflage as there was a huge Warsaw Pact listening post on the Harz Mountains, which recorded all our wireless transmissions. I always felt slightly paranoid about preventing them from building a file on me which would allow an enemy armoured commander to analyse and predict how I would move my formation in a future war.

Surprise is a vital ingredient in free-flowing armoured

battles, so I made it my business to perfect the art of ambush. It is not difficult to work out where to strike an opponent on an armoured battlefield, but I was always amazed at how perfectly intelligent officers came up with overcomplicated plans and then made excuses about the fog of war when the plan failed. There is a very important difference between theoretical work in a sanitised operations room and rough physical distractions in armoured warfare, which demand simplicity and clarity of thought. As Carl von Clausewitz wrote: "Everything in war is simple, but the simplest thing is difficult. The difficulties accumulate and produce a kind of friction that is inconceivable unless one has experienced war".

Fortunately, we did not remain in the boggy beech wood for long and were allowed to hide our tanks in the farm buildings of a friendly village. From there, we reconnoitred our fire positions from every angle and watched the sappers lay minefields on the enemy approaches. Eventually we were called into the delaying positions to engage the opposition known as "Orange Forces". This was a German Leopard tank formation and after holding them for 24 hours, we withdrew in contact at night through the minefields and over the rivers, picking up our attached company of Irish Guards on the way. This phase was not easy to control, but fortunately, no tank was lost and the whole squadron arrived in good order at the reorganisation area 25 miles away.

The tactical focus for the United Kingdom was to demonstrate a series of operational level counter moves. The counter stroke concept had been gestating for 18 months and involved a large force attacking a second echelon manoeuvre group in the flank. We had practised this at lower levels, but now, for the first time, we had the opportunity to attempt it at brigade level.

After a torrid weekend in a quarry, wearing full nuclear biological and chemical warfare protective clothing, we were given a warning order for a move of some sort into the Einbeck Bowl. The operation was complicated by a river crossing, after which my squadron was expected to exploit through on the left and attack the enemy formation in the flank. In the middle of the night we drove to a new area, closed down all our electronic devices and waited.

Suddenly new orders arrived by messenger and we were called forward at best speed. Timing is everything on military missions. There is nothing more frustrating than a delay to an agreed and synchronised time of departure. In this case, we worked out precisely when we needed to move from our hides and reduced our notice appropriately before setting off at full pace to cross the river.

All went well on the move to the assembly area, but then abruptly we were called on the radio and told by brigade headquarters to stop and wait for a group of VIPs to finish their lunch and arrive at the viewing stands. The whole battle group was seething as we pulled into the side of the road in the open countryside whilst we waited for almost an hour. Then with no further notice, we were called forward and embarked on the first brigade level counter stroke on a major exercise. As the sappers finished their safety checks on the crossings, we poured across the bridges and closed with the enfiladed enemy. I was very conscious of our own vulnerable flank, but fortunately there was excellent visibility that day and a Lynx helicopter squadron protected us at long range with their TOW missiles.

Navigating a tank at 30 miles per hour when the hatches are closed is quite disorientating, so it did not surprise me when several tanks drove into ditches and "bogged" in the soft ground while crossing the open fields. It did not help that we had to avoid the numerous asparagus fields cordoned with red and white mine tape. Unfortunately, my regiment had caused front page headlines when a corporal drove his tank 10 metres into one of these precious fields during a previous exercise, so we were very sensitive about any unintentional damage, which might be exploited by the Green political movement.

Despite these hazards, the squadron achieved the mission and waited on the objective for the planned relief at the end of the battle. However, there was an awkward pause when the reinforcements failed to arrive, which made us worry even more about the staff planning and what would happen for real against the Warsaw Pact. The whole adventure reminded us of the two occasions in history when my regiment had been launched into a valley of death; at the battle of Fondouk in the Second World War and the Charge of the Light Brigade at Balaklava.

This failure to reinforce was not the only frustration in the first week of the exercise. Our main complaint was that the American forces ignored the umpires stationed at properly-prepared defensive positions. Against all tactical conventions, we had to physically block the roads and tracks with our tanks to stop them driving straight through. During the weekend, we discussed taking matters into our own hands for the final part of the exercise and decided that we would mirror the Orange forces' approach and play them at their own game.

A key to building momentum in the offensive phase of war is to fight lots of little fights rapidly with overwhelming force, rather than waiting for a pitched battle. Two of the command mantras at the time were "speed saves blood" and "clout don't dribble", which encapsulated this way of making the best of our equipment by fast aggressive action. During the next phase of the exercise, we applied these principles and moved swiftly between enemy platoon positions, before they were reinforced.

For the final three days, the regiment was given orders to capture a bridge over the Salzgitter Canal, having first established firmly defended bridges over the River Fuhse. I returned from the Commanding Officer's evening meeting and issued orders to the squadron. I told everyone to prepare for a hasty move before first light and then handed them a series of map references and control points as their objectives.

To their credit, the sappers did a fantastic job on the river crossing during the night. As dawn broke, my Commanding Officer suddenly called me on the radio, demanding to know where I was with my squadron. He needed me to quickly cross a gap before the sleepy obstacle police arrived. Fortunately, I was alert and had anticipated this situation, so we were able to push through and outflank the enemy's matrix positions. On and on we drove, with no orange marked tanks guarding the route. In my right ear, the Commanding Officer encouraged me to continue until I met with the enemy and in my left ear I heard the umpire pleading with me to pause and allow the enemy to reposition their tanks.

After 30 minutes, I reached the lightly-guarded Salzgitter Canal. I dealt with the enemy platoon and reported to the

Commanding Officer that the objective had been secured. The next hour was full of confusing orders and counter orders. The NATO exercise planners were furious that we had bypassed the German defensive positions.

Surprisingly, the British planners were also not happy that the Chieftain regiment had won the day. They had expected us to be held by the German Leopards and had primed the Challenger regiment subsequently to gain the glory. But they couldn't change the result, so reluctantly they called a halt to the exercise 24 hours before the scheduled time. However our tactical resourcefulness did us no favours in the long term because the NATO staff ordered us to leaguer nearby in a wet muddy field and spitefully arranged for us to be the last troops to return to our barracks the following week.

Success on this exercise did not save the Commanding Officer from being sacked. He will be remembered for his outspoken views, his tactical genius and for his belief that soldiering required total immersion, rather than some kind of osmosis. He was suspicious of the developing trend in fledgling officers to worry too much about their own careers, rather than concentrating on what was in the best interests of the regiment. But perhaps every generation feels the same way about their young pretenders.

By the end of 1984, I had taken an important step towards mastering the three elements of armoured warfare. The first is being able to conceive a plan which pinpoints enemy weaknesses and plays to the strengths of the friendly forces – most professional officers are trained to do this well. The second element is to ensure forces under command know their part in the plan, together with their freedoms and constraints. Clear orders and attention to detail are part of this ability; however, what marks out the best commanders is the talent to instil a level of understanding whereby every soldier knows what his neighbour will do in a given situation. This is all about inspiring total trust in the team.

The final and hardest element is the intuition to win battles after the formation has crossed the line of departure. This is something that cannot be taught and is a gift that Napoleon described as a superior understanding, or *coup d'oeuil*. It is not luck, but luck can play a part in it; anyone can be lucky once, the trick is to achieve success consistently. Thus to my mind, battlefield decisions are the alpha and omega of leadership; everything else can be done by competent technicians and efficient staff officers trained in schools and colleges.

★ ★ ★

After commanding B Squadron in Germany, I was selected to lead one of the first Operation Raleigh expeditions in Central America. The Contra War made this slightly hotter than expected, but our group of 32 young men and women, including a member of the Royal Family, had a wonderful time completing the scientific, adventurous and community projects in the Bay Islands. We all made friends with the cheerful local population, but more than once I had to use the final phrase in my Spanish handbook, "I'm sorry, but in England we do not sell our women".

I returned from the jungle to Münster to work in regimental headquarters. This was a difficult time because the relationship with 4th Brigade was at a low point after the sacking of the Commanding Officer whilst I was away. However, during my tenure, we repaired the damage and after converting the regiment to Challenger tanks and successfully introducing the thermal observation gunnery sight to the British Army, the replacement officer was deservedly awarded an OBE.

As Adjutant, I was always on call. When the *Herald of Free Enterprise* sank on a Friday afternoon in March 1987, I had to work all night to ascertain whether anyone from the regiment was among the 193 people killed in the tragic accident. I am certain that our mandatory parade after lunch saved some of our soldiers and their families, who would otherwise have joined the fatal crossing.

There were no secrets or hiding places during my time as Adjutant. By then, I had developed a wonderful network of friends and colleagues throughout the regiment. They kept me informed about what was happening in the officers and soldiers' accommodation and on the tank park.

It was fascinating to hold both of the principle staff appointments in regimental headquarters. Of the two roles, I preferred that of operations officer, with the associated work to refine the British Army's counter stroke concept. As a result, we were able to outwit the United States forces when they returned for Exercise Certain Strike in 1987, equipped with the latest airborne stand-off radar systems and new Apache attack helicopters.

After two years as a staff officer, I took my promotion exam. The first paper covered International Affairs and War Studies. I chose safely and discussed Mr Gorbachev's policies and NATO credibility. Most of us avoided challenging questions about Islamic resurgence and international terrorism because we had paid scant attention to the never-ending violence in the Middle East and the intermittent clashes between Libya and the United States of America.

At the time, we thought Colonel Gaddafi was a joke, but Washington took him very seriously. His alignment with the Soviet Union and his attempts to become a nuclear power, plus the overt support to violent terrorist organisations targeting Israel led President Reagan to take pre-emptive action. American F-14 Tomcats had shot down a pair of Sukhoi SU-22 Fitters over the Gulf of Sidra. When the United States again sent a Carrier Task Force into disputed waters, Gaddafi sponsored the bombing of La Belle discotheque in West Berlin, killing two United States Army soldiers and injuring a further 79 American servicemen and women.

After passing the exam, I was promoted to command the largest squadron in the regiment, comprising more than 180 soldiers. This included every department and troop outside the sabre squadrons. My war role was to organise the echelon support to cover every eventuality, and this gave me a broad understanding of the logistics burden associated with armoured warfare.

The full training season included one of the last Divisional level manoeuvre exercises in Germany, "Iron Hammer". This was held towards the end of a wet autumn when the Green Party complained about the environmental damage caused by NATO exercises. In response, our tanks were kept in dripping beech woods for most of the exercise and when eventually they were called into battle, they were restricted to driving on roads and tracks. The soldiers in the tank squadrons mischievously nicknamed the exercise "Rusty

Filings", but the constraints did not affect my logistics squadron unduly and we had the best of times.

The frustration of the young officers in the regiment, whose expectations were deflated by the inactivity, spilled out when we returned to Münster. After dinner, they decided to set off their pyrotechnics and took a chainsaw to the ugly parts of the Officers' Mess. The grievous damage resulted in an interview with the stand-in Commanding Officer the next morning, when they accepted an appropriate punishment, rather than being charged under the Army Act. The chief protagonists had to repair all the damage and replace the curtains and carpets and they all had to make a significant donation to charity, so the event became known as the Great Ormond Street Hospital Dinner.

At that time, I knew most of the 500 soldiers in the regiment, having worked in Münster every year of the decade. We had progressed a long way from our arrival in Germany in 1980 and become the best armoured regiment in the British Army. We had the lowest figures of premature release and ill-discipline amongst our peers. Notwithstanding a few errant subalterns, the regiment's professionalism was reflected by consistently high grades in all our tests and inspections and our talented officers and soldiers were picking up influential appointments throughout the Army.

Success on our tanks stemmed from the outstanding support in headquarters squadron. Most of these soldiers had changed career after a short period on the tank park and wished to stay in the regiment forever. In the 1980s, the clerks and truck drivers were very much part of our family regiment. Several of them were commissioned as officers, including the unflappable Assistant Adjutant, John Hodges, who also built the successful cricket team which won the Royal Armoured Corps Cup.

Loyalty to the regiment, forged through shared experiences and filial bonds, laid the foundation of success, which drew envious glances from elsewhere. We knew there were threats because society could not and did not wish to afford its peacetime Army. New technology promised efficiencies, but as a compromise demanded an erosion of the regimental system. My attitude to this situation was pragmatic; I was proud of our past, but not so absorbed in it to lose focus on the future. The future to me was all about operational relevance, so it was with fresh optimism that I departed from Germany to take command of B Squadron in Cyprus at the beginning of 1989.

This was my second visit to the island where Queen Berengaria married Richard the Lionheart in 1191. As a Sandhurst cadet I spent two weeks in the foothills of the Troodos Mountains labouring up the spurs with the platoon machine gun and a five-gallon water container on my back. Much had changed in the intervening years, with many parts of the coast developed into popular holiday locations. Reassuringly however, the Sandhurst exercise had stayed the same, ending the week by waking the irate local residents with a traditional dawn attack on poor old Paramali village.

My primary responsibility as a Commanding Officer in Cyprus was the internal security of the two sovereign base areas in the east and west of the island. This included protecting the strategic signals units and the Royal Air Force base at Akrotiri, where we provided mobile patrols on a daily basis. We also covered the United Nations peacekeeping zone, known as the Attila Line, for more than 10 miles, where it lay in our area.

Throughout this peacekeeping zone, everything remained unchanged from July 1974, when Turkey invaded the island as one of guarantors of the constitution. Our area overlooked an abandoned Greek Cypriot village where tables still set for lunch were covered in powdery dust and walls of buildings slowly crumbled as Nature regained control of the land. Whilst we patrolled our designated route, we were watched from observation posts manned by Austrian peacekeepers, Turkish paratroopers and Greek infantry. They were all friendly to us, but their tolerance towards each other was extremely fragile.

By 1989, the peace process had stalled for many years. Diplomatically, a solution depended on the Turks being magnanimous and the Greeks acknowledging the mistakes of their leadership, in particular the policy of union with Greece, or Enosis as it was known. However, the intransigence of the rival leaders, Spyros Kyprianou and Rauf Denktash, meant there was little hope for a resolution in the short term.

Whilst the Greeks and Turks argued intently over a few inches of turf, the rest of the World turned upside down. George Bush succeeded Ronald Reagan as 41st President of the United States of America and in June, the world focused on the protests in Tiananmen Square. NATO celebrated its 40th anniversary as the Soviet Union pulled out of Afghanistan, and the fall of the Berlin Wall signified the collapse of the Warsaw Pact.

In Cyprus there was a wide range of threats, including espionage and terrorism. We were very conscious that some of Colonel Gaddafi's family took their holidays on the island. The destruction of Pan Am Flight 103 over

Lockerbie and the subsequent attack by American Tomcats on a pair of Libyan MiG-23 Floggers as I arrived in Cyprus increased our concerns. In addition, we had to deal with occasional mortar attacks and shooting incidents, so there was enough to keep my patrolling troops on their toes. However, the biggest risks to life and limb were on the lethal roads and tracks.

We shared our mess accommodation with the Coldstream Guards battalion which I met in West Belfast. Unfortunately, they lost more soldiers in 1989 in Cyprus than in all their Northern Ireland tours put together.

The most tragic incident was when a truck transporting a platoon from Number 1 Company plunged off a precipice and plummeted down the mountain side near the village of Platres. The old Bedford had picked up Lance Sergeant Horsfall and the others in his platoon from their guard duty at the Mount Olympus radar installation and started the return journey to the Sovereign Base Area at Episkopi. They had completed this journey many times and in the back of the vehicle, the tired but relaxed soldiers chatted about their plans for leave and wondered whether the swelling numbers of student protestors in Prague would lead to the end of the Cold War. Suddenly, the driver lost control as he approached a sharp bend and in slow motion, the four-tonne truck slid over the edge. The soldiers sitting on the benches in the rear didn't know what hit them. Eight of those on board were killed and thirteen others seriously injured.

We were all devastated by this incident, which hardly made the news in Britain. It was strange that in the wider Army, Cyprus was perceived as an easy posting. However, the families and friends who attended the tearful memorial service in the Guards Chapel at Wellington Barracks would testify that that was certainly not the case.

Driving in Cyprus was known to be very hazardous. Despite laying down very strict rules for motorcycle owners, I lost Trooper Paul Rogan, who rode a large motorbike off the road near Aya Napa in May 1990. Paul was an experienced driver, having mastered a Sultan command vehicle in Germany before joining the squadron to drive a Ferret Scout Car. His tragic accident reminded everyone of the daily perils on the island.

To mitigate these risks, we sent the soldiers on courses and encouraged them to pass the Heavy Goods Vehicle test. As a result, our armoured vehicles never had a serious accident during my tour, despite covering 20,000 miles per year across every type of terrain. We also drove competitively and after we won the military Land Rover driving championships, my squadron's entry was accepted for the Rothmans International Rally. This was one of the most demanding and notorious in the European season, with a coefficient of 20.

Our contribution to Glasnost was to drive a Lada car, sponsored by a Cypriot dealership with back up provided by the Russian works team. Gaining the security clearances was not easy and the mixture of languages needed to obtain the best engine and gearbox combination made me dizzy. The drivers were two characters in my squadron; the motor transport section commander, Corporal Andy Bolton, and our medic, Corporal Mark Thake.

Several stressful moments littered their gruelling route, with fifteen tyre changes and a broken shock absorber on the night stage at Milikuri. The moment of truth arrived on the penultimate stage when the car stopped with fuel pump problems. However, by running a tube from the windscreen washer and taping a sponge to the pump, they kept the car running until the end of the day, much to the relief of their many supporters. The final leg was televised live to 35 countries and we were all really proud when they climbed the finish ramp in the National Stadium in Nicosia as one of only 34 cars out of the 73 starters to complete the rally.

During my second year on the island, there was a change in military emphasis. Following the collapse of the Warsaw Pact, the fifth pillar of British Defence Policy, out of area commitments, was drawn into the spotlight. As a result, I was visited by the Under Secretary of State, the Earl of Arran, and in April by the Secretary of State, Tom King, after he attended the 75th Anniversary commemoration of Gallipoli. In a prescient interview, he cautioned that despite the lessening of tension between NATO and the Soviet Union, the world was still an uncertain and dangerous place. He expressed particular concern about the proliferation of countries with missile capability and referred specifically to the "supergun" Saddam Hussein was developing in Iraq.

My squadron had an important role as a response force in the Middle East. To practise our amphibious and air portable roles, we routinely travelled from one area to another by sea or C-130 aircraft. At the end of June, we conducted a battlefield survival exercise. Eight groups deployed by helicopter to rugged observation posts, sited at the foot of the Troodos Mountains, overlooking an imaginary front line between hostile forces. During the night, these positions were compromised and the four-man teams had to withdraw over harsh terrain occupied by a mobile hunter

Returning from West Belfast in 1982, my troop welcomed me back for an eventful summer. Sadly, both Corporals Nigel Laycock and "Dinger" Bell (front left) died two years later.

The 17th/21st Lancers Rugby Team that won the Royal Armoured Corps Cup, captained by the redoubtable Mick Holtby. We also won the 3rd Armoured Division Cup and the Hamburg Seven-A-Sides. Chris Ling is second from the left in the front row.

Episkopi, April 1990. The author showing the Secretary of State for Defence, The Rt Hon Tom King, around a Saladin tank, as the United Kingdom's out of area role came to the fore

Al Jubayl - troops cooped up in a large hangar.

B Squadron 17th/21st Lancers on the gunnery range at Akamas with the newly procured T-55 tanks used as hard targets. Three of my troop leaders in this photograph and about 20 soldiers deployed forward on Desert Storm. The remainder patrolled the Forward Mounting Base and carried out a wide range of Operation Granby support tasks.

Kevin Griffin in his "ergonomic" tank turret on the 25th February 1991.

The pennant which led the British armoured advance into Kuwait on 27th February 1991.

Tim Buxton's troop in Kuwait after the ceasefire on 28th February 1991

force. When caught, the soldiers were escorted to an "interview" cell, where they were questioned by my specially trained non-commissioned officers.

This was the penultimate part of my annual training, which included firing our light tanks on the Akamas peninsular and at Pyla ranges. The training was divided into two aspects; the first was to ensure all the individual soldiers maintained high skills in gunnery, signals and driving as well as the secondary skills of musketry, de-mining, first aid, fitness, the law of armed conflict and protection from nuclear, biological and chemical attacks.

The second aspect was developing their crew tactics. As a reconnaissance squadron, we placed much emphasis on perfecting the skills needed in an observation post and especially the accuracy of written and radio reports. We also concentrated on movement across open and close terrain, clearing defiles and routes, calling down indirect fire, replenishment, reserve demolitions and convoy escorts.

We acquired three T-55 tanks from the Sinai desert, which were placed on the gunnery range at Akamas and filled with concrete. This was the first time anyone had fired high explosive rounds there against hard targets. We also worked with the infantry who fired their mortars over our heads to simulate realistic battle conditions and shot at a three-dimensional glass fibre moving target, pulled by wire around a mile-long track. So by the end of July, B squadron was ready for the out-of-area role.

As news arrived of the Iraqi invasion, our notice to move was reduced, while 30 Signals Regiment deployed to provide satellite communication links with the Gulf. The contingency plan was left over from Operation Vantage in 1961, when

British Forces in Cyprus had augmented 24th Infantry Brigade and deployed to defensive positions in Kuwait after Iraq claimed sovereignty over the newly independent state. However, since then, Saddam Hussein had fought a protracted war against Iran and built an Army of one million men and 5,000 tanks and an air force of 500 aircraft, so ground troops from Cyprus were never going to be the answer.

I immediately thought of my 1500-metre running companion serving with the Kuwait Liaison Team, Warrant Officer 1 Peter Barlow. It turned out that all his team had been forcibly separated from their families and interrogated at a divisional headquarters before being dispatched to detention centres around Baghdad. Meanwhile, their families endured a traumatic week, frantic with worry and scared witless about the marauding Iraqi troops vandalising their homes.

After two wives were assaulted, the British Embassy managed to persuade the Iraqi authorities to allow them to join their husbands. Sixteen days later they were reunited in a gas refinery outside Baghdad, before the families were flown out of the country on 2nd September. The men remained in detention for a further three months, but with much relief, they eventually flew back to the United Kingdom on 10th December.

In the meantime, the United Kingdom government sent a squadron of Royal Air Force Tornado F3 air defence fighters and a squadron of Jaguar ground attack aircraft to the Arabian Peninsula. Together with additional ships for the Royal Navy's Armilla Patrol, these aircraft joined the large build-up of United States forces. Many of them staged through Akrotiri, which became the forward mounting base for Operation Granby. The airfield was used for transport flights, tanker support and transit sorties, with Phantom FGR2 aircraft tasked in the air defence role against a possible attack by Iraqi bombers.

Under the leadership of the Commander of British Forces, the headquarters, signals and logistics units in Cyprus had all become "Joint", with the three services working together rather than separately. Merging the Royal Navy, Army and Royal Air Force units together was a huge success and a forerunner for more Joint units across Defence in the following decade. However, the combat troops were still separate, so both my squadron and the Royal Air Force Regiment independently provided security at Akrotiri in our different armoured vehicles

After another short training exercise to validate our out-of-area role, a friend from England, Robert Pearson, arrived on 3rd September just after Iraq declared Kuwait to be its 19th province. He was working in the Ministry of Defence team rallying support for coalition action against Saddam Hussein and conducting a whistle stop tour of eight Middle East countries in seven days. Over dinner, he gave me advance warning about the plans in London and so it was no surprise when we were formally assigned three important roles in the war effort.

The most important role was to send combat troops to the front line. There was some confusion which brigade would deploy until the Defence Secretary announced on Thursday 14th September that it would be 7th Armoured Brigade. This resulted in a request to fly a group from my squadron to Germany and assign them under command of the Desert Rats.

This deployment of a formed troop was complicated by the fact they had to fight on Challenger main battle tanks, rather than the wheeled Saladin and Ferret Scout Cars we drove in Cyprus. Fortunately, I had reorganised the squadron to conform to a Type 57 Challenger regiment earlier that year and ensured that all my soldiers maintained their tank qualifications.

They had to take over and shoot their tanks at the Hohne gunnery ranges in North Germany on the following Monday morning, so there was no time to waste. However I knew this composite troop had to be highly resilient, so it was important to devote sufficient time to blending the best people to ensure the group was more than the sum of its individual soldiers.

I was concerned to avoid any reluctant married soldiers going to war if at all possible. Looking through the names and characters, it was clear there were sufficient single soldiers in the squadron. I also believed that if the leadership was right, everything else would fall into place, so the command appointments of the young officer and his sergeant were my most important decisions.

I sent a senior troop leader, Freddie Elwes, around the squadron to ask who was keen and who felt uncomfortable with the idea of fighting a protracted war in the desert. He set off on his motorcycle to the village of Berengaria, where some of the soldiers lived. On the way down the steep hill at Curium he approached a Suzuki jeep.

Suddenly, he saw a windsurfer board fly off the car and come hurtling towards him. The board hit him square on the chin, broke his helmet and knocked him out. He lost control of the bike, but fortunately, he slid into the side of the road and did not hit any of the posts or fall over the edge of the cliff. Once he had recovered his poise, he returned to my squadron headquarters and told me about the accident. The swelling from the gravel rash on his face and jaw made him look like Desperate Dan from the Dandy comic. More importantly, this prevented him from wearing a respirator, which sadly ruled him out of contention for the appointment of the Gulf Troop Leader.

As a result of Freddie's unfortunate injury, I invited Lieutenant Tim Buxton to take the troop to Germany. He had led the musketry team to success at the Near East Skill at Arms Meeting, winning the Young Officer's cup and beating all the infantry companies, despite firing with iron sights. Qualifying for Bisley does not necessarily translate to success as a tank troop leader, but Tim had also won the squadron gunnery prize at Akamas and performed very well on the tactical phase, so I was supremely confident of his abilities.

A young married soldier, Kevin Griffin, volunteered to be the troop sergeant. He was already very experienced on Challenger and was an outstanding driving and maintenance instructor. This was a vital skill, because vehicle availability was a huge issue in the desert. It did not surprise me that he was commissioned later in his career, since he lived up to all my expectations in the Gulf.

Once I had confirmed the senior leaders, I had to consider the skills needed in the other crew positions. For a Signals expert, I selected a soldier who I knew well from my time as operations officer, Corporal "Marty" Rush. He could build radios from scratch and had the sort of dry sense of humour needed in war, when stress levels rise and people become frightened by isolation and uncertainty. The realities and horrors of war were unknown to these soldiers and I needed phlegmatic leaders who would not flap under pressure.

In choosing the other crew members, I identified the best tank gunners available in the squadron, those who I knew would be top shots with the 120mm rifled guns of the Challenger tanks. I picked the drivers for their understanding of the automotive systems in the tank, as well their instinctive abilities at finding routes through low ground to avoid being seen. Finally, the operators had to be multi-skilled, canny crewmen. They were required simultaneously to handle two or three very high frequency radio sets, load the gun and deputise for the crew commander when required, so they also had to be outstanding team players.

There was only one soldier I selected who refused to go to war, and I was confident that his replacement would not diminish the capability of the troop. Within 24 hours they were flying to Germany and shortly after taking over their new tanks, they had to shoot on the ranges wearing chemical protection suits and respirators. The fact that they achieved the highest scores during these tests was a good start, but it did not mean they could rest on their laurels.

Meanwhile, I had to consider the second role assigned to the squadron, that of security, protection and escorts. The base at Akrotiri had become incredibly busy. We were required to increase our patrolling around the airfield, which was used 24 hours of the day and night, working alongside the Royal Air Force Regiment. I also had to provide escorts for the container ships which carried the British equipment through the Suez Canal. One of the great squadron characters, Corporal "Cres" Cresdee, volunteered for this role, together with a young Trooper, "Chick" Fowler, who had recently joined the regiment.

The third role was logistic support. There were almost 14,000 Operation Granby movements at Akrotiri. It turned out that my squadron held more heavy goods vehicle driving licences than any other unit on the island, except the Joint Logistics Unit. Many of their Royal Corps of Transport drivers had been deployed forward to Saudi Arabia, so I was asked to help the all-night work of cross-loading stores from the Galaxy aircraft to the smaller C-130s during the build-up of materiel in the Gulf. In our logistic effort, Sergeant Alf Smith worked unstintingly in a less glamorous role and ensured that the ammunition and arms stores were kept open whatever time a patrol departed or returned each and every day of the year.

In October, the Ministry of Defence drew up plans to send 4th Brigade, either as a long term replacement for 7th Brigade or as part of a larger British formation. For the second time, I was asked whether I had any spare soldiers. Personally, I was keen to take my whole squadron to the front line, but this could only happen if we were replaced on our other duties and our planned arms plot move to England at the end of the year was postponed.

Eventually, the decision was taken by the Commander of British Forces in Cyprus that we could not be released, although I did manage to send a few extra soldiers to Saudi Arabia, including the young man who had refused at first and then regretted his decision. Ultimately, the whole of my squadron was involved to some degree in the initial stages of

Operation Granby, although only three officers and about twenty soldiers deployed forward into Iraq or Kuwait.

★ ★ ★

After firing at Hohne, Tim took his soldiers to Soltau to dust down their tank troop tactics and armoured skills. Then he had to drive the Challengers onto a train destined for Bremerhaven, where they were loaded onto the ships bound for Saudi Arabia. Once they had said goodbye to their vehicles, the pace of life returned to normal as they waited for further instructions. Apart from taking their Naps tablets as protection from chemical attacks, the next fortnight really did not feel as if they were about to head to war.

When Tim's father heard that his son had been issued with only a 9mm Browning pistol as a personal weapon, he generously purchased a nine-cartridge, pump-action shotgun for each of the 17th/21st Lancer troop leaders, who deployed with their troops to the Gulf to bolster 7th Armoured Brigade. The wide spread of a shotgun cartridge was considered to be a more effective close quarter weapon on a tank being overrun by infantry, but the British Army would never pay for such lavishness.

All the soldiers were relieved when the flight timings were announced in the middle of October and they were reunited with their Mark 3 Challenger tanks at the port of Al Jubayl. However, they felt like battery chickens, as they were forced to sleep in huge hangars, with no privacy in the latrines, whilst they became acclimatised to the heat and modified their tanks for the desert war.

They were immediately challenged by the Americans,

who spent hours every day pumping iron in the gym and insulted the British soldiers for being so scrawny. Two days after arriving in Arabia, Tim took his troop for a run and the second in command of a United States Marine company alongside asked if he could bring his troops too. Tim picked up the gauntlet and they all set off together around the camp early the next morning.

What the Americans didn't realise was that all of my B Squadron troops were not only extremely fit but were acclimatised to the heat, having lived all summer in Cyprus. One by one the Americans dropped out as Tim set a fast middle distance pace which his troop maintained in a tight squad. After three miles, all but three of the Marines had slipped behind, and as they ended the run the British troops paid back the American stragglers for their earlier taunts. Unsurprisingly, the British were never again sledged for their slight physique.

Soon afterwards the battle group moved out of Al Jubayl and set up a non-tactical leaguer in the desert at Al Fadili. At this time, Tim's grandmother came to the fore and sent out food parcels with extra supplements which he shared with his troop. She was clever enough to replace the contents of the vinegar bottle with wine, and occasionally this was savoured with instant effect.

The other welcome gift from his father was a survival shower bag. When the water bowser passed by, they filled this bag and left it on the ground in the midday sun. Once the water heated up, Tim hung it over the barrel of the tank and they all had a quick wash to remove the superficial dirt. It wasn't the same as a good long soak, but it was better than nothing and an enviable luxury, which made a huge difference to their day to day routine and kept morale in the troop very high.

Tim's troop trained hard as part of the plan to attack directly into Kuwait with the American Marines until 15th November, when 7th Brigade was officially declared operationally ready. Then, frustratingly, the financiers imposed a restriction on their tank driving to less than 20 kilometres per week, so there was little to do and many soldiers suffered from boredom as they waited for news from home.

There was still much uncertainty about whether they would fight the Iraqis or return home following a diplomatic resolution. An important consideration about the timing was the fasting month of Ramadan. In 1991, this was due to start in mid-March and sensibly, it was considered inappropriate to fight a war with Muslim countries at that time. Therefore, United Nations Resolution 678, which was approved by the Security Council at the end of November, set 15th January as the deadline for Saddam Hussein to withdraw his forces back across the border.

In December, after 1st (United Kingdom) Armoured Division Headquarters and a composite 4th Brigade had joined the British deployment in Saudi Arabia, Iraq announced that it would use chemical weapons if the coalition attacked its forces. I knew how this would play on the minds of the British soldiers on the front line. Some of my troop in the Gulf had been interviewed by journalists from the *Nottingham Evening Post* and their fears about chemical warfare were right at the heart of the worrying article. I had been offered anthrax immunisation and turned it down because I did not believe the threat in Cyprus was realistic, but Tim and his soldiers kept taking their Naps tablets despite the adverse reaction some of them experienced.

It was not until just before Christmas that the decision was taken to transfer command of 1st (United Kingdom) Division from the Marines to General Fred Franks' 7th (United States) Corps. The wide left hook being considered by the high command to defeat Saddam Hussein's strategic reserve was ideally suited to the British tank formations. Effectively, it was something my regiment had practised often during the past decade, dating back to the exercises in Germany, when we developed the counter stroke concept in the Einbeck Bowl.

Just after Peter Barlow and the other British hostages in Iraq were flown back to England, it was decided to improve the protection of the tracked vehicles in the Gulf. Defence research establishments had designed some new armoured plates, which were bolted over the outside of tracks. The magnificent Royal Electrical and Mechanical Engineers craftsmen worked tirelessly under floodlights with their metal grinders and welding equipment to fit this modification, which was an important fillip to the combat troops in the desert.

After Christmas, Tim's troop flew back to Al Jubayl for rest and recuperation. The camp was very dull, so he hatched a plot with two other subalterns to drive a hire car into Dubai and spend New Year's Eve in a smart hotel. They took their civilian clothes and enjoyed a lavish dinner, but after weeks without alcohol, they became tipsy very quickly and only just made it to midnight before falling asleep.

Tim drew the short straw to drive them back into Saudi

Arabia at four o'clock in the morning. When he reached the border, he spent five minutes trying to persuade the customs official not to look inside the boot of the car, but there was a suspicion they might be smuggling alcohol into the kingdom, so he insisted. Tim opened the boot a couple of inches and suddenly the border guard dropped his jaw as he caught site of the arsenal of grenades, machine guns and ammunition which the troop leaders had brought with them. Much to Tim's relief, he was immediately waved through the fast lane, so they could all return to camp before first parade in the morning.

In the New Year, the training became more intense and they developed their multi-national co-operation through greater interaction with the American formations. The flat, featureless scenery became even more miserable when the cold, wet, windy weather arrived that month. Cries of "Gas, Gas, Gas!" were heard on a regular basis and added to the sense of foreboding. The start of the air campaign on 17th January brought home to them what was about to happen. Those who were not already heavy smokers increased their nicotine intake as the explosions made them think hard about their vulnerabilities.

The 17th/21st Lancer troops attached to the three battle groups in 7th Armoured Brigade were annoyed when they were told to remove their recognition signs. Displaying our beloved motto was an excellent way to reassure friends and family back home when they appeared on television news items, or in the daily press. It was understandable that the chain of command did not wish any units to be identified in photographs, because the operation depended on a complex deception plan along the border. However, this did not stop

Tim from flying his B Squadron 17th/21st Lancer pennant from his antenna during the twelve-hour move to the forward assembly area west of Al Qaysumah and throughout the whole of the ground war.

By the time he came under command of 7th Corps, I had taken the remainder of B Squadron back to Tidworth to join 19th Infantry Brigade as part of the planned arms plot move, but Tim maintained contact through the forces mail system, known as "blueys". Now the British troops became totally tactical in camouflaged squadron leaguers, just as they had practised in Canada. They dug trenches with overhead protection and maintained 24-hour guards, reacting immediately to the frequent chemical alarms and alerts.

The fratricidal engagement at Al Wafra at the end of the month increased their concerns. During a six-hour battle, a Coalition aircraft mistakenly attacked a United States LAV-25 personnel carrier, killing several marines. As a result, a number of preventive measures were taken by the Coalition and Tim's troop painted inverted Vs and displayed brightly coloured panels on their tanks in an attempt to avoid further tragic blunders.

The sense of apprehension continued into February, whilst the probing attacks along the border increased. Frustratingly, the British forces were ready to fight, but had to wait for the American Corps to come up to full strength. In the middle of the month, Tim was on guard in a trench with his outstanding gunner, Lance Corporal "Bunny" Warren, looking north over the border when a stealthy helicopter flew ten feet over their heads on another border raid. It was a reassuring display of military capability which made a big impression on Tim's troop and boosted their confidence about the imminent land campaign.

Eventually, Tim received orders from the battle group commander in a tent during the afternoon before the ground war began. The higher mission was to defeat the Iraqi tactical reserves, in order to protect 7th Corps' right flank. The next day he wrote his final letters home and made preparations for the advance into the unknown, whilst on two hours' notice to move. Finally, the order came and he joined the long line of vehicles which were queuing to cross the border. Although the American bulldozers of the 1st Mechanised Infantry Division, nicknamed the Big Red One, had cleared sixteen lanes, it still took several hours for the seething mass of armoured vehicles to pass across the control line, which was named New Jersey.

Approaching the breach, Tim switched on the green recognition lights of 7th Brigade, which distinguished his vehicles from the red lights of 4th Brigade. Beyond the staging area, he heard the distant rumbling of artillery and saw the flashes of gunfire reflected on the dust clouds, which extended across the horizon. The slow-moving vehicles would have been easy targets if Saddam Hussein's air force had been able to operate with impunity, so all the British troops were extremely grateful to the United States for ensuring they were not attacked from the air at this most vulnerable moment in the war.

Throughout the first night, the fog of war extended across the battlefield. Whilst Tim was crossing the breach, the first engagements with the enemy were being fought. Although the official despatch from the Joint Commander states that the Queen's Royal Irish Hussars' battle group was in the vanguard, a different battle group, under the Commanding Officer of the Staffordshire Regiment, cleared the first position on Objective Copper North.

Another of my troop leaders, Chris Frankland, was commanding a troop in the Royal Scots Dragoon Guards, which was also part of 7th Armoured Brigade. He had taken a Trabbie car on a boat from Cyprus to Turkey and then driven it through Yugoslavia back to the regiment before he joined up with his troops. He was an unconventional soldier, who was very effective in the field and well-liked by his soldiers.

A young Scottish tank commander, Ken Anderson, who later became one of my troop sergeants, suffered a mechanical breakdown in the breach and had to wait whilst his Challenger was repaired by the squadron fitters' section. As evening approached, he attempted to navigate his tank, together with the lightly-protected Royal Electrical and Mechanical Engineers, to the main part of the battle group, unaware that the ground was still held by the enemy because 4th Armoured Brigade had not begun its advance.

After some thirteen kilometres, he suddenly came across a large enemy force in their trenches on Objective Copper South. Night had fallen, so visibility was very poor and he advanced to within range of their hand-held anti-tank weapons before firing his machine gun, then dismounting and walking forward to the enemy position. Realising that he was unsupported, he nevertheless persuaded the Iraqi soldiers to surrender and captured a company strength position all on his own.

Ironically, four minutes after he left with his prisoners in tow, the position came under heavy artillery bombardment prior to the 4th Brigade assault. In effect, Ken managed to prevent the bloodshed that the artillery would have wrought and for this courageous and decisive conduct, he was deservedly awarded the Military Medal after the war.

After Copper came Zinc and a pause until dawn to collect everyone together. Tim gave instructions to his troop face to face and the three tanks drove forward into their over watch positions and settled into a night-time routine, scanning their front through the thermal observation gunnery sight, or Togs.

Togs was a brilliant British invention which changed the way the Army fought. Four years earlier in October 1986, when I was Adjutant, my regiment trialled this new equipment and showed off its merits to the divisional commander on the Soltau training area. Inevitably, the night he chose to visit was stormy, with the rain falling at 45 degrees to the ground. We set up the Commanding Officer's tank with A Squadron in support and arranged a variety of targets at different ranges for the General to view. Rather than squeeze him into the gunner's seat, we fed a remote lead from the computer inside the turret to a television screen in a large tent behind the tank.

During the rehearsal, everything that could go wrong did. The crews in the target vehicles lost communications and drove away wide of the mark. When we finally established a sequence which worked well, the storm picked up the tent and tossed it 25 metres away. Then the rain penetrated some of the electrical connections, so our electrician had to replace the leads.

Everything was sorted by the time the General arrived and so the technical demonstration went without a hitch. On a vile night, when British tanks would normally be blind, we were suddenly able to operate effectively. As a result of this impressive breakthrough, the tactical doctrine of the British Army changed and night fighting, which had depended completely on white light, became the physically exhausting activity which characterised the Gulf War.

* * *

As dawn approached on Tuesday 26th February, Tim waited in anticipation for the advance to contact. Although it was satisfying to have reached Iraq safely, there remained an overriding fear of the unknown because he had not yet encountered any enemy. His task was to rapidly clear a series of objectives by destroying enemy tanks and mechanised vehicles, whilst bypassing dug-in infantry positions, which were allotted to follow up formations to clear.

At the appointed hour, they set off to Objective Platinum, a regimental-sized enemy position. The two waves of tanks in the lead squadron drove across the desert looking for the first enemy target. Everyone was eager to ensure their guns worked, so many crews fired a round to their front, even though they saw nothing but scrub ahead. A sense of anti-climax began to descend on the troops; even the Canadian Prairie was more interesting than this!

Suddenly, an indistinct dot appeared on the horizon. The six tanks in the lead all used their lasers and discovered it was over six miles away; too far to fire their guns. They thought it would turn around, but it kept on coming at them and as it became more distinct in the magnified sights, they saw that it was an Iraqi fuel tanker. After another minute, one of the tanks fired, but the shell landed just short of the target. Then everyone joined in and the driver of the bowser suddenly realised he was under attack. Tim watched him sprint away from his vehicle and reach safety before the fuel exploded in a mighty fireball.

There was a collective sigh of relief at this first action, which helped to settle everyone's nerves after so much build up. The sky was clear, but a vicious wind was whipping up the sand to the level of the gunner's sight, making visibility difficult. His troop stopped about two miles short of Platinum and started engaging the enemy tanks.

Then out of the desert, three camels complete with gun-toting Arabs and soldiers on foot charged towards them. They couldn't bring themselves to shoot to kill, so they fired a warning burst from their coaxially-mounted machine gun, which did the trick. The objective was cleared quickly, and they realised that the Iraqi Army was not as resolute as they had feared. The rest of the day was consumed with many small actions engaging the enemy at long distance, firing and manoeuvring to avoid counter-attacks. By midday, they had started to catch up with the medium reconnaissance regiment, which had been pushed through at the start of the operation to prosecute the depth battle and was then withdrawn for rear security duties.

Tim had been issued with one of four sets of satellite navigation systems in the squadron, so he always found himself in the lead. His tank was hit by enemy fire as they approached the main position, but the wonderful British-designed composite armour protected the crew completely. Occasionally, when he took up a firing position, he would look up into the sky and see the familiar Lynx helicopters only ten feet above his tank, firing their missiles at targets beyond the range of his 120mm gun.

The heavy maintenance work which the troop had undertaken in Saudi Arabia proved to be a wonderful investment. Whilst other troops lost tanks with reliability and maintenance problems, Tim was able to manoeuvre his whole troop throughout the free-flowing battle. The fighting continued all day and into the night as he cleared Objective Platinum 2. By dawn on 27th February, he found himself overlooking Wadi al Batin, a wide valley marking the border between Iraq and Kuwait. They had only managed to snatch a few minutes' sleep here and there, so all his crews were now exhausted and whilst the remainder of the Division caught up, there was an opportunity to be resupplied with fuel and ammunition and to catch their breath.

At reveille, Tim asked Corporal Rush to ensure the crews in the neighbouring tanks were awake and ready to move on his signal. Weighed down by his webbing and wearing his chemical protection suit, this intrepid soldier ran across to the other tanks. The crews needed reminding about the routine, so it took some time for him to complete the task and return safely to Tim's tank.

As they drove across the sand, he heard what sounded like firecrackers outside the tank. At first he thought the noise might be coming from enemy machine gun fire, but then he realised that it was from the anti-personnel mines, which the tracks were setting off. It suddenly dawned on Corporal Rush that his early morning jog had been fraught with danger because he had run across a live minefield. Unsurprisingly, he did not volunteer to dismount from the tank for the remainder of the war.

There continued to be much confusion on the battlefield. Unfortunately, this led to several fratricide incidents, despite the precautions taken before the ground war. A platoon of the Royal Regiment of Fusiliers was hit by an American A-10 aircraft and the reconnaissance troop of the Queen's Royal Irish Hussars was attacked by an American Abrams tank, which had become disorientated in the dust and perceived the British formation as fleeing Iraqis. Mercifully, the Abrams only hit the reconnaissance vehicles with machine gun fire, rather than its main armament, but this was still very distressing. The Irish lost their tempers, boxed in the American tank and attacked it with pick axes and anything they could lay their hands on. The incident escalated to the highest levels and seriously threatened the coalition's unity of purpose. As a result, the most senior British officer flew by helicopter to personally resolve the issue and calm down the situation.

Apart from the muddle on the battlefield, there was also uncertainty about where 7th Brigade would go next. At some point, orders were issued to clear the wadi to the south west, but this was soon countermanded as it became clear that the next move would be into Kuwait. By then, Tim had the only working global positioning system amongst the front line troops, so he was again asked to lead the advance into the unknown.

He launched his troop across the wadi and accelerated to maximum speed. The clouds of dust made visibility very difficult, but he kept his eye on the satellite system and reported the grid reference points as his troop crossed the border, flying the B Squadron, 17th/21st Lancers' pennant. Once they secured Objective Varsity, they paused for the remainder of the brigade to catch up and by late afternoon they had set up a defensive position awaiting a final decision about their limit of exploitation.

That night they heard a rumour of a ceasefire. Everyone was excited about the prospect of peace and went to sleep hoping this would be confirmed in the morning. Eventually, orders were passed down the chain of command for the rapid move to Objective Cobalt astride the Basrah Road. Tim learned that the British Forces had to be there by eight o'clock to conform to a cease fire, so it became a mad dash across the scrubby desert. Leading the way for the battle group, he told his drivers to push the tanks to their utmost speed and they managed to squeeze 65 kilometres per hour out of the 70-ton beasts.

The excitement mounted the closer they came to the road. Everyone scanned the horizon, trying to pick out enemy positions, or vehicles. Then, just before the objective, Tim stopped to allow a reconnaissance helicopter to survey the road and after they assured him it was clear, he drove on to the tarmac surface at 0755 hours on 28th February. It was with a great sense of pride that he not only led the 7th Brigade formation to Objective Cobalt, but did so without losing any of his soldiers or vehicles in the fight.

When the news came through to England, I was thrilled to hear that my B Squadron soldiers had been the first complete British troop to cross the border into Kuwait. However, my pleasure was tinged with a desire to be with them on the Basrah Road and congratulate them in person. It must have been similar for the original leader of the 1953 British Everest Expedition, Eric Shipton, who was prevented from accompanying Sir Edmund Hillary when he eventually reached the summit; a sense of simultaneous delight and disappointment.

When we heard about the casualties, we were sad for the families of the 24 Service personnel killed in action and the other 23 who died during the operation. However, it was remarkable that the whole of the British Army death toll from hostile action in the Gulf War was fewer than the Coldstream Guards suffered during our shared operational tour in Cyprus in 1989.

For his logistics work in my squadron, Alf Smith was awarded the British Empire Medal, but it was disappointing that there was no formal recognition for the part Tim played in setting the standard for all the other armoured troops and leading the United Kingdom formation into Kuwait. It did appear to be a petty and perfidious action to deny the significant contribution of the 17th/21st Lancers to Operation Granby and I believe this was a contributing factor in the decision of several officers to resign after the war.

Handing over B Squadron after two years in charge, I said that I would never again experience such an exhilarating command appointment, but four years later I had to eat my words when I took another independent command to Bosnia at the height of the Balkans conflict.

Gulf War - Extract from Sergeant Kevin Griffin's diary

25 Feb G+1

Going to Zinc. Fire Support!
NBC Dress. Everybody Good Spirits
Advanced All Day All Night No Enemy
Saw First Prisoners Dead + Wounded
Ran Over Bomblets – OK

26 Feb G+2

Attacked Infantry Position Only Injured + Dead Left
Attacked Huge Position Destroyed Several T55's
Fired At 3 Times By Enemy Killing Is Very Impersonal
Over 900 Surrendered In 1 Position
Advanced Well Into Iraq
Letter To Miriam

27 Feb G+3

Attacked Another Position Took More Prisoners
Xed Minefields No Problems
Replened Twice Killed Several Iraqi Infantry
Advanced Into Kuwait Along Wadi Al Batin
US Tanks Engaged 22 Recce Troop
Went Thru Old Kuwaiti Tank Range

28 Feb G+4

Advanced West To MSR 20 Kms North Kuwait City
Cease Fire 0800 Local
T-62, T-63, 2S1, ZSU-23-4, BMP, BRDM, MTLB
Wrote To Miriam
Mines All Over. Windy Day
Cut Eye With Cam Pole No Stand To's!

CHAPTER 3

Bosnia 1995 – Operation Grapple

Seen from the angle of someone about to plunge headlong into it,
the turbulent stream of Balkan history had a new fascination.
Fitzroy Maclean

Dusk descended on the drab dwellings and deserted roads in war-torn Maglaj. The Bosnian Serb gunner scanned the valley to his front using the power traverse in his T-55 tank. He pinpointed the converted school house used as a base by the United Nations and instinctively checked the distance with his laser rangefinder. The commander turned to the loader and ordered him to select the special fragmentation round with the RDX and aluminium high explosive charge. With a clang, the breech shut and the gun settled.

Inside the school, I had just finished my supper and my soldiers were clearing the tables in the canteen. We had said farewell to our predecessors, the Household Cavalry, earlier that day. In taking over as the northernmost British troops in Bosnia-Herzegovina, we had to wear the blue helmets of the United Nations Protection Force, despite the well-reported concerns about its reputation. The talk at dinner was all about the first foot patrols through the shelled streets, the routes used to bring humanitarian aid into the town after the siege was lifted and our pet dog with its insatiable appetite for sausages.

Suddenly there was a deafening noise as a tank shell tore through the reinforced concrete wall. Darkness followed instantaneously as the white hot metal cut through our makeshift lighting system. Dust and plaster mixed with the smell of explosive to add to the confusion. This was no ordinary ordnance but a special round designed to break into fragments of shrapnel and cause maximum casualties in the crowded dining area. Shards of metal ripped through the flesh of six soldiers and buried into the plaster work of the school walls. A thousand red glowing stubs on the floor provided the only light for the soldiers to evacuate the base and head for the shelters.

Everyone knew what to do without the prompt of the alarm. I had prepared the squadron in Germany during an intensive period of training to respond specifically to this type of attack. As sixty soldiers found cover, the Quick Reaction Force mounted their light tanks ready to respond in self-defence.

The first commander into his vehicle was Lieutenant Peter Troup. He had rehearsed the orders I had given earlier in the day and knew them backwards. His job was to cover the move of his troop and the Royal Canadian Dragoon section, as they deployed to their predesignated firing positions. The Canadians were equipped with the tube-launched, optically-tracked, wire-guided, TOW anti-tank missile system, which significantly strengthened our capability.

It was common knowledge that the T-55 tank outreached the British recce vehicles. Our Scimitar light tank was equipped only with a 30mm Rarden Cannon and a machine gun because the British Army had a policy of reconnaissance through stealth, rather than fighting for information. However, during our training, I had designed an exercise to practise firing beyond the battle range of our tanks, so I was confident that our weapons could at least neutralise the enemy tank over two kilometres away.

Apart from the lack of firepower, Peter had another major concern. He knew the aluminium armour of the Scimitar would provide little protection against a direct hit from the enemy tank. For this reason, he adjusted the firing positions to ensure they were behind the concrete barriers, with just enough space to ensure the crest in front was clear.

He turned to his gunner next to him in the turret. Two minutes earlier, Lance Corporal Cowie had been walking into the main entrance of the base. When the tank fired, he ran into the darkness and confusion and snatched his weapon, webbing, body armour and helmet from a rack near the door. He dressed as he ran back outside and by the time he reached his tank, he was fully focused on what he had to do. He climbed into his seat and as soon as he was settled, he peered through the sights at the view ahead.

He had spent much of the day studying the heavy weapon positions on the far ridge line. Even so, it was extremely difficult to identify the T-55 tank, which only had its turret showing above the dug-in emplacement. Slowly, Cowie became used to the gloom and recognised what was known as the teardrop position, a key point of orientation. He laid the aiming point onto the target ahead and reported to his commander. By this time, Peter had switched on the wireless behind his seat to establish communications with the operations centre, where I stood waiting and listening with my head sets.

When the 100mm tank round hit the base, I checked the dining area and then headed straight into the operations room to control the battle. I wanted Peter to start shooting immediately, so I flung open the window and shouted to him to start firing. At moments such as these, it is strange how one's vocal chords can outmatch a 4.2 litre petrol engine being revved in neutral.

Seconds later, at exactly 8.30 pm, we fired the first high explosive round from our tanks. It missed. Carefully, Cowie corrected the point of aim and fired again. With relief, he saw a strike on the tank and instinctively called "target". He knew these rounds would not penetrate the frontal armour and the best we could hope for was to smash the sighting equipment and to achieve a mobility kill before the Canadian missiles came into action. If the Bosnian Serbs had failed to close their hatches and there were unprotected soldiers in the vicinity, then the effect would be greater. The Rarden Cannon had a rapid rate of fire and through a combination of slick loading drills and relaying, Peter quickly used up a belt of rounds, but this was only the start of the response.

On the eastern side of the base, another Scimitar, Call Sign Yankee Two Two, joined the fight, but without its normal crew. Sergeant Goble had been sorting out a problem with the water pump when he heard the explosion. He grabbed his webbing and climbed onto his vehicle, but the internal communications failed to work. He shouted down to the driver, Corporal Sarsfield, to dismount and fetch another tank from the protected area behind the base.

Goble cursed his luck, but then he saw a neighbouring Scimitar was missing a crewman. He ran across and jumped into the gunner's seat, joining Corporal Knight in the turret. Trooper Porter, normally a radio operator, was in the driver's compartment and he rapidly manoeuvred the vehicle into a position at the other side of the school. This part of the building was still being used as a sixth form by the teenagers of Maglaj, but fortunately, they had all returned home earlier in the afternoon.

Goble had already memorised the skyline around the target area. He was a specialist in recognising different armoured vehicles and quickly located the T-55 tank, following the tracer of Cowie's shots. He started firing with his day sight, but after twelve rounds, found he was losing the focus, so he switched to the image intensification night sight. Fortunately, the sky was clear. Shooting at a target two and a half kilometres away with a sight that is designed for only one thousand metres demands the utmost skill from a gunner, but the flashes of orange as the explosive hit the steel of the tank provided ample evidence that both tanks were now hitting their target.

In the meantime, Sarsfield had found another vehicle and had been joined by Lance Corporal "Bunny" Warren wearing his West Bromwich Albion shirt. He was on 15 minutes' notice and had just left the shower when the Serbs attacked the base. He only had flip flops on his feet and a towel around his waist, but this did not stop him from rushing straight to his vehicle and being ready to fire within four minutes, albeit in a strange order of dress.

Sarsfield shouted over to the Canadians, who were mounting their M-113 personnel carrier, and told them to follow his Scimitar to Fire Position Bravo. In the operations room, we registered this important moment, when Yankee Two Three escorted Call Sign Five Seven Hotel out of the compound twelve minutes after the attack. Meanwhile, I was anticipating a second attack from the T-55 tank or another heavy weapons system on the ridge line. Four days earlier, when I was travelling into Bosnia from Croatia, there had been a double strike on the school without a reply from my predecessor. Given these circumstances, it was probable that the Bosnian Serbs would repeat the same stunt if I didn't act fast.

The Canadians were also in the middle of their change over and so only one of their M-113 infantry vehicles was stationed in Maglaj at that time. This was commanded by Master Corporal Rehberg. His section was watching television when the attack occurred, but they reacted admirably and joined the Squadron radio frequency net before following Sarsfield's vehicle to their firing position.

Initially, the target proved hard for the Canadian gunner to locate through the red on black thermal sight. However, as the temperature of the target area increased with the explosions, it became easier to identify. I had already received special permission to use TOW missiles under the very strict United Nations Rules of Engagement, so there was no delay when Rehberg reported his system checks were complete and I ordered him to fire immediately.

The noise in the valley as the first missile set off will always be remembered by those of us there and brought a huge cheer of relief from the soldiers waiting in the hardened shelter. As the 28 kilogram missile sped away from its launcher at 200 metres per second, it left a trail of white smoke, which quickly evaporated into the darkening sky. TOW is not a "fire and forget" missile system, so the operator had to keep the aiming mark on the target all the while. The first missile, fired at 8.41 pm, blew away the emplacement in front of the tank.

Listening to the reports from the troops on the ground, I was not yet satisfied that the position had been neutralised fully and so I instructed the Canadians to fire again. The second missile malfunctioned and veered to the left towards the River Bosna, impacting harmlessly against the hillside. I instructed Rehberg to strike again, while the three Scimitars in the Quick Reaction Force continued to shoot their Rarden cannons at the enemy position. When the third TOW missile hit the target, I issued orders over the radio for all the troops to cease firing and move into hide positions, but to remain on immediate notice to re-engage if necessary.

Two things were clear at this stage of the battle. First, the attack had been sanctioned and co-ordinated at the highest level. This was evident from the jamming of the high frequency radio net, which could only be authorised by Senior Army Commanders. Second, NATO air support, which effectively was the fall-back reserve, would not be committed to the fight. This was made plain from a satellite telephone call with the United Nations headquarters in Sarajevo.

I had under command a New Zealand Tactical Air Control Party, led by Captain Kevin Scott, who had a very personal reason for wishing to join the party. Four days earlier, he had been helping in the observation post on the top floor of the school, when it was hit by the first tank attack. He had just taken over from Sergeant Goble when he noticed some activity on the confrontation line. This was not unexpected as there had been a drifting return to hostilities as the cease fire, brokered by ex-President Carter, approached its conclusion at the end of April.

In the observation post, Kevin scanned the houses occupied by Serb snipers. Out of the corner of his eye, he caught a flash from an area where a tank had been known to shoot into Maglaj. For an instant, he wondered where the target would be, but the next moment, he was thrown backwards into the room when the kinetic energy round punched its way through the corner of the building, three feet to his left. Dazed and confused, he found his way to the entrance and was assisted downstairs by the soldiers who rushed to his aid.

That week, he had also helped to clear the shattered homes in the residential areas. On Monday, a tower block close to the school had been targeted by Bosnian Serb artillery launching three white phosphorus shells at the apartments. The chemical reaction when this element touches human flesh is so ghastly that the Geneva Convention has banned its use as an anti-personnel weapon.

All this was going through Kevin's mind when he pleaded with the air operations centre in Sarajevo, but it was with considerable disappointment that he reported to me that although a pair of F-16 aircraft would be heard overhead, they would not be authorised for weapon release.

Apart from Kevin, the only person with me in the operations room was Sergeant Iain Findlay. As a veteran of the GulfWar, he had seen plenty of action during his military service, but this was different. As well as recording the battle sequence minute by minute, he was required to register the ammunition usage and monitor the evacuation of the base, which was co-ordinated by Staff Sergeant Dave Earp.

Dave was busy accounting for all the soldiers in the base. His job was made harder because there were so many men attached to the squadron who he had not met. Added to the New Zealand and Canadian contingents, there were combat support sections from the Royal Artillery and Royal Engineers and several logistic and administrative attachments which had just arrived and were harbouring in the school overnight.

The Royal Artillery team was completing its work on a new computer-based hostile artillery locating system. This trial had been highly successful and we had conducted a patrol earlier in the day, analysing new shell craters, in order to confirm the location of the long-range Bosnian Serb guns. This team was hosting a visit from their parent unit in Larkhill and changing over personnel.

The Royal Engineer section was clearing a secondary aid route which ran between Maglaj and Tesanj, a Muslim *Opština* in the hills to our west. My squadron's light tanks had to protect them each day because one of their light diggers had been hijacked at gun point earlier in the week.

Apart from these sections, I had a number of combat service support troops in the base. There were cooks from the newly-formed Royal Logistics Corps, clerks from the Adjutant General's Corps and teams from the Royal Army

Medical Corps and Royal Electrical and Mechanical Engineers to support the men and equipment.

* * *

Dave Earp was in his room on the first floor when the explosion rocked the base. He fumbled through the darkness, feeling his way along the corridor, not realising that he was walking through the zone of the worst effects of the devastation. He heard a cry for help and turned into the nearest room on his right, which was the transit accommodation for visiting units.

He peered through the gloom. On the floor in front of him lay a wounded soldier, Corporal Trevor Walker of the Royal Engineers. He was being comforted by his pal, Lance Corporal de Angelis. A large pool of blood was spreading around his legs, which were not where they should have been in relation to his body. Earp knew that the medics were downstairs, so he immediately left the room to hail one of them. On the way downstairs, he met Sergeant Cunningham, who was searching for a torch. Earp briefed him on the injured soldier and told him to help until a medic arrived.

As Cunningham entered the room, he saw the two soldiers on the ground. By now the pool of blood was so large that he realised that it was life-threatening. He pulled out a field dressing and applied it to the back of the right knee, which was the worse of the two, just as he had practised during our training at Sennelager in Germany.

In all his years of service in the Army, he had never come across anything like this. Despite applying successive dressings, he could not stem the blood. Fortunately, Private

Harper, a qualified medic, responded to Dave Earp's instructions and rapidly joined Cunningham and de Angelis. He applied a tourniquet and managed to control the blood flow. Walker was in a bad way, but still conscious. Harper tried to inject him with his morphine, but it failed, so Cunningham offered his syrette, which was inserted into Walker's thigh.

Harper cannulised the left arm and another medic who had arrived in the room, Private Lewin, did the same with the right arm. They ran Hartmann's solution into the veins, which was harder than expected due to the lost blood. Whilst they were doing this, Sergeant Cunningham went downstairs to the sick bay, to pick up some plasma and bandages.

He was met by a scene of chaos. It was fortunate that the sick bay had closed early that evening, because the tank round and a significant amount of shrapnel had caused havoc in the room. Normally, the evening sick parade lasted until 8.30 pm, but a dearth of customers had allowed the head of the Medical Section, Sergeant Wright, to lock his store two minutes before the tank round ripped through it. He was one of many who counted their blessings later that night when the dust settled.

Cunningham returned to Walker and started to apply the bandages as Private Lewin fetched a stretcher. As he descended the stairs, he was confronted with two further casualties. The first was Trooper James, a Scimitar driver with fourth troop. He had been standing in the dining area, queuing to buy some chocolate from the squadron bar, when a large piece of shrapnel hit him in the abdomen and knocked him to the ground. Fortunately, James had been wearing his body armour, which prevented a very serious injury, but he was still feeling as if he had been kicked by a mule. Lance Corporal Armiger, serving in the shop next to the trooper, was extremely lucky as he was not wearing his flak jacket. He helped James across the room to where the other casualties were being treated and Private Lewin placed him in the best position to alleviate the pain.

The next casualty was an artillery gunner scheduled to return to England after his six-month tour that week. He had a six-inch laceration to the head above the neck. Lewin dressed this wound and Sergeant Wright applied a neck collar, but they did not administer any morphine due to the wound's location.

After treating these soldiers, Private Lewin returned upstairs with the stretcher to where Corporal Walker was lying ready to be evacuated. Carefully, four soldiers transferred him onto the stretcher; Lewin carried the right leg, de Angelis held his head, Lance Corporal Johnston, who had arrived after the others, carried the left leg and Sergeant Cunningham carried the drips.

I had three ambulances in my squadron, one wheeled and two tracked. The wheeled vehicle was the fastest and we used this for Corporal Walker. Hauling him downstairs through the darkness and rubble was not easy, but within fifteen minutes of the attack, he was on his way to the operating table in the surgical unit in Zepce, a small Croat town twenty miles south where the United Nations maintained an administrative headquarters.

In the ambulance with Walker sat Warrant Officer Jones, visiting from Larkhill. He had been chatting to the artillery section in the entrance to the school, watching the setting sun as it dipped behind the hills and joking about what their first pleasures would be when they returned to England. This entrance area had been considered safe from attack, but seconds later, shrapnel and glass felled three of the assembled group, including Jones, who was hit in the right arm and left leg.

Private Wallbridge was the medic who dealt with this group. He started by elevating the limbs of the injured and administered his personal auto jet of morphine to Jones, as he had not been issued with one as a visitor. The time of treatment was recorded in ballpoint on his forehead so that those providing secondary care knew when the effects of the drug would wear off.

He attempted to put an intravenous drip into Jones' left arm, but no veins became obvious. As he increased the pressure, he felt a small vein in the forearm, but after two attempts without success, he deferred to Sergeant Wright, who also tried and failed. By this time, Corporal Walker had been loaded into the wheeled ambulance, so they postponed further attempts and assisted the warrant officer into the ambulance.

The road to Zepce was full of potholes created by shells and mines, so the journey was slow and bumpy. However, Privates Wallbridge and Lewin continued to attend Walker and Jones carrying out routine dressing checks, applying another litre of Hartmann's and releasing the tourniquet on Walker's leg, which had stopped bleeding.

As the soldier in charge of the medics, Sergeant Wright's main responsibility that night was to co-ordinate the casualty evacuation. He immediately assessed the priorities and reported to me in the operations room. When he read the names of the casualties, I suspected one was incorrect, so I asked him to check.

The British Army has a swift and efficient means of informing the next-of kin about injuries and deaths on operations. I knew how important it was to have accurate information because I had been the casualty visiting officer only ten months earlier when Corporal Robert Hawksley was killed in what the press described as a shambolic exercise in Canada. Sure enough, my suspicions were correct and it turned out that a wallet with an identity card had been incorrectly handed in to Sergeant Wright, who had assumed the soldier was a casualty.

Once we had transmitted the correct names to Zepce, Sergeant Wright returned to allocate casualties to ambulances. After he had dispatched Jones and Walker, he loaded the next three wounded soldiers into the tracked Samaritan, Call Sign Yankee One Four Bravo. This was one of the inherited vehicles which had been in Bosnia since the first British deployment in 1993. The Samaritan was in a very poor mechanical state and unsurprisingly, it broke down just outside our town. Fortunately, we had arranged this exact location as our ambulance exchange point, so the casualties were immediately transferred to another ambulance and taken to the operating table at Zepce.

Trooper James, who was later found to have bled three pints internally, was riding in the back with two soldiers from the artillery section, Sergeant Ritchie and Bombardier Turton, who had lacerations all over their bodies from shrapnel and flying glass.

The final casualty was the soldier on the reception desk, Corporal Dabell. With blood streaming from both legs, he headed for the two ISO containers which provided our hardened protection. As the first soldiers gathered in the nearest shelter, they saw a jagged hole in one side and a large piece of shrapnel buried in the other. They looked at each other and realised they would not be safe if the T-55 tank fired again, so they moved smartly across to the other shelter, which was better protected. There, Corporal Dabell was treated by one of my troop leaders, Johnnie Russell, before he was driven in the third ambulance to Zepce, where he was flown with Jones and Turton to Gornji Vakuf to have their shrapnel removed and wounds stitched.

As Corporal Dabell was unable to carry out his allocated responsibilities, we needed a volunteer to help clear the building with Dave Earp. Without hesitation, Corporal Packwood, one of the Scimitar crew commanders standing in the doorway, who was mercifully unhurt, even though his trousers had been ripped by the shrapnel and glass, stepped into the breach. First, he called a medic to deal with the casualties around him. Then, he took a deep breath and ventured into the darkness to check everyone had evacuated their rooms and there were no more casualties. Linking up with Earp, he worked from top to the bottom of the school until it was clear.

Back in the operations room, I was still fighting the battle. There were three considerations in my decision to cease fire. First and most importantly, I wished to ensure the total destruction of the T-55 tank. Without the ignition of fuel tanks or ammunition, this was hard to confirm, but after 30 minutes of firing without return, I was certain the enemy was defeated.

I was not able to work around the flank due to the dispositions of the warring factions on the confrontation line. The Bosnian Serbs had other armoured vehicles and heavy weapons on the ridge line and I did not wish to expose my troops to further attacks. The United Nations rules of engagement were very strict and allowed me only to fire in self-defence and not pre-empt any action.

Another constraining factor was to ensure that collateral damage to the civilian population was minimised, so we selected fire positions away from where the townsfolk lived. However, the critical factor was the strategic message I wished to send to the Bosnian Serb high command in Pale that the British Army would not be influenced to leave the country by attacks of this sort.

Although Maglaj was on the periphery of events in Bosnia, I knew there would be a ripple effect following this battle. If the attack in Maglaj was successful today, there might be another on the British troops in Gornji Vakuf tomorrow. The utility of our forces was being questioned by the media, as it appeared that humanitarian aid was reaching most parts of the country without the assistance of armed escorts. Many commentators were equivocal about Britain's role in Bosnia because we had failed to protect vulnerable civilians from the ethnic cleansing.

Acutely aware of the international context during this encounter, I was nevertheless savouring every minute. It is every combat soldier's ambition to lead his troops into battle and test his tactical ability against a real enemy.

Once I was satisfied that we could gain no further benefit by continuing the action, I ordered all the troops to cease fire. I felt it was important to keep an eye on the enemy position and the high-calibre weapons systems on the ridge line throughout the night. I called Johnnie Russell from the shelter and instructed him to take over from Peter and maintain a vigilant watch on the enemy positions.

We checked how much ammunition was used in the battle. Sixty-one rounds had been fired by the three Scimitars in addition to three TOW missiles by the Royal Canadian Dragoons. Our 30mm rounds were quickly replenished from Zepce, but the missiles had to come all the way from Visoko, 40 miles south of us, and it was commendable that they arrived within three hours of the battle.

Although I had taken over the area that day from the Household Cavalry, I was still missing more than half the troops in my squadron. The main party move had been delayed and my second in command, operations officer and sergeant major were all away. Therefore, Sergeant Findlay compiled the reports and returns in accordance with the standard operational instructions.

A number of plans had to be made for the remainder of the night and the following day. I was cautious about returning the soldiers into the school, but there was a very large room protected by two walls of concrete and after I worked out the angles of fire, I was satisfied this would be safe shelter. I asked Dave Earp to assemble the troops so I could speak to them.

There were many apprehensive faces when the group gathered. Corporal Packwood had updated them during the fight, but generally they knew little of what had happened in the past hour. In these situations, it is often easier to be busy and fully occupied than stuck in a steel box feeling helpless to assist, hearing the noise of gunfire and the cries for help.

Already one soldier had been identified as suffering from battle shock and there were clearly others who were at the limit of their experience. It was an old lesson from previous conflicts and made a lasting impression on me.

After summarising the events so far, I turned to the practical short-term requirements. I told Dave to fix the electricity and lighting. The chefs were dispatched to make hot drinks and provide food. Sleeping arrangements were centralised and everyone instructed to fetch their sleeping bags from their rooms. Finally, I told the other troop leader in the base that night, to conduct a perimeter check with his troop.

Soon makeshift light was installed using the emergency generator. By the dim 40-watt bulbs, the true scale of the devastation became apparent. My intrepid Intelligence Corps advisor established the point of entry and its trajectory. This made clear how fortunate we were not to suffer many more casualties. He realised that the path of the shrapnel had narrowly passed the basket of Kenny, the pet dog, who was the squadron's mascot. Intrepid found him outside and it was clear he was suffering from dog shock, so everyone made a fuss over him and fed him sausages, which quickly perked him up. If only humans were that easy to cure!

By this time, the F-16 aircraft were flying overhead to provide some comfort in the base. These were seen from Delta Four, an observation post under my command, overlooking the Blizna hill feature ten miles south of Maglaj. The crew there heard the noises of our battle as they echoed down the River Bosna valley during that chilly starlight night.

Even though it was the beginning of May, the weather was still cold in the Bosnian Mountains. We had been issued tropical wear for the summer tour, but everyone had brought sensible clothing, since we were not due to return until November. Johnnie Russell's troop now gathered their warm equipment together and made their way to their vehicles to relieve Peter and his troop, who were still watching the enemy.

They met about a quarter of a mile from the base, next to a derelict silo. They were good friends and confident in each other as they had spent the previous summer training in Canada together. After a short brief to explain the positions on the ground, Johnnie deployed his troop and settled into his tasks.

The soldiers in the base worked hard and by midnight, some form of order had emerged from the chaos. Most people found it difficult to sleep. Small groups of soldiers were comparing stories in the gloom, drinking hot, sweet tea. There was a video machine and to relieve some of the tension, someone put on a cassette. The choice of *Hellraiser 2* was beyond my logic, but it attracted a good-size audience of soldiers wearing flak jackets and helmets.

In the operations room, I was still formulating the plans for the following day. I ordered a full stand to arms just before dawn, in case the Bosnian Serb Army took the option to attack again. Reveille was set for 4.45 am and I had to adjust the whole operations cycle to take account of the requirement for a permanent protection group on the ground.

I set the priorities of work for the remainder of the squadron with the main effort channelled into clearing the school of rubble and debris and improving the physical protection where we could. The principal problem was the impending arrival of the 40 soldiers in the main party, who would bring my command to its full complement and result in 120 soldiers in the base. Fundamental questions about the accommodation had to be addressed, but for now, there was a hostile enemy to monitor.

After a lengthy period in one static position, Johnnie decided to move his vehicle. His driver had set his cruise control to keep the engine ticking over and fallen asleep. Suddenly he moved his cramped position and knocked the gear into reverse. The revs were so high that the vehicle started to move rapidly through the darkness with no one steering. Johnnie shouted at him to put his foot on the brakes, but the vehicle accelerated through a wooden fence towards an inhabited cottage. Fortunately the driver just managed to avoid hitting the building, but this did not stop the irate owner seeking financial compensation from me the following day.

Johnnie took up a new position and after about an hour, at 3.30 am, he saw a small blip in the sky above the ridge line. At first, it wasn't clear what this was, but from the speed it became apparent that a helicopter was approaching the Serb tank position. He reported to the operations room and we pondered its significance. It was certainly possible that a senior officer with reinforcements was coming forward to issue orders to attack the next day, but it was more probable that the helicopter was evacuating casualties to the hospital in Doboj.

In 1995, the 20-mile road between Maglaj and Doboj formed part of the confrontation line. However, before the war, this had been the main route for holiday traffic from Hungary, Romania and other northern countries to the Dalmatian coastal resorts. In the 1980s, twenty thousand cars a day used it at the peak of the holiday season, bringing with them the economic benefits of their tourism. The road followed the River Bosna through a spectacular valley, which now provided rugged perches for heavy machine gun emplacements overlooking the road like vulture pits. As Johnnie watched, another two helicopters arrived at the scene. It was impossible to identify which type of aircraft landed in the vicinity, or the exact location.

As he looked out of his turret, a mist began to rise from the valley floor. This was not unexpected because Maglaj had been known as a foggy town ever since its name was recorded in the fifteenth century. The locals told a story of an Ottoman ruler in the now derelict castle who believed the cloud would act as a cushion. The result of his attempt to prove this to his courtiers was predictable and his heirs never made the same rash claim.

Before the war, the population was a multi-ethnic community of ten thousand. This comprised 45 per cent Muslim, 35 per cent Orthodox Serb and 20 per cent Catholic Croats. It was described in tourist books as a centre for big game hunting and fishing, but the bears and wolves had long since disappeared and most of the fish had two heads due to the pollution from the industrial steel factory in Zenica. Ironically, one of the benefits of the war had been an improvement in water quality in the past two years.

The mist prevented Johnnie's troop from gaining any further information about the enemy activity. However, it also provided excellent cover for our own work and back in the base, the gas cookers were being lit, reveille was being called by the guard and the soldiers were being shaken from their short slumber.

Before the sun burned through the fog on the fourth

Corporal Gutsell in the Observation Post which was hit by a tank shell on 29th April 1995, the day before I arrived in Maglaj.

The left of arc view from the Observation Post; the tank position is on the left of the ridge line. The school basketball court was unused for three years.

Corporal Mallin with the head of the 100mm 16kg tank shell which caused so much devastation on Wednesday 3rd May, the day I took over responsibility in Maglaj from the Household Cavalry.

Spotty Dog, the checkpoint where the ambulance exchange point was located on 3rd May and which I subsequently used as my headquarters.

Maglaj School at 3.40 pm on 6th July 1995. The Chief of the General Staff, who had been my Brigade Commander in 1983, meets soldiers who defended the United Nations base and evacuated the casualties from the school after the tank attack on 3rd May.

Back in Germany, where Corporal Bunny Warren is introduced to HRH Princess Alexandra.

Maglaj from Route Dobbin in the west. The high ground in the distance was held by the Bosnian Serb Army which pounded the town with rockets and heavy weapons, including white phosphorus artillery shells.

The Tactical Air Control Party's M-113 tracked vehicle and a Scimitar from the Quick Reaction Force in its firing position behind the school.

morning in May, we received our first visit from Bosnian national television, who wished to run an item for their daily news programme. I had just finished a hearty breakfast of bacon, scrambled eggs and the delicious bread baked by local wives in Maglaj. I took a large mug of NAAFI tea outside to meet the Bosnians with their video camera, because I wished to use the opportunity to speak to the people on both sides of the confrontation line.

I was under no illusion about Bosnian television and knew it was politically controlled by the government. However, the message of intent to the Serbs was really important, so I used one of the five interpreters employed in the base. The most experienced of these was a former teacher in the school, Barbara Panic. She was a Croat, but remained in Maglaj when it was isolated because she had an elderly mother who refused to leave her home in the centre of town.

I started by saying to the Serb Commander that we were not there to fight them, but if they attacked us, we would hit them much harder than they hit us. I reassured the local people that Great Britain would not desert them, but before the questions turned political in nature, I took the crew into the base to film some of the evidence of the attack. As the interview continued, I had to stop myself smiling as I was using so many words beginning with R – repulse, robust, resolve, response. These reminded me of the speech in Monty Python's *The Life of Brian* when Pontius Pilate ordered his men to "welease Wodewick".

The departure of the film crew gave me the opportunity to inform a wider network of friends and colleagues at home. After informing the rear party in Germany about the tank battle, my interpreter told me that the Mayor had invited me to visit whenever I wished. Whilst the clear up in the school started in earnest, I set off in my short wheelbase Land Rover for the *Opština*, where the Mayor had his office.

★ ★ ★

Previously, I had become involved in Bosnia soon after the first British troops deployed there in 1993. As Chief of Staff of the Brigade in Nottingham, I had to find a volunteer from the military works force to deploy at short notice to lead some of the civil engineering projects. The best man for the job was a fine family friend, Captain Paul Arsenault; a Canadian officer attached to the British Army. He was tremendously successful and it was a great pleasure to complete the citation for his outstanding work after he returned safely the following year.

The second connection was Captain Milos Stankovic, who worked for me as a staff officer, having previously been an advisor to General Rose. Milos provided me with valuable strategic insights into the work in Sarajevo before he was called back for a second tour in 1994. Before he departed, I organised the announcement of his MBE, which he recorded in his book *A Trusted Mole*.

Milos sent me regular updates from Bosnia. He wrote a long letter after he organised the first helicopter trip to General Mladic's headquarters in Banja Luka for General Rose and the then United States Director of Strategy in the Pentagon, Lieutenant General Wesley Clark. I was greatly saddened when Milos was arrested unfairly by the military police just after he started his Army staff course in December 1997.

The third connection was an officer in the next door Territorial Army battalion, Murray McCullough. He helped set up and later led the European Union administration of Mostar after they assumed responsibility for that town in July 1994. Murray provided me with further insights into the mentality of the Balkans, with a number of transcripts of interviews with politicians and military commanders about the disagreements within the state leadership.

Whilst I was posted to Nottingham I had the idea to send a squadron from my regiment to Bosnia as one of the two independent commands in theatre. The British Army had run out of reconnaissance troops, following the Defence Review cuts after the Gulf War, known as "Options For Change". This deficiency had been recognised by the Army's executive committee, which had agreed to form a third regiment, but funding was not yet available and so a short-term solution had to be found.

The answer, to my mind, was to convert a Challenger tank squadron to the lighter weight Scimitars used in Bosnia. My regiment had re-roled in this way in the 1980s when I was Adjutant, but this time it would have to be done in six months rather than the two-year preparation time considered normal. I had to "walk the corridors of power" in the summer of 1994 in London, Bovington and Germany, to ensure my squadron was selected and then appeal to my Brigade Commander for an early release, so I could supervise the conversion and training, which we completed in record time. Part of the preparation included a comprehensive recce to Maglaj.

On my first visit, the road journey through Bosnia contrasted nature in all her glory with the tragic work of hate-filled armies. We used the safe route created by the Royal

Engineers, which cut through the mountains from Tomislavgrad past the brilliantly turquoise Lake Ramsko to the town of Prozor. Here we were warned that Bosniacs had faked accidents in order to claim money from the United Nations, so we gave the local traffic a wide berth.

After Prozor, we passed the Croat pockets in mid-Bosnia with checkpoints manned by emotional Federation police. The final stretch into Maglaj offered a sad sight. From the abandoned Natron factory, which provided employment for many people before the war, there was increasing evidence of ethnic cleansing. Several houses had been burned after the Washington-brokered agreement and these underlined to me that the relationship between the so-called Federation allies remained tense and fragile.

We left the road at a set of tunnels where three Danish Aid workers were killed in 1993. They were in a crowd of ten civilian truck drivers, delivering aid to the UNHCR depot in Maglaj, escorted by a platoon from The Prince of Wales' Own Regiment of Yorkshire. Foolishly they were gathered around the entrance of the tunnel when the Bosnian Serb T-55 tank fired a shell that impacted on the wall, fragmented and scythed through the group. Ever since that incident, the tunnels had been avoided by local traffic, which sneaked through the back streets under cover.

As I drove in to the town for the first time, I was shocked by the wanton damage to the civilian buildings and infrastructure. The mutilation sustained by two years of artillery and tank attacks was widespread. For example, the famous mosque of Kursumli Dzamija was in a pathetic state with its polygonal minaret looking as if it would collapse at any moment.

We drove the last four hundred yards to the base at full speed, because the road was overlooked by snipers with a reputation as fierce as those in Sarajevo. One had recently slain a civilian planting his vegetables in a field. Allegedly, he was killed with a head shot at eight hundred yards.

It was a considerable challenge for my troops to remain neutral in our situation. Although this was an important principle for the United Nations, our credibility was dependent on what tangible support we provided to our hosts in terms of protection, money, construction and aid. The locals informed me that although the ceasefire was just about holding, as soon as Ramadan was over, the BiH Army would begin a number of offensives in order to regain land lost in the past three years.

* * *

The Mayor of Maglaj, Suleman Delic, had served as an artillery lieutenant in the Yugoslav Army twenty years earlier, so he understood the military mind as well as politics. Apart from one posting to the Adriatic, he had lived his 45 summers in the Maglaj pocket. He was a stocky, muscular man with a full head of hair. The lines on his face were testimony to the stress he had been under for the past three years, but he appeared to have borne it well, as he still had a sparkle in his eye.

He handed me a letter of sympathy for the injured soldiers which my interpreter, Haris, translated. Over a Bosniac coffee, I thanked him for his support and reiterated the message that we were not there to make war, but nor would we shirk our responsibilities. I met Delic many times during the next six months and it was comforting to establish a sound base at this first meeting. Clearly he could make life very difficult for my squadron if he wished, so it was important not to antagonise him. Once he realised that I was not interested in the wider political issues about which I had no influence, such as the arms embargo, our relationship developed well.

I returned to the school to find it swarming with visitors. A pair of European Union monitors arrived seeking sustenance and a delegation from the International Committee for the Red Cross asked about the incident. The public information officer for Sector South West arrived to write a news release. They all asked my opinion about the reasons for the attack.

The failure of the United Nations to secure an extension to the Cessation of Hostilities Agreement was certainly part of the reason, as this was important to the Bosnian Serb Army. They saw the United Nations troops assisting the Federation war effort by sustaining the internal lines of communication, which released scarce resources for troops and equipment.

They also believed this allowed the greater proportion of Muslim men to be drafted for military service and while sanctions were imposed on Serbia, there were no restrictions on Croatia which was openly resupplying the front line. Serbia under Milosevic, faced with political isolation, cosied up to other pariah regimes such as Colonel Gaddafi's Jamahiriya. The irony of the Brotherly Leader aligning himself with Orthodox Serbs against Balkan Muslims was not lost on us in Northern Bosnia.

I did not believe the attack in Maglaj was linked to the

Croatian offensive which had just reclaimed land from the Krajinian Serbs. The most probable scenario was that the head of the Bosnian Serb Army, General Mladic, and his political counterpart, Radovan Karadžic , wished to create the conditions under which Great Britain and France, whose governments were unwilling to take unilateral action, might make a joint withdrawal. This would leave the remaining contributors in an untenable position and cause the collapse of the United Nations Mission.

If the Bosnian Serbs believed they had achieved a partial success by the removal of the Union Jack from the school in Maglaj, this would provide succour to their policy of attacking other United Nations bases. Thus, I saw it as my duty, despite the obvious vulnerability of the school, not to withdraw. The issue then became one of improving the protection of the base, building a capability to deter further aggression and dispersing non-essential troops around my area of responsibility.

Whilst I formulated the plans for this strategy, the most pressing requirement was to prepare for another possible attack at dusk. Before lunch I gathered my troop leaders together and worked out some different firing positions on the ground, just in case the Serbs focused on the ones we had used before.

At 11.50 am, there was a crack and thump as a sniper fired a high-velocity rifle over our heads. For those who had completed Northern Ireland tours, this was a familiar noise, but it was not included in the United Nations training package, so there were many soldiers and officers who appeared quite startled. I was more relaxed and laughed when several of the group with me dived for cover because I knew we were perfectly safe behind the building. With a six-month tour ahead of us, displaying frayed nerves did not gain anyone's respect.

The tension increased palpably as we approached sunset. Communications were checked and Johnnie Russell's troop mounted their vehicles and prepared their guns for firing. The Canadian crew peered through their thermal sight for an indication of tank movement on the ridge line. More importantly, two NATO aircraft arrived on schedule to circle overhead, high in the sky, and this more than anything provided reassurance to the remainder of the troops sheltering in the collective protection.

There was no sense of anti-climax, just relief that the worst case scenario had not been realised. I maintained twenty soldiers at a high alert state through the night, but it passed peacefully and I managed to sleep fitfully for a couple of hours after midnight.

The intense sniping continued throughout the month of May, but the battlefield discipline of my squadron was outstanding and we suffered no casualties. Winning the first fight was hugely influential for the tactical success of the remainder of operational tour. I worked hard on the relationship with Delic and the BiH Brigade Commander, Huzo Durakovic, and as a result we secured privileged access and freedom of movement.

The strategic effect lasted several weeks. During this lull, we rebalanced the squadron and set up a main headquarters location at a checkpoint named Spotty Dog on the boundary between the Croat and Bosniac areas. This white villa, which had been a roadside stop for travellers before the war, received its nickname from the first British soldiers into Maglaj because it was pockmarked with hundreds of bullet holes. All the fixtures and fittings had been looted, so we used United Nations plastic sheeting to cover the windows and a carpenter made a couple of makeshift doors for us.

By 25th May the political situation had changed dramatically. It was explained to me by Mayor Delic that the Federation would prefer the United Nations to leave if it meant the arms embargo was lifted. This message was passed to the highest levels in Sarajevo and soon afterwards, a NATO air attack was authorised on the Bosnian Serb ammunition store outside Pale.

The focus of the world was again directed toward Sarajevo. Like some attention-seeking teenagers, the Bosnian politicians took perverse pleasure from the global media interest that focused on their recently recognised war-torn nation. I was in Zepce when the alert state was raised in case of retaliatory attacks by General Mladic and returned to Maglaj just as three artillery rounds hit the town, one of them causing my driver to swerve around the debris.

The Bosnian Serbs argued that everyone had contravened the ultimatum, but the United Nations only targeted one side. Their response was predictable; apart from the three rounds fired into Maglaj, they also shelled the so-called safe area of Tuzla, killing more than sixty people. Another tactic, used previously, was the seizure of United Nations monitors as hostages. I warned my soldiers about the possibilities of capture and reinforced all the daily patrols to ensure we were not perceived as a soft target. It was disturbing that others did not do the same and subsequently to see peacekeepers being used as human shields and the French soldiers killed at Vbranje Bridge on 27th May.

The next day, I took over responsibility for the United Nations base in Jelah. The Devonshire and Dorset Regiment had a company there which had been re-tasked to join their battle group further south. They managed to withdraw their Warrior fighting vehicles with great difficulty and I could only replace them with the troop led by Lieutenant Ed Carrell, because I was stretched across a very wide area. To reach Jelah, we had to drive through Tesanj, the tough *Opština* run by a brutal chief of police, Semsudin Mehmedovic, who was indicted for war crimes after the conflict.

Jelah itself was no safer than Maglaj, as the base was overlooked by the Bosnian Serb Army. A crater in the road by the entrance served to remind everyone that it was easily in range of their artillery. That day proved to be the longest day of the operational tour for me and the only Sunday when I failed to attend our Padre's ecumenical service in Zepce.

By the time I returned to Maglaj in the evening, word of the capture of British soldiers in Gorazde was reaching us. Information from the chain of command was sketchy, but with the news from satellite television, I passed a timely warning around my squadron. During supper, three artillery rounds landed nearby. One killed an old woman picking vegetables in a field, one split a tree and the third landed on the unused railway line next to Spotty Dog. I was well aware that for us, life returned to normal twenty minutes after the "all clear" was sounded, but for the family grieving a grandmother, it would never be the same again.

On Monday, I met with the BiH Army commander of 37 Division in Tesanj, Nedzad Ajnenadjic. He appeared to be a fair man, with whom I could deal in a straightforward manner. My next meeting was with Mehmedovic, who had a ruthless reputation as a warlord, dominating every aspect of civilian life in the area. His personal vehicle was an M-80 armoured personnel carrier in blue and white paint, which sat in pristine condition outside his headquarters.

I was surprised at his appearance and age, judging him to be under forty. His large office was more European than I expected and was spotless, apart from the ashtrays. I noticed he smoked expensive American cigarettes, rather than the local brand which was all anyone else could obtain.

We had a short discussion. He declared that I would only be allowed to move on routes agreed by him and complained about the damage caused by the United Nations tracked vehicles. I explained that the ground pressure of a Scimitar light tank was less than a soldier with a rucksack on his back and quoted the Status of Forces Agreement, which provided the overarching freedom of movement for the United Nations. He interrupted me and made it clear that he did not recognise this government document and in his area, he made the rules. However, he did agree to allow me to rotate my Scimitars through a routine operating cycle every three days and with this small concession, I departed.

For the next month I was incredibly busy with the stretched span of command, supervising our routine in three patrol bases, three checkpoints and the observation post overlooking the Blizna. The increased patrolling made huge demands on the tank fleet, but the outstanding detachment from the Royal Electrical Mechanical Engineers worked their magic on the ancient vehicles, some of which were older than the soldiers.

There were contrasting rumours about our future role. On the one hand, I provided a detailed assessment of the equipment required to re-role my squadron to full combat operations, in order to lift the siege of Sarajevo. At the other extreme, I was asked to update the withdrawal plans, which had already been leaked to *Newsweek* magazine. This required a detailed recce of the alternative routes out of our area which I might have to use. It took six hours to drive to all the locations where I commanded soldiers in the Maglaj Finger, so the analysis had to be completed over a week-long period. I concluded that it would be nigh on impossible to fight our way out of the valley against a determined enemy who wished to prevent our departure, not least because there were so many culverts on the main roads and tracks.

That week the artillery attacks increased significantly and we witnessed 21 explosions in Maglaj. However, the statistics for machine gun bursts and small arms fire remained consistent at about four thousand in the whole area.

We had a sudden surge of British press arriving in our town. Amazingly, there were not too many misquotes in the articles which followed the five visits. Most of these passed without incident, but the *News of the World* reporting team left a lasting impression. After they arrived unannounced, we provided them with the sort of story they prized, showing off British soldiers helping the local population. They left us just before lunch, but as they drove out of town, they ignored our advice and foolishly stopped to take a photograph in a restricted area. Inevitably, they were spotted by the Bosnian military police, which promptly arrested them and escorted them to the local headquarters.

As they were British citizens in distress, I felt obliged to provide some assistance as soon as I heard about the problem. After a long negotiation, I eventually managed to have them released, but without their camera equipment, worth thousands of pounds, which remained confiscated. The photographs are probably still tucked away in the bottom drawer of some security department in a Bosnian building. However, I did not weep for them too long since their next assignment was in Los Angeles, where they wrote an exclusive article with the front page headline "Hugh Told Me I Was His Sex Fantasy" after they persuaded Divine Brown to expose her "astonishing" story.

I also had to bail out my soldiers a number of times when they were arrested by local police and army commanders. At a lengthy meeting with the Maglaj Mayor, he explained how attitudes were hardening throughout the country. He questioned me about the United Nations Secretary General's recommendations to pull out of the safe areas and withdraw, which I countered with James Bone's opportune article in *The Times*, describing how the Security Council was set to "trample over" the Secretary General's recommendations.

He remained unconvinced and made the pessimistic prediction that the safe area of Srebrenica would fall by the end of the month. Superficially, I brushed this statement aside, but there was something about the intensity of his insistence that came through the interpretation and made me take note of his concern. When I pressed him on this issue, he stated that the BiH Army would not continue their defence of Srebrenica as they considered its loss would result in the Arms Embargo being lifted.

I started to make my departure. Before I stood up, he thrust a piece of paper into my hand. When I looked at it, I saw a bill for 1142 Deutschmarks for six weeks of bread eaten by the first infantry company based in Maglaj the year before. I promised that this and the water bill would be paid promptly, and I was delighted when the efficient Quartermaster in Zepce paid it by the end of the week.

On 15th June another Security Council Resolution was agreed. This allowed a multinational planning team with a reserve force to be set up in Theatre. The Force comprised a French brigade near Mostar, our British 24th Airmobile Brigade, which was already based at Ploce, and a third brigade located out of theatre. However, it was clear that these were never intended to change the nature of the peacekeeping; they were designed merely to provide the United Nations command in Sarajevo with a tactical option between a strongly-worded protest and an air strike.

Despite the worsening situation elsewhere, we continued to achieve great success in the Maglaj area. On 12th June, we sent our first joint patrol along the former confrontation line. I joined Johnnie Russell, who took half his troop to meet with BiH and HVO soldiers at a village called Fojnica. We climbed the steep hills and saw where the fighting had taken place from a series of shallow trench systems.

The countryside was stunning. The sharp contrasts of colour between the golden fields, lush green trees and azure sky reminded me of a Pre-Raphaelite canvas painted by William Holman Hunt. The setting would have inspired Thomas Gray to write some idyll. It was only when one looked at man's contribution to the canvas that reality intervened.

* * *

The much-heralded Bosnian offensive was launched on 17th June. This brought with it a further clampdown on United Nations movement. By delivering children to hospital and other clever ruses, we managed to keep our routes open, but we had to complete a ridiculous amount of paperwork for this to happen.

The key was to relentlessly keep a sense of humour and continuously nag them to allow greater freedoms. Rather like a garrulous farmer walking his boundaries, every day I drove around the area and met as many people as I could. Both the Croats and Bosniacs separately told me that at the local level, they respected us for not tamely accepting the restrictions and as a result, we had greater freedom of movement than any other United Nations troops in the country.

Early in July, we heard about the increasing tension and attack in Srebrenica by the Bosnian Serbs and wondered why the Dutch peacekeepers did not use their TOW missiles, or the Special Forces, which had been so influential in saving Maglaj the previous year. Delic was right. It appeared neither the BiH High Command nor the Netherlands government were willing to continue with the current situation, so General Mladic's forces were allowed into the area on Tuesday 11th July.

We read about and heard the moral outcry from the international media. Commentators repeated all the accusations about the impotence of the United Nations that they published at the time of the hostage crisis. However, when we looked beyond the headlines, no new ideas were presented to avoid the humiliation. French politicians called for a military response. However, from my perspective it was already too late and the next safe area, Zepa, with a small Ukrainian peacekeeping contingent, was also vulnerable.

I was asked to provide a convoy of trucks and escorts to collect civilians from Srebrenica gathering at Potocari, but we were prevented from moving south by the BiH Army. Bosnian television produced images of distressed mothers trying to find their children in refugee camps around Tuzla. However, they did not mention the massive effort of the UNHCR to provide tents, bedding and food, which saved the lives of many.

We were warned that a small village called Biljacici, on the edge of Zavidovici, was being prepared to be used by the displaced families. In Zenica, they were building camps to accept five thousand people. However, it was noteworthy that in both places, the local population did not welcome this prospect because their resources were already overstretched.

It only took a day for the fall of Srebrenica to have an effect on relationships in our area. The Mayor and the Brigade Commander in Maglaj said they would do their best to ensure nothing got out of hand, but there were several people in the town whose attitudes had hardened against the United Nations.

I had to sort out the release of several soldiers from trumped-up detention charges. Fortunately, I had dealt with this sort of thing in a previous job in Honduras when Omani and Japanese adventurers were arrested by the military police in La Ceiba for wearing green trousers, which they purchased in an army surplus store. I knew that anything could be achieved with tact and diplomacy, but I would not allow my soldiers to be placed in a situation where they were being verbally abused by an officious self-important bully.

On one occasion, I instructed one of my Scimitar light tanks to drive to the police station from the north and another from the south and sent in my second-in-command to speak softly, but make them fully aware that we were not there to play games. After a ten-minute discussion, the soldiers were released and the matter was closed. It was another example of how a robust stance was the best way of dealing with the warring factions. Again, I could not understand how this vigorous approach was not implemented by the United Nations in Srebrenica.

As the tragedy to our east unfolded and the mass graves were exposed in newspapers around the World, the Croatian war machine rolled into action in the south. Tons of Teutonic tourists clogged the coastal routes as they scrambled home to Germany. With 100,000 well-armed troops on call, the result was inevitable and very rapidly the confrontation line was re-written as the Bosnian Serbs retreated across the Krajina.

Elsewhere, the Federation captured the Komar feature near Dornji Vakuf and eyed up Jajce, with its electricity power station and radio communications, as the next important objective. This historic town was where the last king of Bosnia lived before he was executed by the Turks in 1528. It also played a vital part in the resistance movement against the German occupation in the Second World War, being the location where Fitzroy Maclean made contact with Tito when he headed the British mission sent by Churchill to Yugoslavia.

A sure sign of the changing intent of the international community came with the decision to pull out the British troops from Gorazde. We were warned about all sorts of possibilities by our chain of command in Gornji Vakuf. In the meantime, I continued with my set mission and our programme of patrols and humanitarian work. In the final week of August, my squadron recorded 700 explosions and 11,000 machine gun bursts, as well as small arms fire. Everywhere the confrontation line was ablaze with fighting. Casualties mounted as more men were drafted into the three fighting armies, while their women and children worked the fields in what was a prolific harvest that year.

Unfortunately, there was another headline accident when the vehicle carrying the American negotiators for Richard Holbrooke's team ran over the edge of the infamous road on Mount Igman. I am uncertain whether they were involved in the NATO planning, but soon afterwards we hosted a visit from the Deputy Commander of Land Forces and at nine-thirty that night we received a telephone call to expect air strikes in our area.

Shortly before 0200 hours the twelve soldiers on duty in my squadron, and a few others awake at that time, became aware of a noise like rumbling thunder from the night sky. These were the EF-111A Ravens and EA-6B Prowlers jamming the air defence systems and the F-16 and F-18 strike aircraft destroying them with their anti-radar missiles.

The well planned attack of fifty three aircraft against forty two targets was in response to an incident in the Sarajevo market square the previous day, when thirty seven people were killed and another eighty wounded. Inevitably, the Bosnian Serbs denied responsibility for the mortar bomb which caused this tragedy. Certainly, there was conflicting evidence about the source. The artillery locating team, which had done so well in Maglaj, was now in Sarajevo and they subsequently informed me that their computer system did not identify a launch site from the Bosnian Serb positions.

Nevertheless, with the complete withdrawal of the United Nations troops from the safe areas, including the British troops from Gorazde, there was little the Bosnian Serbs could do to retaliate. Once the air defence systems were neutralised at a cost of only one French Mirage, the subsequent waves of attack concentrated on the heavy weapons and ammunition dumps using laser guided and conventional bombs.

These attacks changed the attitude of the Bosniacs in our favour again. I was always surprised how well informed many of the soldiers on the checkpoints appeared. They were all interested in whether NATO had bypassed the United Nations chain of command and in particular the senior envoy, Yasushi Akashi. Fortunately, I could confirm from my own knowledge that the United Nations military commander, Lieutenant General Janvier, had worked closely in concert with the NATO commander, Admiral Leighton Smith in the planning. However, it was abundantly clear that this action had projected NATO as the new enforcer of peace in Bosnia.

After 3,000 sorties, which was half the number flown in the Gulf War by the Royal Air Force, Richard Holbrooke secured Bosnian Serb agreement to withdraw their heavy weapons from Sarajevo. Shortly afterwards, the first aircraft to fly to Sarajevo since April touched down to the cheers of the French soldiers, who unloaded a symbolic cargo of wheat flour.

This effect was also felt in my area of operations. The BiH Army seized Route Duck, linking us directly to Tuzla. The Bosnian Serb Army in the Ozren Mountains withdrew north of Zavidovici and a large Bosnian flag was seen flying on top of the Blizna.

There was no doubt the Holbrooke plan heralded the beginning of the end of the United Nations peacekeeping operation. Attitudes were typified on 2nd September, when an American soldier refused to serve with the United Nations. Instead, the proposed NATO peace implementation force had an extra dimension and held more credibility with the locals.

As I was writing a letter in my cabin at one of the bases, I heard a noise which sounded like a diesel train approaching from the south. I looked at my watch and saw it was 9.20 pm. I went outside, where a group of a dozen soldiers had gathered. The railway line had been inactive for two years, so we were doubtful whether there was a train running from Zenica.

Immediately, I became aware that the noise was coming from above, but that it was slower and quieter than a jet engine. We all agreed that it was a remotely-piloted drone, taking photographs of the damage caused by the air attacks. About the same time that we discussed this, the same noise was heard above one of my checkpoints and they had a good view of the UFO, which they confirmed was definitely not a light aircraft.

The rest of the night passed quietly and the following morning, I prepared to meet with the new commander of 37 BiH Division to discuss the extraction of my troop from Jelah. On the way, I checked with the troop in the school as I did whenever I stayed a night away from there. When I entered the briefing room, the television was tuned to Sky News. There was great excitement due to the attack on Banja

Luka and it suddenly dawned on me what had flown over our area; we had witnessed the first use of Tomahawk cruise missiles in Bosnia. Fortunately, the guidance system was much improved compared to those used against Saddam Hussein in the Gulf War.

A fierce debate started on the television about the morality of the escalating NATO attacks. I didn't bother listening, but set off with my interpreter just as the sun burned through the morning mist. On the way, we passed a T-34 tank broken down at Novi Seher and I just managed to take a photograph and put away my camera before a police vehicle drove around the corner towards us.

The NATO attacks were exploited by the Federation. Their offensive redrew the map of the country again, with the inevitable suffering which accompanies population movements. On the one side, 40,000 displaced Serbs moved east and on the other side, 11,000 Muslims who left their houses in May 1992 started their return journey home. Sadly, further tragedies occurred as many eager civilians were killed as they walked onto the land mines outside their houses. The hatred on all sides appeared to be a massive chasm to bridge.

As a result of the NATO intervention, our freedom of movement opened up completely and the Bosniac authorities allowed me to travel almost anywhere I wished. We were taken to a number of sites by the Mayor and arranged several assistance projects with our combat tractor to clear the after-effects of war. My driver and I were shaken, but not stirred, as a number of close rounds struck near our Land Rover whilst we were exploring the area. Although we were caught in the lethal splinter range a few times, we continued to ride our luck as we said our farewells to the locals and to thank those who had assisted us so loyally, such as the interpreters.

In late September, Maglaj appeared to explode as we witnessed the highest levels of activity around the town during our tour. We recorded more than 43,000 machine-gun bursts and small arms fire and 1500 explosions in the area. As usual, there was no mention of this activity in the British press, which concentrated on the first convoys driving out of Sarajevo through the Serb controlled area of Kiseljak. As we prepared to remove our blue berets and become part of the NATO peace implementation force, the fighting around Maglaj continued. Despite the optimism of the Brigade Commander, the Bosnian Serbs did not give way and still held the high ground overlooking the town, reinforcing their domination with frequent rocket attacks.

On 21st September at 2 pm the school was targeted for about the fifth time on the tour. After the loud explosion, we sent out a foot patrol and on this occasion they discovered the remains of two three-foot-long fuel pods which had provided the propulsion unit of a rocket which had exploded in our grounds.

We were incredibly lucky that none of the indirect fire attacks caused any casualties either in Maglaj or Jelah. That is not to say we did not have people injured frequently, including the soldier who sleepwalked over a veranda edge and fell ten feet into a razor wire entanglement. But even he was considered fortunate because he received only 40 stitches rather than being impaled on the four-foot steel picket, which he missed by only four inches.

At one of the conferences I attended, we were told that we might have to extend our tour by a month. For a short time there was some confusion about the handover, but the arrival of the Fusiliers in their Saxon vehicles confirmed that we really were going home after what had proved to be an immensely satisfying operational tour, which offered everything I wished for as an independent commander.

Only one non-government organisation stayed in Maglaj after the tank attack, Médecins Sans Frontières. However, we continued to deliver humanitarian assistance with the gifts organised by my wife, Perry, in Osnabruck, as well as the food and building materials sponsored by the United Nations High Commissioner for Refugees. My troops entered wholeheartedly into this activity and as a result made many friends. Despite being woken early by crowing cockerels and kept awake at night by the Bosnian guards' flip-flop music we actually got on very well with the locals.

Clearly we witnessed a turning point in the conflict when the international community took the collective decision to become more authoritative. Before we departed, there was a symbolic change as the white vehicles were painted with camouflage colours and our Queen's Royal Lancers motto replaced the United Nations' blue badges in our berets. As the conflict headed towards a *dénouement*, some argued that all that had happened had been an extension of the unstoppable process of border formation and ethnic homogenisation already experienced by the rest of Europe and that the good works of the international community since 1993 had merely delayed the inevitable.

Soon after my return, I travelled to the USA. Whilst I was there the Dayton Agreement was signed. President Clinton announced he was sending 20,000 US troops to Bosnia together with 150 M-1 Abrams tanks, 250 M-2 Bradley fighting vehicles and up to 50 AH-64 Apache attack helicopters. The following month an Airborne Battalion began arriving at Tuzla air base on C-130 transport aircraft after the predictable heavy blanket of fog delayed the landing. These troops took over responsibility for the area around Maglaj.

On the withdrawal of the British from the town, the *Opština* submitted a bill for a quarter of a million pounds for the damage caused by the Bosnian Serb tank attacks and the follow-up operations. To many of us, this summed up the approach of the Bosnian authorities towards the international community. No doubt the new troops who arrived as part of the NATO Force quickly learned about their ungrateful attitude.

The events of the tour divide into four distinct parts. It began with a baptism of fire which preceded a month of frantic activity. Just as we were settling into some sort of routine, the hostage crisis provided new challenges, which stretched the squadron's limited resources. In July the fall of Srebrenica became the catalyst for a period of intense hostility from the Bosnian authorities, who brought United Nations operations to a halt. Finally, the NATO air strikes in August restored the international community's credibility, whilst allowing us to extract safely from the region.

In looking back at the magnificent achievements of the soldiers I commanded, with thirteen different cap badges and three contributing nations, it was clear that we made a huge difference by defeating the Bosnian Serbs in battle. Even without the tank attacks at the beginning of the tour, there were enough incidents to keep the soldiers on edge. The level of sniper fire in Maglaj, the 500-pound rocket bombs and artillery attacks which landed near our bases, the shooting incidents in Jelah and the open hostility following Srebrenica's fall were all particularly memorable.

Inevitably, there were a number of adverse consequences following this tour. Sadly, Corporal Walker's injuries failed to heal properly. After seven months trying to save his right leg and thirteen operations with indescribable pain and trauma, he made the agonising decision to have the leg amputated at the mid-thigh point on 26th January 1996. The subsequent issue of his financial compensation was debated in Parliament, but never satisfactorily resolved even though the case went to the Court of Appeal.

In addition, the strain of the tour resulted in the breakdown of a number of marriages, although these were fewer than we had anticipated. At this time, the Regimental System came into its own. By maintaining a sense of purpose and setting a full programme, none of my soldiers were diagnosed with post-traumatic stress disorder during the following year. However, this is a very complex condition and symptoms can take a long time to gestate. For example, Combat Stress reports that veterans wait on average 13 years after discharge before seeking help.

What disappointed many of us was the failure of the British Army to formally recognise the exceptional gallantry of the soldiers who fought Britain's biggest defensive action for twenty years. This was an action that reverberated throughout the country, inspiring those who were faltering in their commitment to stiffen their sinews and strengthen their resolve.

It was also extraordinary that the superb medical response which saved Corporal Walker's life and evacuated the casualties in Maglaj so outstandingly well was ignored. However, this did not diminish the high morale which existed within my command, as we showed when breaking tank gunnery records at Hohne ranges and winning troop tests the following year. What really counts for soldiers are relationships built on mutual trust and shared experiences. These provide a richer reward than any material gain.

PART 2

No More Just War

CHAPTER 4

Bin Laden 2001 – Operation Veritas

No single conflict can be used as a model to find
the solution to other conflicts.
David Trimble at the Nobel prize-giving ceremony Oslo 1998

The cricket pads were a size too big, but the gloves fitted perfectly and he was throwing in a snazzy green bag and a flowery Jimi Hendrix shirt. I raised my arm with two weeks' pocket money in my hand and bid at Prince Mirwais' school-leaving auction.

"Sold to the boy with the big nose and thick glasses!"

Walking away with my spoils, I felt sorry for the son of King Muhammad Zahir Shah of Afghanistan, who was holding this hurried sale in July 1973 because his father had been overthrown after ruling the country for 40 years.

I was one of the few boys who could find Afghanistan in the atlas. My father had inspected his American company's office in Kabul only a few months before the coup. The pictures from his Rollei 35 camera during a leisurely morning drive from Peshawar through the Khyber Pass were spectacular. The famous regimental stone plaques carved into the hillside conjured up images from the past battles of a chastened history.

My father also sent a sightseeing guide from Kabul and a postcard of the famous Noon Gun. His photographs of the exotic camel station at a green oasis in the desert also whetted my appetite for a visit. However, when I left school in 1977, the deteriorating security situation made a lone journey to this historic Asian city inadvisable.

Coincidently, the 17th/21st Lancers had received their clearances to send an overland expedition through Afghanistan to Nepal for an onward trek to Everest Base Camp. My best man, Jamie, was one of twelve soldiers who set off from Germany just as the King's successor, President Mohammed Daoud Khan, managed to upset his neighbours to the north and east.

The regimental expedition took a 48-hour break in Tehran to repair the main bearing of one of the four new blue Land Rovers before entering Afghanistan. They saw very little traffic as they drove on the highway through the extreme heat of the Afghan desert and slipped almost unnoticed across the border into Pakistan. Apart from a minor accident with an indestructible donkey, they were not delayed unduly on the homeward journey. Having travelled 61,000miles on a three-month journey of a lifetime, this gallant band of men returned to the regiment on 1st December 1977, only one hour later than the appointed time.

Soon afterwards, the President was assassinated in a coup known as the Saur Revolution. The new socialist government imposed changes which stirred the religious Mujahedeen to action. In turn, their success as insurgents ignited the Soviet invasion in December 1979, two weeks after I was commissioned into the 17th/21st Lancers. For British Army officers, it became almost impossible to travel west of the Durand Line, but Jamie gave me a copy of Eric Newby's captivating book *A Short Walk in the Hindu Kush*, which kept Afghanistan as a priority destination in my mind.

Young officers in my regiment were all keen to understand how our enemy operated, so we avidly watched *The Beast* when it was released in 1988. The film about a lost Soviet tank crew, caught in a deadly game of cat and mouse with the Mujahedeen in the desert became a cult film in the British Army. It provided an inkling of the Afghan code of honour; however, in reality, I knew very little about the country before 9/11 brought it to the world's attention.

★ ★ ★

Most people remember where they were when the aircraft hit their targets in America, killing almost 3,000 people from 60 nations. However, not everyone recalls what they were doing when the World Trade Centre was first attacked in 1993. I was staying at Patrick Air Force Base on the Florida Coast for a memorial service in the week when the truck bomb detonated under the north tower. Back in England, this event was lost in the news about the mass murders and rape in the campaign of ethnic cleansing in Bosnia.

Usama bin Laden's next high-profile atrocity was to plan the twin assaults on the American Embassies in Tanzania and Kenya, which killed 224 and injured over 4,000 people in August 1998. However, the scale of these attacks was dwarfed by the floods in China which killed 12,000 people at the same time. Both of these tragic events were relegated quickly from the front pages when the Real IRA's bomb exploded in busy Omagh a week later.

In Britain, few people treated bin Laden seriously in the 1990s. His 1996 *fatwā* entitled *Declaration of War against the Americans Occupying the Land of the Two Holy Places* passed largely unremarked. However, when Al Qa'eda hit the USS *Cole* whilst it was refuelling in Aden in October 2000, we started to sit up and take notice and by the end of that year, the United Kingdom's Ministry of Defence agreed to fund a research programme into asymmetric war, unaware that the unthinkable would occur within 12 months.

I was delivering a presentation to the Army's staff course when the 17 sailors died on the USS *Cole*. Soon afterwards, I was posted to Shrivenham to one of the posts in the joint doctrine and concepts centre, where asymmetric war was being researched. I was excited about my first job away from soldiers; there was a vibrant atmosphere in the newly-formed centre, where I rapidly made friends amongst an inquisitive group of like-minded officers.

My first main task in 2001 was to evaluate the operating procedures used in the Defence Crisis Management Organisation, or DCMO, located deep underground in Whitehall. This coincided with a NATO crisis management exercise, testing the full range of political-military decision making mechanisms in government, from the Whitehall

Steering Group to the Current Operations Group. The scenario for this exercise, which stemmed from the Kosovo Crisis, was set within a United Nations Peace Support Operation and NATO intervention, mandated under a Chapter VII Security Council Resolution.

The political-military circumstances incorporated tenuous links to the European Strategic Defence Initiative. It connected to all the high-level NATO institutions including the North Atlantic Council, the Military and Political Committees, the Policy Co-ordination Group and the Senior Civil Emergency Planning Committee. Exercise instructions included ten NATO political and military objectives, such as the practice of civil military co-operation at the highest levels.

Within the DCMO, a current commitments team, led by the Director of Military Operations, was maintained on a 24-hour basis. There was also a strategic planning group, led by the Director of the NATO branch, which worked from 0600 hours to midnight. The permanent joint headquarters at Northwood provided officers for each of these teams and I had a roaming remit to wander where I wanted, in order to rewrite part of British Defence Doctrine.

The exercise started on 14th February 2001 and it was immediately clear that the new arrangements had upset the old order. During the Kosovo and Sierra Leone operations, the strategic planning groups came under command of the Assistant Chief of Defence Staff (Operations). However, for this exercise, an alternative chain of command was created using the civilian Director General of Operational Policy. There was also confusion about the boundary between the strategic planning group and the strategic policy group, owned by another two-star officer, who worked in the Policy and Commitments areas.

The central players were all relatively new in post and still earning their spurs, so the creative tension was exposed on the second morning of the exercise. The Chief of the Defence Staff's planning directive, written hastily during the first evening, was disparaged by the representative from the joint headquarters at the early morning meeting. Unfortunately, they had not been consulted because the call-out system failed, and this gave them an excuse to pick holes pedantically in the text.

Feathers were smoothed and a new directive issued to the commands later that morning. The remainder of the exercise was a huge success. Everyone was impressed with the new mechanism for information operations and the lessons-learned process was highly effective. These identified a plethora of technical upgrades and amendments which I took forward when I returned to Shrivenham. One key recommendation suggested by the Deputy Chief of Defence was that an additional team might be tasked from the concept centre to conduct "out of the box" thinking in some situations.

The aim was to make use of the programme on asymmetric war being developed under the title of *Future Issues for Defence*. On a range of websites, we had invited people to "think the unthinkable" and envisage credible, low-probability but high-significance events focusing on a timeframe of 2020 to 2030. Overall, we received 700 responses before we presented the results at a lively meeting exactly eight years after the first attack in the World Trade Centre.

This conference was attended by the Chief Scientific Advisor, the Chief of Defence Intelligence, the Head of Defence Research and the senior officers responsible for equipment capability, commitments and personnel. Inevitably, some officers tried to promote their pet projects, but overall there was consensus that the work should be taken forward as a high priority. The result, published in March 2003 as *Strategic Trends*, became an enduring and authoritative source of strategic security analysis and has been updated regularly, with a fifth edition benchmarked on 30th April 2014.

What was particularly significant about the £25,000 original study was that more than 25% of the suggested shocks were caused by terrorist action. Apart from the likelihood of a global Islamic threat to Western culture, we also assessed the significance of a collapse of the global economic system with a prolonged recession. We identified a global pandemic, and this too occurred within ten years of the study (avian 'flu).

It is heartening that not all the high-impact, low-probability events transpired and we remain a long way from an ice age in northern Europe, or a global conflict initiated between China and India. However many ideas, such as attacks on water and energy infrastructure and the nexus of organised crime and terrorism, are now part of the realities of modern war.

This conceptual work fed into the United Kingdom Joint Vision published on 15th June 2001, which presciently predicted:

In the future, modern weapons will be widely available and potential adversaries will have increasing access to advanced technology, including weapons of mass effect, with many ignoring the laws and moral conventions of war... There will be an increasing tendency for conflicts to involve non-state actors, who might not be clearly identifiable. They may operate independently or openly in league with, or as covert surrogates for, state forces or the remnants of former-state forces. Adversaries may well use asymmetric attacks [against] our strategic and operational Centres of Gravity.

No one can say that the United Kingdom did not think about the sorts of attacks seen by the world on Tuesday 11th September. The problem was not a failure of imagination, but a lack of application, as this was simply not the priority for defence funding.

During the summer, I continued helping the DCMO in its attempts to join up the government lines of activity. I set up a working group with the Foreign Office and Department for International Development and briefed some of the staff in the Cabinet Office. This was linked with the campaign to improve the United Nations' structures and capabilities associated with mounting and sustaining peace support operations. We built on the progressive report of Lakhdar Brahimi's panel, which was presented as the headline initiative at the United Nations Millennium Summit. His 57 substantive recommendations were received well in London, although some states believed they reinforced the so-called north-south divide and were suspicious about creating a United Nations intelligence capability slanted towards Western needs.

Developing an international consensus on Britain's approach to military operations took me to Norway and

Sweden, which were two of the top five contributors to United Nations deployments. I also addressed some of the staff at the United Nations college in Turin, which was located at the university on the edge of the city. The peeling paintwork, rusting metal and tired 1960s architecture did not disguise the unmistakable scenery of *The Italian Job* and I took great pleasure following some of the route used by Michael Caine when he escaped from the Italian police in Mini Coopers.

In late July, I travelled to New York as part of a four-man team following up Kofi Annan's call on the Secretary of State on 21st June. We were charged with advising the Department for Peacekeeping Operations and our team included an officer from the joint services staff college and two from the permanent joint headquarters. After we drew up a five-stage strategy with the British military representative, he took us to a cacophonous concert in Central Park, where we listened to Weil's Seven Deadly Sins, played a bit of touch rugby and enjoyed a delicious picnic with ecstatic revellers. Life in New York seemed pretty idyllic in the summer of 2001.

Six weeks later I was back in the Ministry of Defence in London. I had booked Room 114 of Metropole Building, in order to host representatives from the Cabinet Office and other government departments. We were preparing for their arrival when the first aircraft flew into the north tower of the World Trade Centre.

The room was next to a media operations office, so I watched the television screen as the second aircraft hit the south building and the towers tumbled to the ground. We immediately cancelled our meeting and hung around the policy area, speculating who might have committed this crime. At the same time, a commitments team was summoned to the DCMO.

Early the next day, the Policy Director called Shrivenham and asked us to send a group to London in line with the February recommendation. By then, we had developed sufficient expertise to provide a Tri-Service team of six military officers, led by the civilian head of policy, a sharp geography graduate from Leicester. We were all approached individually and volunteered without a moment's hesitation.

★ ★ ★

An impenetrable organisation is not a prerequisite for dealing with a crisis, but a secure location to assess the options and plan the response is essential. The authors of the United Kingdom response to 9/11 worked in the central control rooms, underground in Whitehall. I was surprised that the Emergency Planning Chairman, Brian Ward, briefed the media about "Monmouth", as this complex was called, and such a comprehensive piece was published in the *Sunday Times* that month.

On 13th September, I descended into this bunker and met with the head of the DCMO to establish how the concept team would fit into the battle rhythm and where it would work. Space was tight because half the area was taken up by the group working on Operation Bessemer, a highly successful 16 Brigade deployment in Macedonia to disarm the Albanian National Liberation Army.

Once we had agreed the protocols and sorted out a suitable area large enough for our work, I called the remainder of our team, who joined me half an hour later. We all sat around the table in our allocated room and looked at each other expectantly. Then everyone started talking at the same time, gesticulating and making suggestions about what we should do. Our astute civilian leader called for silence and sensibly proposed that the first urgent task we needed to complete was to draft our own terms of reference.

We knew that the overall lead for the United Kingdom response was given to Sir David Manning, so we drew up our riding instructions in such a way that our work was focused at the highest strategic level. Most importantly, we needed to avoid treading on the sensitivities of the "home" teams in the Ministry of Defence. They would be very wary of our presence and critical of our ideas if they were not consulted and brought into our thinking in a tactful way. We also wished to avoid amalgamation with the amorphous mass of augmented staff officers, so we carefully crafted the terms with an exit strategy and a specific end date on 19th September.

By the time we sorted all that out, the United States had reassuringly reopened their airspace and the North Atlantic Council had declared that 9/11 was a breach of Article 5, treating it as an attack against all members. In solidarity, the United Nations had adopted Resolution 1368, calling on all states to bring to justice the perpetrators of the horrifying attacks in New York, Washington and Pennsylvania. Most remarkably, the French newspaper *Le Monde* captured a global sentiment with its headline *We are all Americans now*.

In the United Kingdom, arrangements for senior political military meetings, civil contingency planning and airport security measures were adjusted according to the decisions taken at the meeting in Cabinet Office Briefing Room A, or

Cobra. The Foreign Office reviewed all the security arrangements in countries where there was a risk from hostile intelligence services. Separately, they considered advising United Kingdom nationals to leave Pakistan due to the Taliban presence. This made the Defence Attaché very nervous about having to organise a non-combatant evacuation operation.

The Chief of Defence Staff met the heads of the three services for their 21st meeting of the year on the 11th September, when Operation Veritas was initiated, and agreed to meet daily thereafter. These meetings began with the Chief of Defence Intelligence updating everyone on the current situation and the Policy Director summarising the political-military issues.

On 13th September, representatives from the Foreign Office and Cabinet Office also attended the meeting and a video conference link was established with Brussels, Washington and the permanent joint headquarters. The Policy Director reported the clear resolve and determination of the United States to deal with international terrorism. He was concerned that despite the Article 5 declaration, NATO had not established a battle rhythm because the military committee was stymied by process and bureaucratic log jams.

By then, the DCMO had established good planning linkages with the United States, but it was clear the Pentagon was still dealing with the fallout from the attack on their site, so they were working at half pace. In scoping our military options, three themes were emerging on both sides of the Atlantic. The first was to really understand the meaning of war in the current context. The second was to acknowledge that this would be a long, hard fight. Finally, we were both focusing on a campaign approach, not a quick fix; "no hiding place" became the mantra.

The Chiefs focused on four immediate concerns. Number one was dealing with a copycat attack which might require a quick reaction aircraft to intercept any airborne threat. The Chief of Defence Staff had confirmed the Royal Air Force was able to launch a fighter, but there remained questions over timeliness, rules of engagement and command and control, which needed to be sorted out along with the civil contingencies to handle the aftermath. The Chief of Joint Operations was asked to produce a force options paper to deal with the second and third concerns about conventional and unconventional military capabilities.

Finally, the Chiefs were briefed that our free-thinking strategic think-tank would introduce relevant out-of-the-box ideas under the leadership of the Director General. To avoid any confusion, he was given a new appointment as Assistant Chief of Defence Staff (Plans). My role, as his military assistant, was to integrate the conventional strategic estimate with the wider think piece and produce a coherent package for the Chiefs of Staff in three days' time.

The deadline for this combined product was dictated by the Prime Minister's planned trip to Washington on Thursday 20th September, but I had to be prepared to submit the work earlier if President Bush's war council at Camp David called forward the visit. Since a first draft was to be ready on Monday morning, everyone in the group called their families to inform them we would not be returning for the weekend and I told my son I would not be on the touchline for his soccer match.

That evening we all ate supper together in Smollensky's in the Strand, opposite the hotel which the Ministry had booked as our accommodation. London was still in shock and the hotels and restaurants were empty. There was a palpable sense of fear as the national alert state was still at Amber. Many people were cancelling their travel arrangements as they hunkered down in a state of semi-paralysis.

Early starts and late endings were required in order to fit in with the operational battle rhythm. I produced a daily situation report and sent this at midnight to the officer co-ordinating the input for the Prime Minister's morning brief. One of the irritations for those of us working in the bunker was that the main building was being refurbished. This meant that the daytime offices had relocated to the Metropole building in Northumberland Avenue, or to the Old War Office Building in Whitehall.

On Friday morning, I accompanied my general around these buildings to ensure our work was coherent with other lines of activity. Everyone agreed how critical an effective information campaign would be to support any United Kingdom response. In one call on a senior officer, we were informed that the Pentagon did not believe Central Command was the right headquarters to deal with this problem. It was not just that General Tommy Franks' headquarters in Tampa focused on other regions such as Europe and the Horn of Africa. It was also that their approach was primarily to use military force, whereas Pacific Command was more inclined to use diplomatic, economic and information levers, as well as military coercion when dealing with Asia, which was their sphere of influence.

Arguably the course of history would have been very different if Donald Rumsfeld had asked Pacific Command to deal with the problem. One of the advantages lay in their knowledge about Pakistan, which was inexorably linked to Afghanistan. However, they were not so familiar with the Middle East, so there was no flawless solution.

At 11 o'clock on Friday, we stopped for three minutes' silence to think of the 75 British citizens presumed dead and other victims of the attack and their families. Then we returned to the bunker for the midday update and to consolidate the information we had gathered in the morning.

The three Veritas teams in the bunker worked independently of each other. The *primus inter pares* current commitments team, under a Royal Navy captain, was responsible for co-ordinating minute to minute responses and the daily briefs for senior officials. They delegated some responsibilities to the permanent joint headquarters and other top level budget holders; for example the plan for the defence of Canary Wharf and other key points, such as the Channel Tunnel, fell to the regional chain of command under the Commander in Chief, Land Forces.

Separately, another Royal Navy captain led an ad hoc strategic planning group, charged with producing the grand strategic estimate for Operation Veritas. Finally, there was the concept team from Shrivenham, which was already sticking dozens of yellow Post-It notices on the wall as they came up with out-of-the-box ideas for the strategic think piece.

Over the next couple of days, everyone worked flat out to produce three outstanding documents. The current commitments team submitted a menu of United Kingdom offensive military capabilities available for operations against

Afghanistan. This made nine assumptions about over-flight agreements and the approval to set up military bases from our international partners.

There were other caveats. Early decisions about issues and capabilities, including air-to-air refuelling tankers, needed detailed planning. However, the elements available by 27th September included a Special Forces task force with two parachute battalions and a squadron of Tornado aircraft. These could be augmented by early October, with two submarines ready to fire Tomahawk cruise missiles and more carrier-based aircraft in the Gulf.

We all had a hand in the brief to Sir David Manning about the consequences of the Taliban failing to comply with an ultimatum. For this, we assumed that the Taliban would reject any demand on the basis they faced a reduced internal threat with the onset of winter and the assassination two days before 9/11 of the "Lion of Panjshir", General Ahmad Shah Massoud. He was the charismatic leader of the internal resistance to the Taliban regime, respected for his moderate version of Islam, who had warned the West about the possibility of 9/11 when he addressed the European Parliament in Brussels.

The strategic planning group produced a summary of their estimate. This focused on the elimination of Al Qa'eda in Afghanistan and beyond as part of the fight against international terrorism. The team highlighted the extensive support within the Muslim community for extremism and suggested this was likely to expand with an increasing teenage population and the endemic unemployment in the Arab world.

Presciently, they suggested that targeting bin Laden

directly was unlikely to prove decisive and could arguably be counter-productive. They were thinking of the words of the Danish philosopher, Soren Kierkegaard, who wrote "The tyrant dies and his rule is over; the martyr dies and his rule begins". Whilst acknowledging the need to provide clear support to the United States, they considered any action must neither alienate moderate Islamic states nor impair the peaceful integration of ethnic minorities into a multi-cultural Britain.

They also highlighted the importance of political stability in the Persian Gulf region and the Middle East Peace Process. They covered our new shared interest with Russia, the influence of India and Pakistan and the need to reduce organised crime and the flows of Afghan drugs and people in the Balkans. Two particular warnings were included about the potential to de-stabilise the existing pro-Western regime in Pakistan and an opportunistic military campaign into the Gulf Region by Iraq.

There was a strong expectation that punitive action would be taken. Not to do so would be seen in the Muslim world as evidence of weakness. However, right at the start we recommended that a broad political coalition needed to be constructed.

Consensus was required to bridge potential religious and ethnic divides between the West and moderate Muslim states and to legitimise subsequent military actions. We also recommended that a comprehensive cross-government counter terrorist strategy should be produced. Any military action needed to be placed within the context of a sustained diplomatic, economic and legal campaign across the entire spectrum of Al Qa'eda capabilities.

The work of the Shrivenham team got bogged down on Saturday. Our general was concerned about the apparent friction in the team and asked me to resolve the fraught situation. The problem was caused by tension between two of the older lieutenant colonels and the civil servant who led the team.

Within the Ministry of Defence, it has always been felt that military officers should take the lead when it comes to military operations. Most civil servants are aware of their lack of front-line experience, so they do not venture into the bear pit of an operations centre. However, when it comes to strategic analysis about national security at the highest level, civilians hold sway over the military and in this case, our civilian had the brightest brain in the team. Once we focused the military minds on the higher level of work, using the seven dimensions of the strategic environment, the team produced an excellent submission.

We did not dwell long on the academic debate about definitions. The teams all agreed to use the endorsed NATO meaning of terrorism and describe the special characteristics that qualified 9/11; the scale of the suicide attack and the use of unconventional weapons of mass effect.

In fact, there was plenty of material written about international terrorism. There were twelve existing conventions dating back to November 1937. I remembered Question 15 of my promotion exam in 1988, which asked how states should attempt to combat international terrorism. At that stage, the focus was on attacks sponsored by countries such as Libya. However, the agreements covered everything from piracy on the high seas and hijacking in the air to hostage taking and nuclear terrorism. To pull them all together, the United Nations drafted a comprehensive convention in August 2000, but this had not been ratified by the General Assembly.

We also assessed the three causes declared by Usama bin Laden: American basing in Saudi Arabia; the failure of the Middle East Peace Process and the Iraq containment policy. Attempting to understand the cultural aspects, we were very aware that our planning groups comprised middle-aged white men, with little diversity. To compensate for this weakness, we reached out to academia and trawled the available research sites about extremism and terrorism. However, we avoided the sources used by Britain's intelligence services because these had been heavily criticised for their failures to provide timely and actionable information.

On Monday morning, the Secretary of State, Geoff Hoon, visited us in the bunker. He showed particular interest when we said that we had discarded several options because they were illegal. His view was that, as a trained lawyer, he could make up his own mind about what was legal and what was not, so he instructed us to put them back in the document. The Policy Director picked up on this later and asked what shifts in the law were required to provide an appropriate legal base for success.

In the afternoon, we presented our emerging thoughts to the Deputy Chief of Defence Staff. He was worried about the immediate pressure emanating from America to hit as many targets as possible. He questioned the presumption that Al Qa'eda had no discernible centre of gravity, but no one could offer a feasible alternative, other than ethereal ideology.

Ignoring the oversimplified Pearl Harbour analogy, he suggested that focusing on Al Qa'eda was already too narrow.

He asked us to widen the aim to include the mindset which drove people to commit collective suicide acts of terrorism on a scale using weapons of mass effect. It was really important to us to avoid the accusation of focusing solely on the Muslim world, so we looked at how other international networks linked to organisations, including Aum Shinriko, FARC, ETA and PIRA. However, once we created a matrix of known terrorist organisations, it was very difficult to identify any current non-Muslim cells employing suicide bombers for their political purposes.

We worked through Monday night incorporating the guidance into the two submissions. On Tuesday, the level of activity increased again. Every hour, there were at least two meetings to attend. The Chiefs of Staffs' meeting was brought forward from the afternoon to 0900 hours. They were particularly concerned with the operational security around the Special Forces plans and authorised the procurement of secure mobile telephones to ensure nothing was intercepted by the media. They were also sensitive about one of our General's links to Pentagon thinking, which was closer than the politicians realised. The Chief of Joint Operations was straining at the leash and the Permanent Under Secretary was turning white as the costs mounted.

At 1715 hours, I sent version 4 of the Grand Strategic Estimate to the two-star Assistants working for the members of the Chief of Staffs' committee. I asked for their observations by 1200 the following day, so we could incorporate these in the Wednesday review before the Prime Minister's departure for Washington. In fact, the document was discussed at the highest levels that evening and a copy was passed to the Chief of Defence Staff after his dinner engagement.

It came back to me with his hand-written notes. There were two big ticks against the need for an effective information campaign and international co-operation on the grandest scale. Given his high level guidance, it seemed strange that one week after 9/11, the cross-government implementation group had not even met and no draft information campaign was being circulated for comment. He also underlined the advice in paragraph 12 that Usama bin Laden, as an individual, must not be the primary target. His comment about considering the United States' end of the telescope acknowledged the reality of the Prime Minister's direction to everyone that we should provide all assistance to America.

Wednesday 19th September was a very busy day putting together the papers for the trip to Washington. At the morning meeting, the pros and cons of mounting the planned major overseas exercise, Saif Sareea (Swift Sword) 2, were discussed. My regiment had already sent D Squadron's tanks to Oman as part of the 20,000 troops taking part in the largest deployment since the Gulf War. They were not due to return until November, so the potential for it to be targeted by terrorists was highlighted by the intelligence staff. Quite rightly, the decision was taken to continue with everything despite the risks. Everyone realised that it might be useful preparation for the impending war.

In the afternoon, we met with the Policy Director and Deputy Chief of Defence Staff again to review progress on our strategic analysis. They confirmed that our contributions would feed into the Blair-Bush discussion, although the General asked us to remove regime change from decision point 6. This prompted a long discussion about our aims, which I incorporated into a new pair of Powerpoint slides, articulating the strategic objectives as follows:

To eliminate terrorism globally as a force for change in international affairs.

To that end:

- To bring those responsible for 11 September to account.

- To dissuade any terrorist groups from any similar scale action.

- To deter states from harbouring such groups.

In order to achieve these objectives:

- Create an international consensus and will to act against international terrorism whatever origin.

- Bring about a step-change in the international capability to act effectively.

- Construct a new effective international law for long term control.

- Break the links between terrorist groups and organised crime.

And as a continuing precaution:

- Enhance the national capability to prevent, predict and manage the consequences of such attacks.

In line with the consensus, not one of the objectives mentioned bin Laden. That evening I completed the submission for the Prime Minister's trip, which comprised the strategic estimate and the concept team's think piece entitled *Building a Longer Term Strategy against International Terrorism*. They had produced 36 building blocks, which looked beyond any military responses and highlighted some of the consequences of our actions and the strategic ways and means of dealing with the phenomenon facing the world, emphasising the need to strike in a way that would avoid coalescing Islam against us.

Securing the Gulf States' agreement to the objectives would be a challenge and needed a sophisticated diplomatic effort. The key issue of harbouring terrorists was seen by many in the Arab world as hypocritical. Many of their opposition groups, committed to political violence, were based in London. Our diplomatic efforts were not helped by the continuing use by senior Americans of inappropriate terms such as 'crusade'.

Our General flew to Washington on the Virgin flight at 1130 hours the next morning, whilst I checked my To Do list:

- Resolve tension between the permanent joint headquarters and the MoD commitments area over the ownership of the strategic estimate.

- Share thinking with the Pentagon, which was still in a state of flux, via the British Defence Staff in Washington.

- Develop the Al Qa'eda concept of operations and the strategic objectives agreed at the meeting on Wednesday.

- Start a strategic estimate on international terrorism using the same methodology as the estimate on Al Qa'eda.

- Work out how and when to engage the other government departments.

- Generate the strategic information requirements.

- Discuss wider think piece with Army, Navy and Air Force before the weekend

- Prepare a presentation to the Chiefs of Staff covering the two submissions.

- Update the unclassified rolling brief for wider dissemination.

The team from Shrivenham was in fine fettle after producing a timely, relevant and valuable think piece, which already had influenced much of the United Kingdom response. However, it was clear that we had failed in our attempts at an exit strategy after the first week of the operation. We were extended in our posts with a review point set at the end of the month, so I telephoned my wife again to tell her that I would not be returning for the weekend. Then I cancelled my appointments for the following week and started to work on the presentation for the Chiefs of Staff.

★ ★ ★

As we started our second week in London, we received some good news from the manager of the Marriott Hotel across the Thames. She was a friend of one of our team and had received many cancellations from American clients. She offered to accommodate us at the same price as the noisy hotel on the Strand and we jumped at the chance.

I was caught in the rain walking over Westminster Bridge with my suitcase, but the journey was worthwhile for the view alone. Although we worked throughout that weekend, there was time to watch the new *Planet of the Apes* film in Leicester Square and to enjoy an excellent dinner in a packed Chinese restaurant in Soho. The resilience of the capital was remarkable, despite the shortage of American tourists.

On Sunday, I introduced two new objectives to the strategic work. The first was to prevent Al Qa'eda from committing similar acts again and the second was to reintegrate Afghanistan into the international community. At another afternoon review meeting, we again debated the importance of keeping moderate Arab opinion on side to avoid a conflagration, which might provide a catalyst for World War III. Some people suggested that we should conduct a rapid demonstration of force, such as the ineffective missile strikes of the Clinton era, but they could not articulate the overall good this would achieve.

At the Monday update, there was spurious talk about Usama bin Laden travelling to Chechnya to meet Mullah Omar. We received formal feedback from the "sombre, but purposeful" Washington trip, which confirmed there was no clear strategy coming from the United States. They appeared to believe that another atrocity was inevitable and it was a case of not if, but when. A senior officer on the visit said that we must make the Prime Minister more aware of the real nature of the threat. He asked for an update on basing in Uzbekistan because we were not being welcomed in Pakistan.

Again the discussion revolved around the tension between the advocates for "strategic patience" and the instinct of several military officers who were keen to strike first and ask questions later. Everyone agreed that the first move was critical with the mantra "start as you mean to go on", but there remained uncertainty about the relationship between Rumsfeld's Department of Defence and Colin Powell's State Department. Although the American Administration wished to maintain as much freedom of action as possible, it appeared that the argument to build a coalition had been won.

The priority issue that day was a scare about chemical and biological attacks. This required the reprogramming of the Joint Nuclear Biological and Chemical Regiment to ensure it was able to deal with any incident in the United Kingdom. The challenge remained inter-agency coherence. New domestic arrangements were needed because the Home Defence command and control architecture had been removed at the end of the Cold War. We were fully aware that the military was only a small part of the solution, but it seemed that our ability to move seamlessly into crisis mode was not replicated in the other government departments, so we ended up reluctantly filling the void.

This was also a major issue in the United States with millions of dollars allocated to improving their homeland security capability. The British Defence Staff in Washington kept us informed of the new Cabinet appointment to be held by the Pennsylvania Governor, Tom Ridge. They also provided us with sight of activities in support of "domestic preparedness" and the four principles in their emerging counter terrorism policy. It was heartening to see that our ideas had already influenced their thinking.

In the afternoon, I listened to the Chiefs of Staff meeting in the old War Office building. The information domain continued to be a major concern. The intelligence services were still not providing timely and relevant assessments and the information campaign was nowhere to be seen. They were also concerned about media reports on impending military action and the structure of our bunker, so the Director

General of Corporate Communications was asked to speak to the editors through the D Notice Committee.

This anachronistic group was established in 1912 when the Official Secrets Act was created in the build-up to World War I. Its purpose is to form a point of liaison between the government and the media on delicate issues of national security. In this case, it was used to minimise speculation about clandestine operations in Afghanistan. It was inevitable that this would fail to stop the news editors who believe that when journalists are not briefed on operational detail, they have every right to speculate. From our perspective, we realised the aspiration was unrealistic, but the D Notice bought some vital time to protect our troops on the ground.

On Tuesday 25th September, the planning group produced the military strategic estimate on Al Qa'eda. The analysis used the handrail of United Kingdom Operations Doctrine. This describes the campaign planning tools and decision making methodology, but doesn't cover mundane policy, such as the seating plan for the morning meetings. After 50 pages of analysis, the estimate concluded with three courses of action: attrition, military coercion and large-scale humanitarian and information operations linked to precision action. Based on the advantages of each, the author recommended the third option to the Chiefs of Staff.

On the same day, we received a timely update from the Department for International Development about the Afghan humanitarian crisis. They reported that the Taliban had entered the United Nations offices in Kabul and Kandahar, seized control of the World Food Programme's remaining stocks of about 1,400 metric tonnes and locked away all communications equipment.

My team at Shrivenham had established very close contacts with the humanitarian community during the summer of 2001. In the same way that the media are not a single institution, there is a vast range of benevolent companies involved in this area. These range from large international organisations to local enterprises. Whilst in London we contacted our Shrivenham colleagues, who provided us with valuable advice to help shape our work. They sent me a summary of the relevant Afghanistan work, including details about the three years of drought, which had compounded the effects of the civil war and international isolation.

It was estimated that Afghans already accounted for 2.6 million or 10% of the total refugee population in the world. Now the United Nations estimated that up to 200,000 were newly displaced in the third week of September. By early November, when winter closes the country, they suggested that 5.5 million people in Afghanistan would be dependent on the World Food Programme shipments. Of course these were only estimates, but even if there was a 25% variance, the scale of the problem was still enormous.

After several humourless days, the mood lightened at the Wednesday morning update. It started with a gloomy briefing about the attitude of other countries to military action and then the media brief discussed the idea of introducing identity cards in Britain. When someone said "they don't need ID cards in China", there was a sudden crack of laughter, which lifted everyone's spirits and energised the remainder of the meeting.

Concerns about Central Command in Florida continued to be raised in the meetings. Senior officials in the Ministry reminded the permanent joint headquarters that requests for United Kingdom assistance from America must be passed from Washington to London, not direct from Tampa to Northwood. Some senior officers in the Pentagon were not comfortable with Central Command's approach and there was plenty of scope for enthusiastic exchange officers to promise more than London could deliver.

The exercise in the Omani desert became a concern, with a shortage of air filters for Challenger 2 tanks. This risk had been accepted as part of the financial limitations of the exercise several months before. Now the reality of the dust and sand ingested into the engine had to be managed by the frustrated Brigade Commander.

Despite its excellent availability record, the squadron from my regiment was withdrawn from training. Their filters were "cannibalised" so that the remaining 53 tanks of the Royal Dragoon Guards could complete the exercise. Although this was a disappointment to the crews, several of them remained active and an excellent young soldier from my Bosnia command, Corporal Rumsey, was awarded a commendation by the General Officer Commanding 1st Armoured Division for his prompt response to a medical emergency.

The rehearsal for the ten-minute presentation to the Chiefs in the Old War Office Building became pedantic. Having created the first Army Presentation DVD in 2000, I knew how important it was for each of the three speakers after my General to keep their briefs within their allotted time, but they all overran by several minutes. To solve the problem, we removed the complicated cancer analogy, which took too long to explain. I also found two minutes from the conclusion, which I split between the Royal Navy captain presenting on the strategic estimate and the Army colonel briefing on the military approaches.

I returned to the bunker to finish off the script. In the evening, we received a fax from Sir David Manning attaching the seven refined objectives for defeating international terrorism. These had been cleared by the Foreign and Commonwealth Office officials and were distributed to Cabinet Ministers for their endorsement. It was pleasing to see they were unchanged when Jack Straw announced them to Parliament in his statement to the House of Commons in October.

Of these campaign objectives, two now specifically mentioned Usama bin Laden and four focused on international terrorism. The final objective was the "reintegration of Afghanistan as a responsible member of the international community and an end to its self-imposed isolation". It was fully recognised at the time that this could take over 10 years to complete. The cost of reconstructing Bosnia was $5 billion and Afghanistan was much more complex in terms of the tribal population and the damage caused by 23 years of civil war. We all knew that only sustained international development effort had any chance of ridding Afghanistan of heroin and domination by war lords.

On Thursday 27th September, we were ready to communicate our thinking to wider audiences. Apart from the briefing to Chiefs, the Policy Director spoke to the Prime Minister and a select group of defence and diplomatic specialists and at midday, the Secretary of State addressed Members of Parliament about Operation Veritas. His main message was that the fight against international terrorism would be a long haul. His speaking notes highlighted extended campaigns against Napoleon and the Provisional IRA and the need to act because of the very real threat to British citizens at home and abroad.

Following our briefing, the Chief of Defence Staff complimented the strategic teams on the quality of their work and directed that the Cabinet Office should be informed. He called for the options to be fleshed out into tangibles that would strike a chord in the United States. In rebalancing the ideas from the conceptual to the practical, we needed to shape thinking about the first strike.

The sentiment about linking the first strike to the long-term strategy was echoed by the Policy Director, when he returned with the Prime Minister's political military intent. He was concerned about our engagement in Washington and the need to improve direct liaison. To sort this out, I spent a couple of hours with the Defence Secretary's staff and composed the job specifications for a one-star Chief of Defence Staff liaison officer, together with a lieutenant colonel to support him in the Pentagon. I was aware that these posts would not be welcomed by the British Defence Staff in Washington, but as I explained to the first incumbent, the current system was not producing the right level of information for the Chiefs.

On Friday 28th September, the second United Nations Resolution, 1373, was adopted by the Security Council. The robust language was welcomed by everyone, as it provided us with a Chapter VII mandate to use military force and covered the important legal and economic direction to all states to deal with international terrorism. In particular, this was a vital key to unlock support from Pakistan because we

New York City, summer 2001. A working breakfast for the United Kingdom Armed Forces' planning team at the United Nations.

In front of the Non-Violence sculpture on 16th July 2001.

were pushed to achieve what we wanted to do in the east of Afghanistan without their basing agreement.

Preparing for a visit from the planning branch in the Pentagon, we received a copy of the internal draft of the goals and objectives of their broad campaign. The strategy to 'adopt a comprehensive approach employing all instruments of national power and influence in a co-ordinated manner for sustained national campaign against terrorism including its organisations, networks, finances and access to weapons of mass destruction' was slightly convoluted, but nevertheless coherent with our thinking.

Inevitably, there was more emotion in the words than we would use in London. The phrase "eliminate terrorism as a threat to our way of life and to all nations that love freedom" could only have been written by a very senior American unhindered by Sir Ernest Gowers' *Plain Words*. However, the important point was that they were sharing their thinking at all levels. This was a major victory for all of us who worked so hard to persuade the United States to build a coalition, rather than take unilateral action.

The Prime Minister became extremely engaged with the humanitarian situation and spoke with Kofi Annan over the weekend. It was estimated that 56,000 tonnes was needed every month and 75,000 tonnes had to be prepositioned for the Afghan winter. The International Development Secretary pledged £25 million on top of the annual commitment which Great Britain had provided since 1997. The important issue was to pull disparate organisations together, so we recommended that Lakhdar Brahimi was given the lead over all the United Nations lines of activity, including the aid requirements.

On Monday 1st October, the concept team produced their magnum opus entitled "eliminating terrorism as a force in international affairs: towards a coherent strategy". The work was designed to support the Ministry of Defence input to Sir David Manning, as well as the campaign development work and the exchanges with the Pentagon. It built on the first submission of 19th September and drew on the views of many of our external contacts in the civilian sector, including Middle East and Islamic experts and representatives from non-government organisations.

It started with the question – "Are we walking into a trap?" The main part analysed the nature of the long-term battle, differentiating between terrorist groups and rogue states. The focus was on coherence between the role of the military with other levers of power and the sequencing of national and international action to engage agile, diffuse opponents. After providing guidance for the information campaign, the paper then addressed the underlying causes of international terrorism. These were stated as the imposition of the nation state system, globalisation, and the demonisation of America following the failure to deliver a new world order as promised by President Bush's father in his speech on 6th March 1991.

The paper highlighted the fact that all thinking to date had been aimed at treating the symptoms. Therefore, it recommended we should develop and maintain the ambition to tackle the underlying causes, including rapprochement with Iraq. Unfortunately, this course of action was ignored by the politicians of the day.

The fast tempo of work continued during the first week of October. There was laughter when the Directorate of

Overseas Military Activity put up the flag of Taiwan when briefing about the Chinese military visit to London. The main concerns at our level were the same issues as before: basing, the lack of a cross-government information campaign, the response to United States' requests, and the failures of the intelligence services. In response, the Defence Intelligence Services decided to compulsorily call up some of their reservists to bolster their human capability.

We began tracking the increased fighting between the Northern Alliance and the Taliban. A priority was placed on broadening the coalition. The Prime Minister met with President Putin in the Kremlin before showing the evidence about Usama bin Laden's involvement in 9/11 to President Musharraf of Pakistan. At the Thursday update we were informed that Saudi Arabia had agreed to the United States proposal to expand their air operations centre.

The concept team stood down that weekend when the Chief of Defence Staff issued his directive to the Joint Commander of Operation Oracle, but a few of us continued to work in the DCMO. After two weeks of prevarication, the Taliban failed to comply with the ultimatum to surrender bin Laden and so the United States and the United Kingdom struck at thirty military targets across Afghanistan. Our Tomahawk cruise missiles were targeted at the Al Qa'eda network and Taliban infrastructure. In addition to the three Royal Navy nuclear submarines, the United Kingdom deployed Royal Air Force tanker and reconnaissance aircraft and Special Forces moved covertly into the region.

The Prime Minister announced the start of the new operation, Oracle, with great enthusiasm. However, the feedback we received through the Afghan non-government organisations after a week of bombing was gloomy. Afghans believed this was having minimal effect. Statements about not having an argument with the ordinary people appeared hollow because we hit several housing estates in Kabul where Taliban leaders were hiding. We read the local prediction that if Kabul fell, the Taliban would simply move to their Logar and Wardak strongholds, with the hardliners based in Kandahar.

Following the start of military operations, the early morning operations brief in the bunker became steely affairs. There was considerable annoyance at the press speculation about the deployment of troops straight from Exercise Saif Sareea 2 to Afghanistan following the Prime Minister's visit to Oman. This caused the Secretary of State and Chief of Defence Staff to deny there were any plans to use them operationally on 11th October.

The information directorates were totally consumed by the here and now and admitted they had neither read our advice nor received a strategic information campaign from Alastair Campbell by 15th October. It was no wonder that the London newspapers were producing mixed messages. *The Telegraph* and *The Times* were generally supportive, *The Guardian* cautious, the *Daily Mail* alarmist and the *Daily Express* critical of government attempts at censorship.

There remained many unanswered questions about what we were trying to achieve and how this operation fitted into the wider thinking about international terrorism. However, in the United States, moderating voices were given short shrift and a very senior British military officer returned from his visit to Donald Rumsfeld with a disappointing report.

The situation was summarised by a representative from

a non-government organisation when he stated that the bombing was drawing together what was a fairly disparate mob. We were also beginning to lose our international support with several Muslim countries, led by Indonesia, which condemned the continuing blitz of Kabul.

The Foreign Secretary addressed the House of Commons on 16th October, informing them of the seven campaign objectives which we had written. Later that day, I was asked to examine a potential peace support operation under the United Nations mandate as part of the Government's seventh objective, the reintegration of Afghanistan into the international community. The United States was keen to involve Turkey as a friendly Muslim state. The Foreign and Commonwealth Office representative told us that there would be no United Kingdom troops involved and everyone agreed that we did not wish to march into Kabul with our hands tied by United Nations Rules of Engagement.

On 19th October, despite the intelligence services claiming that the Taliban was unlikely to collapse, we all focused on the impending peace support operation. The Director of Special Forces was particularly unhappy with the lack of operational security over his deployments. This was a result of the Prime Minister's pronouncements, which lifted the temperature in the news rooms and raised expectations about an increase in Britain's involvement.

In the Ministry of Defence, there were six big issues exercising the minds of the senior leadership. The first was to keep focused on the strategy, not the side issues. The second was to develop our understanding of the problem by analysing options in the short, medium and long term. The third was to discover more about the dynamics of the Northern Alliance, including their capabilities and coalitions. The fourth was to work out the effect of Ramadan in November. The fifth was to be prepared for an enemy attack, either abroad or in the United Kingdom. The final concern was presentation handling; we needed to move the media away from the notion that the military campaign was working in isolation from other government lines of activity.

On 22nd October, the Chief of Defence Staff launched one of our publications at the Royal United Services Institute. British Defence Doctrine had been revised by an irreverent matelot who took account of 9/11 and turned it into a stylish read. It was not a set of rules, but an articulation of enduring themes and the British way of applying fighting power in support of national policies.

Before this event, I attended the early morning brief in the bunker. The assessment of the battlefield damage and Taliban reactions were sketchy. A Cabinet Office paper seeking input to the strategic plan set a number of hares running. Basing was still being discussed and there were concerns about Pakistan, because President Musharraf had cancelled the elections due to his personal safety concerns. The United States formally requested that their troops should take over the security of Diego Garcia and Malacca.

In the afternoon, I met with the civil contingency secretariat, when we discussed the resilience of the United Kingdom. The Prime Minister was at last able to shoot down any rogue aircraft over London. We were most concerned about the response to a biological attack. We talked about the need to rebuild the old regional government centres and alternative military headquarters in case of a dirty bomb attack in London. In searching for ideas to help local government education officers understand how they could contribute to the overall mission against international terrorism, I was asked to scope a new doctrine publication for Homeland Security.

The last two weeks in October continued in the same vein with heavy attrition from B-52 carpet bombing, which had not been seen since Vietnam. In London, the focus of the military was on operational issues rather than strategic direction. It was frustrating that the good ideas produced by our teams in September were being ignored, but we were now very much on the coat tails of the American response, Operation Enduring Freedom, which effectively meant that we had given up our independent thinking.

★ ★ ★

The Secretary of State visited Exercise Saif Sareea 2 in Oman on 27th October and raised the prospect of deploying the Royal Marines to find Usama bin Laden. On the same day, the Commanding Officer of the regular Special Air Service regiment travelled to Afghanistan, whilst the battle raged for control of the town of Mazar e Sharif. Unfortunately, the Commander of 3 Commando Brigade expressed his concerns about the readiness of his troops for military action, and this caused a mini-storm in the media. The result was an exchange of semantics between Geoff Hoon and the Opposition Defence spokesman in the House of Commons, which put no one in a good light.

To my mind, the problem was caused by the lack of a joined-up information campaign, which played into the hands of mischievous media moguls. Editors did not enjoy being in a situation where they were not setting the agenda. They continued to conjure up spurious scare stories surrounding issues such as anthrax and highlighted distant incidents, including the massacre by masked gunmen of eighteen Christians at prayer in precarious Pakistan. At this time, the *Telegraph*, *Times* and *Financial Times* could be relied on to be factual, but the *Guardian, Mail, Independent* and *Mirror* were all consistently negative. Television news was normally neutral but occasionally played the sensational, such as when they carried bin Laden's broadcasts.

Two companies of 40 Commando deployed from Diego Garcia to Bagram in early November to support our Special Forces operations. At the same time, I flew to Argentina with Sir Marrack Goulding, the former United Nations Under-Secretary General for Peacekeeping, who handed over to Kofi Annan in 1993. The declared purpose of my assignment was to explain the United Kingdom's approach to peace support operations at conferences in Buenos Aires and Montevideo. However, a more important task was to discuss the possibility of Argentina participating in Coalition operations with the United Kingdom.

The Argentinean Head of Operations, Lieutenant General Carlos Zabala, told me that I was the first British Army officer since the Falklands War to enter the operations department in the Defence Ministry. Nine other senior officers sat with him around a long table in a panelled room, with a well-thumbed copy of a British Army manual by his side. The first thing I did was to present him with a copy of our latest, unclassified, joint warfare publication.

After I described our recent operations, I was quizzed as

if I was in a Mastermind chair. Two hours later, the General gave me an undertaking for Argentinean forces to participate in operations alongside the British Army. He stopped short of committing troops to Afghanistan, but we agreed that the Balkans would be a useful stepping stone.

The problem he shared with his military counterparts in Uruguay was that the politicians were very reluctant to deploy their troops on anything other than a Chapter VI operation. After our experience in Bosnia in 1995, Britain was keen to broaden the freedom of action in peace support operations by insisting on Chapter VII mandates. This widened the use of force from merely self-defence to the ability to prevent desperate situations such as ethnic cleansing.

Sir Marrack Goulding was vibrant company during the week in Argentina. His tales of the period when he had run United Nations operations and political affairs were inspiring. He was a strong advocate of a United Nations standing army, but I disagreed with him about its practicalities. The idea had many merits, but in Britain we believed it was unrealistic whilst NATO provided a viable military Alliance.

However, the headlines about the Alliance's prevarication with regard to Afghanistan were not flattering. My favourite was Bronwen Maddox's *NATO is nowhere and Russia loves it.* The United States was disappointed with the Alliance's decision-making processes, which were insufficiently responsive to its needs. The European Union was quicker off the mark, developing arrest warrants and other counter-terrorism initiatives, but their defence programme was too immature to be of value for military operations.

Despite these disappointments, by mid-November the Coalition had extended across the world, with several Muslim countries, including Turkey, actively participating. Even Muammar Gaddafi expressed sympathy with the victims of 9/11 and called for Libyan involvement in the War on Terror against Militant Islamism.

I returned to England for a very poignant Remembrance Service on Sunday 11th November. The next day, Kabul was captured and the United Nations adopted its third resolution on international terrorism since 9/11. As soon as the Taliban regime collapsed, I was called to re-join the strategic planning group. We had to produce another paper for the Chiefs of Staff to form the basis of discussion at their meeting on 5th December. For this enterprise, two officers travelled over from the Pentagon in Washington to assist our work.

The strategic estimate was being updated after we received a copy of the draft United States strategy for the Global War of Terrorism. This was due to be passed to Donald Rumsfeld on 15th December. In the American strategy, a number of further operations were proposed, specifically in Iraq, Lebanon and Palestine.

Iraq was described as a sponsor state with weapons of mass destruction, and the United States course of action was regime change with the creation of a military governate to manage the transition. However, Iraq had actively distanced itself from any association with Al Qa'eda and the Arab states had expressed concern about any attack on one of their core states. Our response was that the United States assessment of support in the Gulf region was optimistic and did not meet with the United Kingdom perceptions, so we recommended that this should potentially be one of our Red Lines.

We compared and contrasted all the American priorities with our national priorities and offered four choices: support the United States unequivocally; discuss with United States potential areas for action and select only those that match Her Majesty's Government's policy goals; provide the United States with United Kingdom Red Lines on potential operations; and contain United Kingdom operations within Afghanistan.

Apart from this analysis, I also updated my previous work on campaign objective 7, the reintegration of Afghanistan into the international community. This was a political, not military, task that required a comprehensive, global approach under the direction of the United Nations. However, no detail had emerged from the Cabinet or Foreign Offices and we were very concerned about the risks of mission creep.

I set out four choices for the government to consider. The first was to return to our previous policy on Afghanistan and remain at arm's length, with a minimal amount of intrusion by military forces, acting only as observers. The next level, which I described as a partnership, was modelled on the successful mission in Namibia, where international forces provided security in the capital and a few other major population centres.

The third level was similar to the United Nations operation in Cambodia, where the international community took control of government functions and assumed responsibility for basic services. The final option was based on our recent operations in East Timor and Kosovo, when we assumed full executive and legislative responsibility in a transitional administration.

I suggested that the decision and force structure should depend on the outcome of the Bonn meeting of Afghan leaders and listed seven military tasks to enable the civilian sector to play its part in the reconstruction efforts. I highlighted the scale of the social problems, which dwarfed the challenges faced in Bosnia. There were several other strategic risks, including a lack of a clear exit strategy and the perceptions of the broader Muslim community about the invasion. However, the biggest hurdle was the potential confusion with other government objectives.

We had already committed significant resources to the hunt for Usama bin Laden and the fight against Al Qa'eda and the Taliban. I wrote that it may seem politically attractive to have United Kingdom troops involved in both war fighting operations and the reintegration of Afghanistan. However, I suggested that a static mission in theatre would prove counterproductive when viewed against the broader campaign objectives and would confuse our target audiences and extend time lines. Some organisations would have difficulty working with United Kingdom troops, if they were also perceived as belligerents in the war against terrorism.

I concluded with the following advice:

The strategic risks of becoming fixed in Afghanistan should not be underestimated. The need for the right intervention force, supported by a clear mandate and the capability to deal with a deteriorating situation are key imperatives for any military force deploying to the region. Sending United Kingdom troops to Afghanistan to support humanitarian activity is likely to confuse the situation. It may be preferable to limit [our] involvement to training and influence roles with the intervention ceded to an Islamic coalition of forces.

The sombre memorial service in Westminster Abbey on 29th November for the victims of 9/11 preceded a plethora of international conferences in December. The principal meeting took place in Bonn, where the Algerian diplomat, Lakhdar Brahimi, who had been appointed as the Special Representative for Afghanistan, agreed the role of the United Nations in establishing the interim authority and subsequent *Loya Jirga*.

The Royal Air Force flew a dozen representatives of the Afghan United Front, formerly the Northern Alliance, on a Lockheed C-130 Hercules to Germany, where they agreed with other prominent Afghans to the transfer of power on 22nd December. I tracked the daily progress of this conference through the morning meetings in the DCMO. My advice on the arrangements for the international security force was to limit its sphere of work to Kabul and the surrounding area, in order to avoid potential confusion with the war fighting operation.

There was also an Afghan women's summit for democracy in Brussels which came up with a range of demands with respect to the reconstruction of Afghanistan, which they sent to Brahimi. They were most irate that women were only mentioned twice in the first draft of the Afghan agreement and claimed that this did not represent the move towards gender mainstreaming agreed in Resolution 1325.

Some of the consequences of 9/11 were not anticipated, including the thawing of relations with Russia. On 7th and 8th December, I attended an undeclared conference with the Russian and French military in Sussex. The delegation from Moscow was led by the Deputy Chief of the General Staff and the French sent their Vice Chief of Defence Staff, who spoke about co-operation between the European Union and Russia in the spheres of security and defence. The keynote address was delivered by the Minister for Defence Procurement.

There was a strong sense of co-operation throughout the talks, although this did not necessarily translate to the lower levels of our respective ministries. Occasionally, there was an outlandish intervention from a particular officer who declared that NATO enlargement was a German plot against Russia. He also suggested that the campaign in Afghanistan was a British colonial plot, which raised a hearty laugh. Despite his conspiracy theories, there were some really useful exchanges about nuclear security and shared insights about tackling international terrorism, which we subsequently used in our policy work.

On 10th December, the Chief of Defence Staff used our grand strategic advice in his address at the Royal United Services Institute. The cautionary tone was cleared with Number 10, but someone briefed newspaper editors against him the next day, which resulted in an ill-informed editorial in the *Telegraph* on 12th December. It appeared that newspaper owners remained unhappy that we were reluctant to deploy United Kingdom conventional land forces; because it meant that they were unable to reinforce their jingoistic headlines about "Our Boys".

We were still not getting it right with the media. Unfortunately, the Downing Street communications unit had lost its reputation when Jo Moore infamously described 9/11 as "a good day to bury bad news". Rather than fulfilling its responsibility to produce a coherent strategy for government departments, Number 10 played games with a frantic media eager to set the agenda and be first with the scoop that would sell more copies than their rivals.

On 11th and 12th December, we ran a joint military civilian workshop to bring together discerning representatives from the media, non-government organisations and United Nations practitioners for 3rd Division. They had been warned about deployment to Kabul and we wished to help them understand the latest developments in the grey areas of peace support operations.

Almost all our recommendations involved information sharing, communications and liaison. When we interviewed the force commander in Kabul five months later, he confirmed that the Department for International Development contact had proved valuable. However, the civil-military group had a limited capacity, which meant that their quick implementation projects were restricted to force protection purposes, rather than reconstruction.

The next day, I flew to Geneva for a meeting with the International Committee of the Red Cross. This was the first time in their 138-year history that they had invited a serving soldier into their headquarters. They placed enormous importance on their impartiality. However, since the mid-nineties their people had been targeted directly in Africa and Chechnya and the Red Cross and Red Crescent symbols no longer offered complete protection.

Tentatively, they wished to develop civil-military co-operation protocols and invited me to discuss their proposals, along with representatives from the European Union military staff and an American officer from NATO. I had already established warm relations with the head of one of their divisions when I addressed a conference in Oslo earlier in the year, so the two-day workshop achieved a great deal.

Just before we departed, a young ICRC director who I had never met asked for a private talk in an adjoining office. He explained that he had seen reports from the Red Cross personnel in Kabul about the Coalition's prisoners who were disappearing in Afghanistan. He provided me with the details of several cases of wounded detainees who were flown out of the country and held either on a ship in the Indian Ocean or in Diego Garcia. The ICRC also gave me the contact details of the National Bureau of Information and asked me to ensure that our armed forces conformed to international obligations.

On my return to England, I discussed the extraordinary rendition issue with the commitments team in the bunker. They agreed to instruct the Special Forces to keep within the boundaries of international law. I also emailed the Chief of Staff of the United Kingdom division deploying to Kabul and asked him to set up an information-sharing mechanism with the Red Cross.

Whilst I was in Geneva, the commander of 3rd Division travelled to Bagram and conducted a reconnaissance of Kabul. At the same time, Task Force 58 occupied Kandahar airfield. Then on Monday 17th December, after the attacks on the Tora Bora caves concluded, Donald Rumsfeld visited Bagram and announced that an international stabilisation and assistance force of 5,000 troops would deploy to the capital. Fortunately, the chairman of the interim administration, Mr Hamid Karzai, stated that ISAF, as it became known, should be robust and able to defend itself. This was very helpful in achieving the desired Chapter VII mandate, which ensured the hands of our troops were not tied behind their backs by obstructive rules of engagement.

On 21st December, the United Nations adopted resolution 1386 authorising ISAF's mandate. Soon afterwards Headquarters 3rd Division and the remainder of the British contingent for ISAF journeyed to Afghanistan on Operation Fingal. Once we verified the viability of Kabul International Airport for the use of ISAF forces, they built a tented camp at a nearby fertiliser plant, which was named after the only survivor of the 1842 battle of Gandamak, Captain Souter.

ISAF's intervention was considered beneficial and extremely effective by many commentators. The commercial bustle of Kabul returned quickly. Markets were selling meat, fruit and vegetables, so there was ample food for the population. Televisions and kites, banned by the Taliban, arrived by the lorry load. Burqas were discarded.

However, there were many challenges faced by the ISAF leaders. The force generation of 17 nations and ad hoc groupings without a NATO framework led to confusion. The lack of common doctrine and equipment limited the scope of the patrol programmes, which in some cases were ponderous and achieved very little. Security remained fragile and a critical concern of the commander.

Progress was hindered in many ways and deployments were delayed. The Parachute Battalion was not complete in theatre until February, five weeks after the lead elements arrived. Rubble around residential areas resembled Dresden after the World War II bombings, and reconstruction was slow.

Then a powerful earthquake hit the Hindu Kush on 3rd January and diverted humanitarian assistance from other areas. ISAF responded to several earthquakes that winter by flying tents, supplies and humanitarian aid co-ordinators, carried by Royal Air Force Chinook helicopters, into the mountains and by providing medical assistance from Kabul. This brought home to the Afghan people the beneficent aspects of the international presence in their midst.

The task of raising and training an embryonic Afghan National Army with an appropriate ethnic mix was torturous, with only 300 volunteers for an Army of 50,000. Demobilisation and disarmament were distant prospects. Most fighters remained steadfastly loyal to their patrons and paymasters. However, ISAF established a location and sourced funding and equipment so that the process could be controlled by the Afghan government when the emergency *Loya Jirga* took place in July.

There were also deep cultural misunderstandings about issues such as blood money. Following the killing of a civilian, when a British patrol was shot at by a gunman, a taxi was impounded. The family of the dead man and the taxi driver demanded compensation. ISAF had to wait for bureaucrats in London to authorise payment, but this was simply not understood by the Afghans, who saw it as evidence of a rich country suppressing the native culture. It took a visiting Minister to finally cut through the red tape and resolve the problem.

ISAF imposed a disciplined law and order regime in the city, but they did not have the scale of resources or remit to deal with ordinary crime. This propagated the perception among some Taliban supporters that the new regime was no better than the Russian occupation. This view was reinforced by the predictable confusion with the war fighting outside the capital. The United States message of "surrender or die" was wholly incompatible with the ISAF themes of stability, normalisation and regeneration. Countering the black propaganda that ISAF was merely a front for the United States and would stay longer than the six-month mandate was a challenge, which required the Commander to designate information operations as his main effort.

The ISAF chief of staff confirmed to us that the distinction between their role as United Nations peacekeepers and the Coalition's role in the war on terrorism was lost on Afghans. The principle of conducting war fighting, peacekeeping and humanitarian assistance all in the same operation was set out by General Charles Krulak in his seminal article *The Strategic Corporal: Leadership in the Three Block War*. However, the lessons were lost in London and Washington and so the seeds were sown for the subsequent strategic failures which consumed billions of dollars and thousands of lives.

Britain's armed forces are regularly heralded for their sacrifices on operations, but the dedicated male and female civil servants who deployed alongside their military colleagues to Kabul are equally deserving of special praise. Our government departments varied in their responses to 9/11, but one ministry which came up trumps was the Department for Trade and Industry. In particular, Edward Lidderdale's elegant series of papers on aid and reconstruction in Afghanistan early in 2002 should not be forgotten.

* * *

In January, the New Chapter of the Strategic Defence Review took over my life. I had been tracking this since 23rd October, when I met with the Policy Planning branch leading the project. Subsequently, I became involved in the qualitative research to gain an understanding of British people's perceptions, opinions and attitudes in the light of 9/11.

The main findings were presented by a tall, middle-aged, balding consultant. He explained the method of research and the profile of the diverse sample groups, who came from across the whole of Great Britain. Knowledge of the armed forces amongst younger people was very limited, but there was strong resistance from the majority of respondents to the suggestion of a higher profile in the United Kingdom. The respondents agreed that any increased military activity or presence in civilian life would generate panic and increase anxiety and not act to reassure the public.

There remained a greater awareness of the threat of terrorism in peoples' lives. An underlying feeling existed amongst some citizens that the United Kingdom had exposed itself to greater danger than its European counterparts by allying itself so closely with America. However, those outside London perceived a low threat and those in London were simply more sensitised to the potential for an attack.

The return to normality had enabled most respondents to reconcile their own fears and insecurities. Many associated our involvement as making the United Kingdom more of a target, especially families living near Asian Muslim areas in cities such as Birmingham. There was a broad understanding that some of the Taliban volunteers were British Muslims. However, there was a very positive response to our operations in Afghanistan and a desire to use our armed forces to facilitate the stabilisation of the country and in support of humanitarian aid efforts.

I fed much of this analysis into working group 4, which held responsibility for countering international terrorism abroad. In December, we had developed a strategic effects framework, which was used as the conceptual base for new capabilities. On 14th January, I circulated the first draft of our report and offered wider consultation with other government departments, academics and non-government organisations.

There were a number of political tensions which we had to finesse. There was a strong sense that our posture should change to one of necessity, rather than benevolence. However, the perceptions of dropping the well-regarded refrain 'Force for Good' were mostly negative, so we kept the headline whilst improving capabilities to wrest the initiative from international terrorist organisations.

The deliberations about Defence Planning Assumptions generated radical ideas about replacing our peace support operations terminology with stabilisation operations. This was more than just a semantic discussion about perceptions and presentation. There were important implications for our organisations and equipment choices, which hinged on the detailed analysis of the roles and missions in Afghanistan and other counter-terrorist operations.

On Wednesday 30th January, the Director of Médecins Sans Frontières wrote an irate letter to our Secretary of State. He complained about the British Special Forces based at Kandahar who were claiming to be on a humanitarian mission. He protested that both the United Kingdom and the United States were contravening the Geneva Convention, which requires military forces to distinguish themselves from civilians. The consequence of these actions was that volunteer humanitarian workers' lives were put at greater risk.

This was not the only ethical dilemma facing us in London. There was a fierce debate about the use of torture which stemmed from the FBI policies. They argued that if they knew the man in front of them had critical information that would enable the United States to prevent a catastrophic atrocity from taking place, they would torture him and take the consequences.

Many people used similar arguments of proportionality to justify the idea of assassinating bin Laden. In November, the International Security Information Service produced a security briefing for Parliamentarians, which concluded "that there could be a morally just assassination, with Usama bin Laden as a prime target". In London, the Royal United Services Institute organised a conference on morality in asymmetric war. Here, the most powerful counter-argument came from a former commander in Northern Ireland. He highlighted four important reasons why it is vital that counter terrorists stay within the law, and summarised these by commenting that remorse is an uncomfortable companion in life.

Whilst I was working on the capability implications of the defence review, I also maintained a keen eye on the urgent operational requirements for the Royal Marines, who had deployed to Afghanistan. On Friday 15th March, the United States formally requested the deployment of a British combat force to reinforce their offensive, Operation Anaconda. The Americans had been surprised at the ferocity of the battle and had lost eight men killed in action.

We had an inkling of what was happening through the Newhouse News Service, which reported verbatim from inside the 10th Mountain Division command post at Bagram

Air Base. These exhilarating exchanges, as they hunted for bin Laden, taunted many British senior officers. The "stabbers and stranglers" were itching to become involved in the war fighting, rather than participate in the peace support operation. However, when I read the dialogue, I couldn't help feeling that this approach of whoopin' and hollerin' when they blew up a truck was a catastrophic mistake in the making.

Soon afterwards, about 1600 troops under the command of 3 Commando Brigade deployed on Operation Jacana. Unfortunately, they took over five weeks to reach full operating capability and suffered from a serious outbreak of disease in 34 Field Hospital at Bagram. Their complaints about weapons and equipment added to the sense of farce reported in the London newspapers.

The media called for the sacking of the Brigade Commander after a series of information gaffes. In fact, this story was planted by a senior Army officer who briefed a journalist that the commando leader had lost the confidence of politicians, junior members of his brigade and the American commander. An intense rivalry existed between the Royal Marines and the Parachute Regiment. Professionally, they both wished to be the principal British rapid deployment force and their officers took every opportunity to censure their opposite numbers whenever a chance arose.

In response, the Chief of Defence Staff sent a message to all personnel defending the manoeuvres of 45 Commando, which had been placed under command of 10th Mountain Division. They were inserted into remote regions and conducted four search and destroy operations to attack Al Qa'eda and Taliban forces. In total, they captured an enormous amount of territory without any casualties and dispelled any lingering doubts about the United Kingdom's commitment to war-fighting. However, the lack of any real combat was an anti-climax and prompted more criticism from the media, who had been promised spectacular battlefield victories.

My team from Shrivenham visited Afghanistan at the end of May and spoke with Lakhdar Brahimi and the commander of ISAF, Major General John McColl. Unfortunately, 3 Commando Brigade refused to accept their visit, but many other political and military leaders were willing to provide information to update the United Kingdom strategy. The Operation Veritas current commitments team closed down on 28th May and their work became normal business for a newly formed international terrorism section in the Ministry of Defence.

Turkey took over the lead for ISAF in the summer as the Iraq War began to take priority in London. I completed two submissions for the Strategic Defence Review, which was published on 18th July, before starting work on an unclassified pamphlet about international terrorism.

After ten months, Operation Veritas was replaced seamlessly by Operation Herrick. Remarkably, each of the three elements of Veritas (Oracle, Fingal and Jacana) had been successful in achieving one or more of the seven original objectives announced by the Foreign Secretary back in October 2001. Progress was seen across the campaign, except for the attempt to bring Usama bin Laden to justice. More importantly, this success was achieved without any British Service man or woman being killed through hostile action.

The main British contribution for the early years of Operation Herrick was the Provincial Reconstruction Team, or PRT, at Mazar e Sharif. We were alerted to this initiative through our contacts with the British Agencies Afghanistan Group. The concept was drafted by a British Army officer embedded with the Americans at Bagram air base. His idea for the creation of what initially was termed a Joint Regional Team was passed to us at Shrivenham. We refined the concept trying to avoid any similarity to the Soviet Union's equivalent teams in the 1980s. We came up with a new name and suitable tasks for the military, including engineering projects for the local economy and security sector reform.

Reality in conflict doesn't always match the theory. In practice, each of the countries which led one of the new PRTs approached its task in a unique way, according to their national caveats and local conditions. The British PRT in Mazar was organised into six-man military observation sections. Most of their work involved stabilisation tasks, including prisoner security, rather than major reconstruction projects.

The responsiveness and adaptability of the military and their civilian counterparts meant that the PRT programme was considered successful. They certainly helped to return the country to some form of normality and thereby achieved further progress in the campaign objective to reintegrate Afghanistan into the international community.

It is a terrific testament to the commanders of the PRT that only two British soldiers were killed by hostile action in Afghanistan before 2006. Sadly, Private Jonathan Kitulagoda died in a suicide bomb attack in Kabul in January 2004 and

Lance Corporal Steven Sherwood was shot dead in an ambush near Mazar e Sharif in October 2005. However, in the light of what happened subsequently in Helmand and compared with other British deployments over the past 30 years, these numbers were low.

Early in 2003, I supported my director at the sixth oral evidence session of the House of Commons Defence Select Committee. Their report into the Strategic Defence Review New Chapter was equivocal in its support, but given the composition of the Committee this was not surprising, and overall, I believe their findings were fair.

There followed another working visit to New York to persuade the United Nations to offer more support to counter international terrorism. Then I deployed to Sarajevo and planned NATO special operations, hunting for the war criminals indicted by the international criminal tribunal. After an exciting six-month tour, I returned to England to work for the Quartermaster General, supporting British operations in both Iraq and Afghanistan.

The hunt for Usama bin Laden fluctuated for ten years. Pakistani forces had their best chance of capturing him when they launched an offensive along the border with Afghanistan in 2004, but they lost the trail. When eventually he was killed in the American raid in May 2011, many commentators expressed relief. However, 33 years after he founded Al Qa'eda with Ayman al-Zawahiri, his martyrdom made little difference to the prospect of peace and confirmed our original assessment that his pursuit was a distraction, which would not address the causes of 9/11.

By then I had read Mullah Abdul Salem Zaeef's biography, edited by the only two Westerners living permanently in Kandahar in 2008. Zaeef was the former ambassador to Pakistan and inmate of Guantanamo prison whose account contradicted many of the previous assumptions about the Taliban. For those seeking reconciliation with extremists intent on political violence, it is worth remembering his solemn caution: *Afghans do not back down – If they are in a weak position, their thoughts will be consumed with fighting for their rights and plotting their revenge.*

CHAPTER 5

Baghdad 2008 – Operation Telic

It would be child's play for a decent man to run Mesopotamia.

T E Lawrence

A large hand blocked the way to my breakfast table. It belonged to what seemed to be a twenty-stone boxer masquerading as a nightclub bouncer. I tried to skip around, but the pugilist was surprisingly quick on his feet. Bravely, I spoke to the hand.

"That's my breakfast table."

"I don't care, you can't proceed any further."

"But there is no one sitting at it."

"This area is now out of bounds."

"Says who?"

"Says the next President of the United States of America. Would you like to meet him and shake his hand?"

"Not if he won't allow me to eat my cornflakes at the same table I have used for the past six months."

Disgruntled, I padded outside the cookhouse with my cereal and cranberry juice and joined another table of British officers breakfasting in the grounds of Saddam Hussein's palace in Baghdad. I complained vigorously. They ignored my curmudgeonly rant and scuttled in to have their photographs taken with the smiling Senator Obama, who was visiting Baghdad before returning to Chicago the following day to record his vote in the Presidential polls.

★ ★ ★

The war in Iraq remains so contentious that anyone attempting to write about it in a positive manner has to accept that their story will not sit easily with all sections of society. Several journalists assigned to Baghdad revealed to me that their paymasters in London would never screen a positive story on the television or publish an optimistic article in the newspapers. Despatches had to be placed within the controlling editorial master message that the war was illegal and we could no longer trust what the government told us. Their subsidiary themes were either that British troops, issued with inadequate equipment, were being killed needlessly by bad planning and mismanagement, or that the same soldiers were abusing Iraqi civilians. The implied conclusion was that we were unwelcome in Iraq and should bring our troops home as soon as possible.

I have the utmost sympathy for the families of the fallen and the civilian casualties of war. I disagreed with the decision to invade Mesopotamia and groaned aloud when I read Richard Perle's keynote address to the Foreign Policy Research Institute in November 2001, which attempted to link Al Qa'eda to Saddam Hussein. However, I was not among those in the Services who refused to serve on Operation Telic.

There were two sorts of conscientious objectors in the armed forces. Malcolm Kendall-Smith was typical of the first group when he suggested that the questionable legitimacy of the invasion allowed him to refuse the order to deploy. There had been a forthright discussion in the British Army in the 1990s about when an officer should disobey an order, but in no sense did Kendall-Smith's argument fit one of the manifestly illegal categories proscribed both in national and international law. Apart from anything else, as a junior doctor, he was not being asked to do anything which violated his Hippocratic Oath and so there was no surprise when he was found guilty of disobeying lawful orders and sentenced to eight months in prison.

In contrast, I respected the second type of objector typified by Ben Griffin, who had an excellent record as a soldier, but became disillusioned with the way the war was conducted. At least he had served in Baghdad alongside American forces, so he knew what he was talking about and had the courage of his convictions to speak out when others might have been more circumspect. I would have welcomed him into my command in 2008, when perhaps he might have changed his view about the lack of any cultural sensitivity when dealing with Iraqis.

* * *

My involvement in the invasion was insignificant. Although the British response to 9/11 was penned in Whitehall, the work on Iraq was conducted mainly in the permanent joint headquarters at Northwood. Underground, in the bunker, operational staff officers beavered away, liaising with their American counterparts in General Tommy Franks' headquarters in Florida and issuing warning orders to Royal Navy, Army and Royal Air Force commands.

On 1st July 2002, I represented the Ministry of Defence at a round table discussion on American Foreign Policy in London. The United States Under-Secretary of State, John Bolton, delivered an uncompromising address. He explained that the immediate political-military response to 9/11 against the Taliban and Al Qa'eda had been refined and the long-term approach was now focused on the fusion of the war on International Terrorism with their Weapons of Mass Destruction objectives, including the pre-emptive use of force for regime replacement against rogue states.

In Whitehall ministries, there were many concerns about the consequences of war in Iraq. However, Number 10's determination to achieve a further United Nations Security Council Resolution, with robust language about Weapons of Mass Destruction, overruled everything else. I attended a gathering at Wilton Park to discuss best practices in post-conflict reconstruction and participated in a Foreign Office workshop on nation-building, led by the Parliamentary Under-Secretary of State, but this turned into a pointless discussion about policy officers' pet projects. There were also plenty of desk level meetings with the Department for International Development, but tight operational security limited the number of people who could influence Telic planning and constrained any real comprehensive planning from taking place.

However, there are always ways to discover what is happening in the British Army, and in October I travelled to Germany to brief the key leaders of 1st Armoured Division at their Study Day in Herford. The commanding general opened the event before flying to the United States for Iraq briefings later that day. Over lunch, the main planning team, which comprised the Deputy Commander, Chief of Staff and Deputy Chief of Staff, informed me that the Division had been given a warning order to deploy to Iraq but up to now, they had been planning in isolation. Since the International Committee for the Red Cross and the United Nations in Geneva both sent representatives, I have no doubt that they also knew about the invasion plans well before the House of Commons passed the motion to authorise military action by 412 votes to 149 on 18th March 2003.

The pivotal military planning was completed by the staff at the Quartermaster General's headquarters at Andover. They used a computer model to analyse the northern and southern invasion scenarios and calculate the amount of equipment and materiel needed to support different land fighting formations. The northern option involved a strategic lift into Turkey, followed by tactical movement on difficult lines of communications through snow-capped mountains. The sea line of communication for the southern option was over 6,000 miles, but the subsequent land supply route was shorter and the requirement for tactical air transport was less. It took some time to come up with the answer, but on the advice of this team, the force generation order issued on 13th December 2002, based on an approach through Turkey, was changed, as we replaced an armoured brigade with an air assault brigade and attacked from the south, rather than through Kurdistan.

I was acquainted with some of the Iraqis in exile through the Al-Khoei family. Ayatollah Al-Khoei was the spiritual leader of much of the Shia world and supported the uprising against Saddam Hussein in 1991. He died under house arrest the following year. His son was a moderate leader who led a family foundation in several countries, with strong connections to the United Nations.

The Al-Khoeis came to prominence when they unrolled a banner about martyred Shia Muslims at the Royal Institute of International affairs in 1999 during the interfaith visit of three senior clerics from Baghdad, organised by the inspirational Canon Andrew White. At the end of January 2003, I chaired a panel of experts at their 'Muslims in Europe' conference in London. My distinguished co-panellists included Stephen Lawrence's family solicitor, Imran Khan, a commissioner of the Metropolitan Police, and the QC defending the Algerian who had recently murdered Detective Constable Stephen Oake in Manchester.

Introducing this eclectic group, I explained why the military must stick to the rule of law and talked about attitudes to security, covering both physical protection and the emotional response to the prevailing environment. I was particularly impressed by HRH Prince Hassan of Jordan, who chaired the final interfaith panel, and the keynote speaker, Professor John Rex, who summarised people's concerns when he said: "For those of us who have made efforts to find a place for Islam in society, these are tough times".

The head of the foundation, Sayyid Abdul Majid Al-Khoei, travelled out to Iraq soon after the invasion with plans to revive the holy city of Najaf to the position it had held under his father. Sadly, he was assassinated on 10th April 2003, close to the Imam Ali Shrine. Subsequently, Moqtadr Al-Sadr took control of the area and used the mosque as a military base for launching attacks during the civil war in 2004 between his Shia Mahdi Army and the Sunnis, led by Abu Musab Al-Zarqawi.

Divisions in the Arab World over Iraq were exposed before the war began on 20 March. At the beginning of that month their leaders gathered for a summit at the Red Sea resort of Sharm el-Sheikh to rally around the cause of peace. Colonel Gaddafi was photographed looking worried and subsequently was influenced to decommission his chemical and nuclear weapons and renounce Libya's possession of weapons of mass destruction. This resulted in the European Union ending their sanctions the following year and the United States removing him from their list of state sponsors of terrorism.

★ ★ ★

As a result of my work on peace support operations, I was telephoned from the Joint Headquarters and invited to join the Phase 4 Post Decisive Action planning team in Qatar. This provided the foundation for the Office of Reconstruction and Humanitarian Affairs, which was set up initially to deal with the provision of basic life support for displaced people. However my Director General refused to let me go because I had to support him at an imminent session with the House of Commons Defence Committee, which was taking evidence on the Strategic Defence Review New Chapter.

I was content with this decision, because it was already clear that the political leadership on both sides of the Atlantic did not understand their implied responsibilities and obligations under international law and the Geneva Convention. A friend who was a senior associate at the International Peace Academy in New York confirmed the unwillingness of the United States Administration to engage in nation-building. It did not surprise anyone in the peace support sector that despite the good ideas and valuable experience of reconstruction practitioners from the Balkans, ORHA failed so badly to match the expectations of Iraqi local leaders in the month after President Bush declared combat operations were over.

On the day of the invasion, I was preparing to address the Wyndham Place Charlemagne Trust, a diverse group of people with a wide range of political and religious opinions from different cultural and professional backgrounds. However, it was difficult to concentrate on this task because I was thinking about two familiar tank squadrons fighting in the desert with the First Fusiliers. These were B Squadron, which I had commanded on Operation Granby, and C Squadron, which I had taken to Bosnia in 1995. The Brigade Commander of the Desert Rats had judged them to be the best sabre squadrons at the end of the previous training year, so it was not surprising that he selected them to be the first through the breach at 0307 hours on 21st March 2003. It was ironic that a troop from B Squadron, 17th/21st Lancers had been the first complete tank troop into Kuwait in 1991 and twelve years later, a troop from the same squadron led the second advance into Iraq.

Both squadrons endured a sustained period of fighting over several days. They moved rapidly to capture the Shatt-Al-Basrah canal, but C Squadron lost two soldiers on Bridge 3, known as Objective Leicester. They had set up a defensive position overlooking the canal facing north east. To their south, B Company of the Black Watch had pushed one of their attached Challenger 2 tanks from 2nd Royal Tank Regiment over the canal at Bridge 4. The squadron leader sent a liaison officer to co-ordinate the arcs of fire with the Black Watch headquarters, in order to ensure they would not interfere with each other.

Despite this precaution, at 0320 hours on 25th March, the crew in the Royal Tank Regiment Challenger acquired what they believed to be a stalking party armed with anti-tank weapons 750 metres away and asked for permission to engage the position known as Truck. Unfortunately, the commander of the tank was disorientated and he fired two high explosive squash head rounds out of his arc at C Squadron's tank 1300 metres away on the western side of the canal. The second round destroyed Call Sign Charlie One-Two and killed the commander, Corporal Steve Allbutt, and the driver, Trooper Dave Clarke.

This fratricide incident hit all the members of the regiment hard and brought home the hazards of war, but the troops rallied well and continued to carry out their tasks with tremendous resilience. After Basrah was secured on 6th April, the squadrons transitioned to Phase 4, the peace support operation. They were both given large areas of responsibility, but in reality, the daily attacks in April and May prevented them from undertaking the complex stabilisation tasks required in the immediate aftermath. By the time the six Royal Military Policemen were killed at Al Majar Al Kabir on 24th June, it was already clear that the British Army's successes in the Balkans and Sierra Leone would not be repeated in Iraq.

I had to deal with the regiment's destroyed Challenger 2 when it was returned to Britain and pieced together at Kirkcudbright ranges. We always conducted a detailed investigation after these sorts of incidents, so we could understand forensically how to improve our armoured protection. Dedicated technical experts pored over the ballistic path of a projectile in their attempts to keep us one step ahead of the enemy. For me, it was an honour to lead the team at the heart of the rapid procurement of land and rotary wing equipment, during the most demanding period of the war in Iraq.

My regiment missed Telic 2, which is probably just as well since there were 1160 heat injuries with a quarter of those affected requiring hospitalisation and many returning to England for medical treatment. Insufficient acclimatisation for our soldiers, who had to conduct dismounted patrols in 50-degree heat wearing body armour, was another example of poor planning to add to the strategic mistakes made by the occupying forces. Chief amongst these was the disbandment of the Iraqi Army, which allowed Islamist militias to fill the security vacuum and pushed many Sunnis into the enemy camp.

Although there were good days, such as the raid on Saddam's sons in Mosul and the subsequent capture of the tyrant, there were many more bad days as the United States quickly lost its reputation as a proficient liberator. In preparing for my tour, I sought the advice of Hilary Synott, who was the regional co-ordinator for the four southern provinces in 2003.

Hilary told me how the fledgling Baghdad ministries failed to provide timely guidance, which contributed to the sense of an incompetent occupation. The suicide attack on the United Nations headquarters, which killed the head of mission, was a severe blow to the Coalition Provisional Authority. The withdrawal of the International Committee of the Red Cross, after they suffered a similar attack, added to the sense of despondency. However, the military allies held together well throughout the first year, with Poland becoming the third country to run a sector of the country, when they took control of the five provinces in the central-southern stabilisation zone on 3rd September.

This area contained a dozen of the most important cultural and historical sites in Iraq. These included Babylon, which had been fortified during the war and Najaf, where Sayyid Abdul Majid Al-Khoei was assassinated in April. In the eastern part of the Polish sector, Wasit Province held special significance for the British Army. Following its defeat by the Ottoman Army at Ctesiphon in November 1915, 6th Division under General Townshend was surrounded at the provincial capital, Al-Kut. Despite the heroic efforts of Gerald Leachman, who led the escape of 5,000 troops and two batteries of guns under the cover of darkness, the General surrendered after a siege of 147 days, with 11,000 prisoners marched into captivity.

Italy provided the fourth largest contingent of over 3,000 troops and ran the difficult area around An Nasariyah in Dhi

Qar Province. They suffered their worst incident since the Second World War, when a suicide attack in a truck on 12th November 2003 killed thirteen Carabinieri and fifteen others. After three days of national mourning, the Italian forces rallied and continued their operations with some success. In April 2004, they rescued a 37-year-old British contractor, who had been taken hostage. By then, the first cracks had appeared in the coalition after the Madrid train bombs killed 202 people in March, resulting in Spain pulling out of Iraq a month later.

After the bodies of four contractors were dragged through the anti-American heartland of Fallujah, it was clear that reinforcements were required. We had already been told that the planned reduction to small scale in Iraq had been put back a year. Then on my birthday, the United States formally requested that we took over the Spanish area of operations at Najaf by the end of April. This was turned down by the British Government, just as the first graphic images of the prisoner abuse scandal at Abu Ghraib were released.

The following month, I had to produce a submission on six different courses of action, which were being considered by the Chiefs of Staff. The extreme option was to send NATO's Allied Rapid Reaction Corps, or ARRC as it was known. However, after much wrangling, the Secretary of State announced only a small expansion, with the addition of 40 Commando and the Black Watch in July.

In the meantime, the other two squadrons in my regiment had deployed for the tough tour on Telic 4 from April to October 2004. A Squadron was based at Camp Abu Naji near the city of Al Amarah close to the border with Iran. They experienced the rising tensions in Najaf and the deteriorating situation in Maysan Province. This resulted in a change of role from training the Iraqi Police Service to fighting Moqtadr Al-Sadr's militia during the two major uprisings in April and August. They were mightily relieved when we turned around the ship with 242 vehicles and equipment, so they could take over the Challenger 2 tanks which would withstand the rocket-propelled grenade attacks, now commonplace in southern Iraq.

A Squadron was intimately involved in the operation to reassert control of Al Amarah after the spike of enemy activity in April. It also responded to the multiple weapon ambush of a vehicle patrol on the Basrah highway at the Iraqi Police checkpoint named Danny Boy on 16th May. Call sign Alpha One-Zero suppressed the enemy depth position with its 7.62mm chain gun, whilst Call sign Alpha One-Two fired a single high explosive round to neutralise another militia position and enable the infantry to extract themselves and return to the safety of Camp Abu Naji.

Back in England, we were inundated with requests for equipment modifications and urgent operational requirements to meet the new threats emerging in southern Iraq. My award-winning team was intimately involved in these procurements. For example, our logistics convoys were increasingly coming under fire on their way from Shaiba to Basrah. We had to produce new protective armour and a pintle mount for the top of the trucks to stabilise the machine gun and improve the accuracy of the weapon. We found an obsolete piece of equipment in our stores and set about adapting it to fit all the wheeled vehicles used on Telic. This required three independent project teams to pool funds and work together on the design, never an easy task. One of my outstanding staff officers, Major Taniya Dennison, a Lynx helicopter pilot in the Army Air Corps, discovered that the solution was being designed for a six-foot-tall guardsman. She assiduously pointed out that many logistics operators were less than five foot six, so the design was changed to allow short female soldiers to use it effectively.

Then on 29th June at the NATO Summit in Istanbul, the Prime Minister announced that he was sending the ARRC to Afghanistan. We immediately realised that this would cause a huge problem because we knew there was not enough equipment for the predicted commitments, which not only involved Iraq and Afghanistan, but also a high readiness brigade for the 6th rotation of the NATO Response Force. Moreover we still had to sustain our troops during the marching season in Northern Ireland and peacekeeping in the Balkans. Only three months earlier, we had supported the short notice deployment of an infantry battalion to Kosovo following violent disturbances between ethnic Serbs and Albanians. They required 24 Snatch Land Rovers, which we had to borrow from Northern Ireland because most of the fleet was being used in Iraq.

However, it was impossible to persuade decision makers to conduct only one major land operation at a time and meanwhile, there were more pressing problems facing us in Iraq. There had been a catastrophic failure of Warrior tracks, which resulted in 80% of the fleet being downgraded as non-taskworthy. And for the first time, the frontal armour of a Challenger 2 tank had been penetrated by an enemy weapon system, so we had to airlift this back to Britain and replace half a dozen Warriors and eleven Snatch Land Rovers which had been damaged beyond local repair in the fighting.

At this time, part of my regiment was living in the former residence of the Maysan Provincial Governor, built on the confluence of the Tigris River in the centre of Al Amarah. There were constant gun battles at what was known as Cimic House until it was handed over to the local authorities in September. During a two-week period in August, the soldiers in fourth troop witnessed 495 mortar attacks, 37 rocket-propelled grenade attacks, seven incoming rockets and frequent shooting incidents, before a relief column of Challenger 2 tanks and Warrior infantry fighting vehicles fought its way into town as part of Operation Hammersmith, just before they ran out of rations. Afterwards, the Chief of the General Staff admitted publicly that we were back at war. However, to most Army officers, it seemed we had not stopped fighting since the invasion.

Meanwhile, D Squadron was based at Az Zubayr on the western outskirts of Basrah City and the port of Umm Qasr. They had a more successful time training the Iraqi security forces and through the initiative of a young captain, they created the Ports Joint Security Centre. This became the focus for all land and maritime security operations and enabled the strategically vital ports to begin handling the $18 billion reconstruction effort and to bring in two thirds of all the grain needed to feed the population.

At the end of October, the two squadrons returned to England as the Black Watch deployed north to Camp Dogwood, under direct command of the United States forces. They were the first battle group to receive the newly designed bar armour on their Warriors; a simple lightweight solution to the problem of stand-off attack. However, it did not take long for the enemy to counter the improved protection and on 17th November, we had first sight of the Iranian PG-7 tandem rounds which were capable of defeating our new armour.

Back in Catterick, A and D Squadrons discovered two important changes were being implemented in the regiment. The first was the conversion from heavy to light tanks as we became a force reconnaissance regiment, which was more relevant to contemporary military operations. The second coincidental change was taking effect throughout the British Army. Up to then, the first priority in my regiment had always been the tanks (and before mechanisation, our noble steeds in the stables). Now, people had become the priority as we shifted to a deliberate policy of equipping the soldier, rather than manning equipment.

One of the main catalysts for this change was the death of Sergeant Steve Roberts of 2nd Royal Tank Regiment on Telic 1. The pathologist's report of 17th November 2003 and the forensic evidence established in all probability that Roberts would have survived had he been wearing the enhanced combat body armour, rather than the basic protection he had been given.

It must seem dreadful to many people that investigations and inquiries after tragic events continually expose our equipment as a contributory factor to the death of Service personnel. There were more than a dozen reasons for the shortage of enhanced body armour, but it was shameful that so much of it was unused in an ISO container in the desert. The worst aspect was that this accident could have been avoided if the gunner had been trained properly on the weapon he fired and the crew had carefully practised their actions at vehicle checkpoints.

Part of the resulting change of priority included the introduction of whole fleet management. This concept was promoted by an opportunistic staff officer who convinced policy makers that armoured vehicles could be treated like taxis and passed from unit to unit. The theory proposed that a training fleet was located on the edge of our armoured manoeuvre area and a pristine fleet was stored and only issued after an operation had been announced.

Apart from ignoring the cost, time and manpower that is needed to maintain complex land equipment, there was a very straightforward political reason why this theory would not work. If the Treasury under Gordon Brown could not afford to keep our gold reserves, it was simply inconceivable that any government official would allow the Army to keep a fleet of a thousand unused armoured vehicles in pristine condition waiting for a rainy day!

★ ★ ★

My regiment took a well-deserved break for one year from Iraq. During this time, the first elections took place on 30th January 2005, but this did not stop the casualties from mounting. I was with a group of Royal Air Force transport pilots when a Lockheed C-130K Hercules crashed after enemy ground-to-air fire hit the outboard starboard wing, whilst it flew low from Baghdad to Balad on the afternoon of the elections. They were inconsolable when they heard about the deaths of the crew, which resulted in a change of policy about daylight low flying and the fitting of explosive suppressant foam to fuel tanks.

We delivered the first tranche of new Snatch 2 Land Rovers to the extremely high readiness battalion which deployed over the election period. The majority of drivers had extensive experience both in Northern Ireland and on Telic 4. They identified a number of issues, such as the reduced space in the front cab, but their report concluded "Snatch 2 is undoubtedly a major improvement to existing Force Protection measures. It has been well received by the troops on the ground and held in high regard by all that have used it thus far".

Air support was another critical issue for our operations in Afghanistan and Iraq. Throughout the year, I worked on the calculation of logistic factors for the new Task Force deploying to Helmand. It was essential to make people understand the consequences of expanding one front at the expense of the other.

A main part of the analysis centred on rotary wing. The commander of the British Army's new Apache helicopters was very keen to show off the full operating capability by taking his regiment on operations to demonstrate that these £30 million aircraft were value for money. He was frustrated that the in-service date had been delayed.

At the same time, there was a vigorous debate about the need to order extra missiles, engines, rotor blades, windscreens and all the other consumable items which take up to six months to manufacture. Then on 21st July, two weeks after the suicide attacks which killed 52 people on the London transport system, the Prime Minister endorsed the recommendations for the deployment of the Task Force, together with the attack and support helicopters, and this allowed us to place the relevant orders just before the contractors' deadlines expired.

★ ★ ★

There were two iconic images of the British Army in Iraq that year. The first brought joy to millions of people. A spoof video of the song *Is This The Way To Amarillo*, performed by members of the Royal Dragoon Guards, became an internet sensation in May. It certainly lifted everyone's spirits even before it caused the Ministry of Defence central computer system to crash.

The second image was the picture of a soldier in flames jumping from a damaged Warrior after it was hit by a petrol bomb in September. This occurred when the commander of 12th Mechanised Brigade decided to storm a police station after it transpired that two SAS soldiers were being detained. Their subsequent rescue demonstrated that the British could still pack a decent punch, but it also showed that we controlled the area in name only.

To my mind, this was the watershed moment when we lost our authority in Basrah. Only 18 months earlier in 2004, the judicious governor, Wael Abdul Latif, had complimented the British Prime Minister during his visit for the improvements to the conditions of life. People could assemble freely, the lights were on, scarce commodities were plentiful and cheap and the main religious leader reported that Ramadan was a success. It was sad that in the space of two summers, we were no longer welcomed by the local politicians.

Although my regiment did not deploy on Telic 6, one of my subalterns from the 1980s commanded the Coldstream Guards in southern Iraq. Nick Henderson had been my best troop leader in B Squadron in 1984 and also my 2IC when I commanded the squadron again in Cyprus. In 1989, we shared a wonderful Officers' Mess with the Coldstream Guards in Episkopi and worked very closely on operations with them and this was a key reason why he was appointed to command the battalion fifteen years later. Nick had a very successful command, but the pride in his soldiers was tinged with sadness due to the casualties, which included Sergeant Chris Hickey from Bradford, killed by a roadside bomb only a few days before the end of the tour in October.

The continuing failure of the British occupiers to establish effective security sector reform programmes was apparent to Nick when he arrived in Basrah. The lack of continuity caused by frequent changes in personnel prevented the British forces from developing the meaningful relationships which are so important in a Muslim country. There was a perception amongst the local media that the British Army was interested only in killing Iraqis, and the brigade did nothing to counter this view. Fear and military ambition stalked the staff and distorted decisions.

There had been a significant increase in the level of sophistication of the improvised explosive devices in 2005. Nick had not employed his Saxon section vehicles, which were too lightly protected, and had asked for the spare Warrior armoured vehicles in Shaiba. He was not alone in believing that the Snatch Land Rovers no longer offered adequate protection. After a number of heated arguments with inexperienced staff officers, the Warriors were eventually adopted as standard procedure, but their complexity exposed a shortage of armoured expertise.

In response, A Squadron from my regiment was told at short notice to deploy in Warriors with 7th Armoured Brigade on Telic 7. They were given four weeks' training to convert from their formation reconnaissance role to their new vehicles. During the tour, these infantry "tanks" became the vehicle of choice and were used so extensively that they completed the same mileage in two weeks as they normally drove in a year. However, it was not particularly satisfying for the crews from my regiment because the task of escorting convoys effectively meant they acted as "bullet catchers" for whoever transited across southern Iraq.

We had to fight for extra money to buy more sets of the Warrior additional protection, or Wrap as it was known. The handover of this armour normally took four men almost two days to complete. This comprised half a day to remove the bar armour and eight hours to remove the special armour and Wrap, with sixteen hours taken to re-fit everything onto the new vehicle.

This was really heavy work for soldiers who had just arrived in theatre and had not acclimatised. There were several other modifications including improved visibility driver hatches, updated electronic counter measures and drivers' environmental cooling units. After explaining the problem to the Treasury, we were given half a million pounds to buy the extra Wrap, which eased the situation in theatre.

I attended the contingency planning group meeting in London on 9th March 2006 to discuss the priorities between Task Force Helmand and Telic. There were several positive equipment stories. The success of the latest electronic counter measures was acclaimed, as was the delivery of many improvements for individual soldiers, such as the three-litre camel pack hydration system, with a filter that could remove bacteria and poisons from 300 litres of water. The production of the Osprey body armour was being finalised and we had started to send the upgraded Land Rovers with new engines, chassis and running gear. My team had worked hard on the transition plan to draw down in Iraq, but no one knew how the Secretary of State would play this with the United States and through Parliament. We had already refused the American request to bring forward the takeover date in Helmand from 1st July to 20th April.

Two days earlier, I had delivered a presentation to 16 Air Assault Brigade covering the end-to-end support from the United Kingdom to sustain the Task Force. By then, we had despatched six container ships loaded with their equipment, which sailed six and a half thousand nautical miles to Karachi. From there the containers and vehicles were transported by road another 1,500 miles through Pakistan and Afghanistan in unmarked convoys of low loaders and jingly trucks.

The airfield and accommodation at Camp Bastion were almost complete and support to the preliminary operation was deemed a success. The key shortfalls, as in Iraq, were the provision of protected mobility vehicles and heavy lift helicopters, but there were also many other niche capabilities which both theatres needed, including protected heavy equipment trailers, surveillance equipment and the rough terrain cargo handler.

An arbitration panel for land environment support and fighting systems was created on 4th April to make decisions about which theatre held priority for scarce equipment. I attended the inaugural meeting, which was chaired, surprisingly, by a Royal Navy officer. The Apple, as it was affectionately nicknamed, became a useful way to highlight problems in advance, but the owners of vehicles were never happy when their assets were transferred to another user. There was a similar panel for battlefield helicopters which was attended by all three Services.

A month later, a Lynx helicopter from 847 Naval Air Squadron was shot down over Basrah with the loss of four officers and a Marine. Army units deployed immediately to secure the area, but the civil disorder which followed led some television pundits to conclude that southern Iraq was rising up against British control, when in reality it was only about 300 people out of a population of 1.5 million in Basrah. This painful incident was all the more poignant because each of the three Services lost personnel and one of the Royal Navy officers was female.

Soon afterwards A Squadron returned to Catterick at the end of their taxi tour. They curtailed some of their leave to assist in the training of the remainder of the regiment, which had been warned for Telic 9. This was to be our first operational deployment in a reconnaissance role for more than ten years. It was remarkable that the troops would be mounted in the same type of vehicle that I commanded in Norway in 1980 and in Bosnia in 1995, albeit they were now painted in desert camouflage, rather than white.

Our worst case scenario occurred when Task Force Helmand deployed to Afghanistan, whilst we were still supporting the medium-scale war in Iraq and many other commitments around the world. Evidence in Basrah suggested that the enemy were concentrating on the iconic targets of Challenger 2 and Warrior. In August, we lost two of the former and five of the latter. On Friday 25th August a tank from the Queen's Royal Hussars was penetrated by a rocket-propelled grenade through the frontal armour, with the driver losing his foot. The incident took place in the east of the city whilst the crew was providing protection for another Challenger 2 that was being recovered by the light aid detachment.

In Afghanistan, the situation was no better. I now had a Parachute Regiment major under my command and through him we received regular updates from one of the company commanders of the 3rd Battalion. He had been in theatre for four days before deploying into a fire base and in the next month, there were only three days when he was not in contact with the enemy. He provided a comprehensive report of the Taliban onslaught and Corporal Bryan Budd's death on 20th August, which resulted in the award of the Victoria Cross. Commanders in both theatres needed our full attention and it was fortunate that I had three outstanding officers working for me, who ensured there were no delays in the support to either force.

These operations had a severe effect on our equipment because the attrition rates were much higher than anticipated. Generally, our helicopters were affected more than the tracked or wheeled vehicles. Rotary wing life is measured in very rigid flying hours, whereas increasing the track mileage for land vehicles was less problematic because we could bring forward their base overhaul. However, the Treasury only authorised limited numbers of urgent operational requirements and this paucity of specialist vehicles limited our flexibility.

The Scimitar fleet was a good example of how we had to carefully husband our resources. We were losing significant numbers both in Afghanistan and Iraq and could not build any new vehicles because the Alvis production line had ended many years before. These light tanks had been put through a significant upgrade programme with a new diesel engine and gearbox.

A number of them had other operational modifications. These included a thermal imagery sight, the Bowman communications system, electronic counter measures and three extra armour systems. The troops did not see much of this new equipment during their pre-deployment training, which made the first few weeks in theatre much harder than necessary.

In 2006, we also deployed a new tracked personnel carrier, named Bulldog, which was well received by the troops in Iraq. In fact, this was the old 43 series fighting vehicle, which had a full automotive upgrade, including drive train, secondary braking system, additional armour and electronic counter measures. We also procured a replacement for Snatch, which had become unpopular with the soldiers patrolling the dangerous routes.

Almost as soon as 16 Brigade deployed to Helmand, a Defence Minister asked us what we could buy for £50 million. The options included the Bushmaster, the Cougar and a Turkish section vehicle manufactured by Otokar. The Minister demanded that it should be delivered by the end of the year and this became the critical factor, which resulted in the Cougar being selected.

The initial buy was for 108 vehicles, with 54 destined for Telic, 36 for Helmand and 18 as a training fleet in the United Kingdom. We just managed to ship out four to Iraq before January, although these were not up to full specification as we procrastinated over the vehicle camera modification for several months. In April, we sent the first 16 to Afghanistan, but within a month the suspension hangars had broken and there were problems with the braking system. Force Protection and NP Aerospace upgraded the vehicles, but the costs overran by double the original amount. Despite the teething problems, this rapid buy was deemed highly successful and so we ordered another 140 in 2007, after it became the vehicle of choice for the troops on dangerous road patrols.

The introduction of Bulldog and Mastiff in 2006 was only the start of a new fleet of vehicles for the Army which were given animal names. This "pack of dogs", as it was known, included the Ridgeback, Husky, Coyote and Wolfhound, which were all variants of Mastiff and were purchased with money allocated from the Government's reserve funds. A command and liaison vehicle was also brought into service using the normal procurement process, but this was delayed due to extensive reliability problems and to mark the difference, it was called Panther instead of another canine appellation.

★ ★ ★

For my regiment in its rural role in Maysan, the winter conditions were very different from their previous summer tour in 2004. The weather changed from sweltering heat to hard frosts and driving rain. The troops had to patrol a vast area, roughly the size of Wales, which included 175 miles of Iranian border. Much of the desert became marshland and living standards were austere because the vehicles became the soldiers' homes, as well as their protection and transport – so much for slipping them down the list of priorities!

Air drops, helicopters and tactical air landings were the principle sources of logistic support for the dispersed troops. Throughout the tour the support was outstanding, but the fantastic work of the light aid detachment, repairing and recovering broken vehicles under enemy fire, deserves special recognition.

The regiment's mission was to undertake intelligence-led interdiction in order to secure the Iran-Iraq border. They worked with the newly-created Department for Border Enforcement and achieved a reputation similar to Gerald Leachman, who had kept the peace in the Western Desert with the Anaiza tribe 90 years earlier. The United States Corps Collection Manager described the battle group as "the only bunch of guys in Iraq integrating the assets given to them and exploiting them fully". Their ability to use the surveillance and target acquisition systems was rewarded with many finds of weapons, which were destined for use against coalition bases and mobile patrols.

We lost three soldiers on Telic 9. Sergeant Wayne Rees was killed in January when his tank overturned during operations west of Al Amarah. Then on 19th April 2007, another Scimitar was destroyed when it was struck by a roadside bomb. Both the driver, Trooper Kristen Turton, and the commander, Corporal Ben Leaning, were killed instantly.

This incident, more than any other, led the Chief of the General Staff to advise Clarence House that HRH Prince Harry should not deploy with the Blues and Royals for Telic 10. There had been a sense that the operations in the desert were somehow safer than urban operations, but this was not the case. The decision to stop Harry from deploying was entirely sensible because the threat assessment for southern Iraq that summer was extremely bleak.

At the beginning of that year, the United States had initiated a new strategy by sending 21,500 soldiers to counter the insurgency in the north of Iraq. This surge built on the success of the tribal sheikhs of the *Harakat Al-Sahwah Al-Sunniyah*, or Sunni awakening movement, who had turned against Al Qa'eda. Together with enormous financial resources allocated to the head of the stabilisation command, real progress was occurring in the north.

Unfortunately, the British government did not replicate this change of strategy in the south. The declared position was that Telic was still the top priority for the Ministry of Defence. However, the reality was that the substantial force in Helmand left the Army without sufficient troops for any surge in Basrah. Furthermore, the stabilisation funds allocated by the Treasury were minuscule compared with the money Congress provided for the north. There was a short diversion when a group of Royal Navy personnel humiliated themselves in front of the World media after they became Tehran tourists; then the serious fighting started again on Telic 10.

Having reduced the British forces in Basrah City to a few hundred soldiers, it was inevitable that they would be attacked by the Iranian-backed militias. The Rifles battle group suffered eleven killed in action and 63 wounded over the course of three months. Eventually, the commanding officer received instructions to hand over Basrah Palace to the local security forces and withdraw to the airport. The media headlines in September generously reported that our forces withdrew with their heads held high. However, the reality was that the British Army had lost control of the city, with the Chief of the General Staff having to explain after the end of Operation Telic why Britain had failed in southern Iraq.

The situation in Baghdad was entirely different. British officers embedded in the multinational headquarters were valued for their timely and wise advice by the United States decision makers and "one-nation" Iraqis. There was still widespread fighting in northern provinces, but with prodigious numbers of military and civilian officials, the tide was beginning to turn.

The surge became far more than just boots on the ground. By seizing the initiative, the strategic geometry of the whole campaign changed. The military commander, General David Petraeus, and the civilian ambassador, Ryan Crocker, were united in their purpose. This provided inspiring leadership for the empowered commanders, who were encouraged to develop and exploit all opportunities to defeat the enemy. For this reason, when my work on the urgent operational requirements ended, I volunteered to take over as the commander of the British contingent and Chief of Staff of the NATO Mission, which held the lead in the Iraqi national command and control centres and ran a wide range of education and training programmes.

★ ★ ★

My journey to Baghdad took three days. After pre-deployment training at the NATO command headquarters in Naples and a regimental parade to commemorate fallen colleagues in London at the beginning of May 2008, I reported for a flight from the Royal Air Force base at Brize Norton. The chartered airbus picked up a battalion at Hanover and dropped them in Kuwait, before we landed at Al Udeid in Qatar. I emerged from the aircraft blinking in the morning sunlight like the spring mole which had caused so much devastation in my garden.

The 45-degree heat was stifling. At the British military reception desk, I was told that I had to wait 36 hours for a connecting flight and was allocated a bunk in the transit tent with thirty other soldiers. This rubberised accommodation was part of the administrative camp offering rest and recuperation to American troops during their breaks from duty. The facilities for our troops had improved dramatically since one of my team, visiting Iraq in 2005, had alerted the Army Board that they were a health hazard.

Whilst acclimatising to the heat, I took the opportunity to explore the enormous American base where air, land and sea operations were planned in the Gulf region. I was so engrossed in the pink architecture, which reminded me of a certain resort in Florida, that I nearly missed the reporting time. However, I needn't have worried because there was another long wait once our names were checked on the manifest.

The flights into Iraq were all timed to avoid the threat of surface-to-air missiles. Eventually we were loaded onto the British C-130 and ascended into the darkening sky. An hour later, we landed at Basrah airport to drop off a group of civil servants in their chic blue body armour, helmet and jeans. The first thing I noticed was the smell. Sanitised Al Udeid lacked any scent other than the occasional wafts of aviation fuel. At Basrah, there was an unmistakeable fragrance emanating from the open sewer system close to the runway.

After a quick turnaround, filling the plane with mail and other supplies, the Royal Air Force Loadmaster shouted his garbled instructions at us and we strapped ourselves in for the 75-minute flight to Baghdad. Most people sat on their body armour in case a bullet came through the floor. The pilot climbed steeply to avoid any potential threat and I settled in to the journey, listening to the music my children had recorded for me on a Zen stone. Fortunately, they included some Van Morrison tracks as well as their favourite *Noah and the Whale.*

I am not sure why the pilot discharged his chaff and flares over Baghdad, but it looked very pretty from the porthole as we approached our destination. The sharp descent preceded a noisy thump as we landed hard at the international airport. We said goodbye to the people posted to the headquarters in Camp Victory, who travelled by bus to the other side the airport. Those of us destined for the international zone struggled with all our possessions across the airfield to the helicopter landing zone, where we waited patiently for the British Puma helicopters to fly us into the centre of Baghdad.

It was almost midnight by the time I met the officer handing over to me. He took me to my "hootch", a small cabin in the grounds of one of Saddam's many opulent palaces. After dropping off my bags, we walked over to the Green Bean, which provided sustenance for those on the night shifts and talked eagerly for a couple of hours before retiring for four hours of refreshing sleep.

I awoke at dawn and went for a run around the grounds, orientating myself to my home for the next six months. It was

My regiment sent two squadrons with 1st Armoured Division on Telic 1 in 2003. Their Challenger 2 tanks were fitted with improved armour protection in theatre by civilian contractors deployed on operations (CONDO).

Bar Armour was attached to the Warriors of the Black Watch Battle Group in 2004 before they deployed on Operation Bracken, to Camp Dogwood where they assisted the Americans fighting in Falluja.

Convoys travelling from Shaiba to Basrah came under regular attack. The pintle-mounted General Purpose Machine Gun which Tanya Dennison helped design in 2004 and the Webley Eagle armour around the cab significantly improved the protection of the logistics vehicles.

Snatch 2 with improved transmission, protection and communications was well received by the troops when it first deployed in 2005.

By the end of the year Snatch 2's reputation had plummeted, as it was attacked regularly by the Iranian-backed militias with passive infra-red, explosively-formed penetrators.

Snatch 2's vulnerability to sophisticated improvised explosive devices earned Snatch its media nickname as a "coffin on wheels".

There is nothing more emotional for a soldier on operations than a ramp parade, when a dead soldier is carried on the shoulders of his comrades in arms into a waiting aircraft to be flown home to his family.

Mastiff was procured as an Urgent Operational Requirement after the Minister for Armed Forces demanded a better protected vehicle for the troops in June 2006. The 22-tonne Cougar with a 7.2 litre turbo diesel Caterpillar engine was shipped from America to NP aerospace at Coventry, where it was modified before deploying to theatre. The initial vehicles deployed to Iraq before the end of the year, with the first 16 for Afghanistan arriving in April 2007.

Italian Carabinieri training the Iraqi National Police at Camp Dublin. There was always a marksman on duty covering the Iraqis in case a rogue policeman attempted to shoot the trainers.

Army officer graduation at An Nasariyah. We organised simultaneous ceremonies at the four military academies at Zahko, Qualachulon, Nasariyah and Rustamiyah on Victory Day, 14th July 2008.

The Iraqi Prime Minister's National Operations Centre in Baghdad. We ran a series of command and control exercises to prepare senior Iraqi staff for their role in securing the national elections in 2009.

The author showing NATO's Deputy Supreme Commander around Ar Rustamiyah during Ramadan in 2008.

a sparkling morning and the birds were chattering in what remained of the palm trees. Cheerful contractors greeted me around every corner. Many of these were migrant workers from Bangladesh, but some were Iraqis who had passed the testing security clearances needed to satisfy the strict American authorities.

After a quick breakfast, we drove to the NATO headquarters at the Cultural Centre in a park next to the zoo. This was once the largest animal centre in the Middle East, with more than 600 creatures. In 2003, there was fierce fighting all over this site between the Republican Guard and the Unites States 3rd Infantry Division. Unfortunately, this resulted in many animals being released and later stolen by looters.

My office was in a building between the Iraqi Defence Language Institute and the National Defence University. I was given five computers, four identity cards, three mobile phones and a partridge in a palm tree. At least, I would have had a nesting bird outside if the tree had not been decapitated by an air-bursting artillery shell.

The Americans insisted on lengthy handover periods which took at least a fortnight to complete. British officers were more relaxed. Knowing their successors would ignore all advice, they sensibly concentrated on introducing them to influential people. First impressions are very important, but when meeting over a hundred people in rapid succession, it is difficult to remember names. However, working sixteen hours each day meant the handover sped past and it only seemed a few hours after arriving that I bade farewell at the Washington landing zone to my predecessor and drove to the NATO headquarters to address the staff in the dining hall.

I arrived in the middle of a campaign of rocket attacks launched mainly from Sadr City. The multinational staff in the NATO headquarters appeared to be very nervous. There were some who refused to work and would not leave the hardened shelters due to their anxiety. My first task was to sort out these officers, who were a negative influence and focus everyone on the vital task of professionalising the Iraqi security forces.

My American commander was double hatted as he was also in charge of the Multinational Stabilisation Command – Iraq, or Minsticky as it was known locally. This coalition headquarters was also in a fretful state. Although it was inside the Green Zone, it was close to Sadr City and just before I journeyed to Baghdad, a 36-year-old Major, Stuart Wolfer, was killed in a rocket attack. The staff were still grieving for this popular and hardworking reserve officer, who left a wife and three children under six years old behind in Idaho.

It didn't help that the strident sirens were constantly set off when a radar system detected an incoming artillery attack. There was a standard procedure known as "duck and cover". Anyone in the open had to move smartly to one of the dozens of concrete shelters scattered around the Green Zone where the international community lived and worked. Some people overreacted to these alarms and this fear spread insidiously through the staff; however in reality I never felt the situation was as bad as Bosnia in 1995.

The British Deputy Commander of Minsticky gave me some useful advice during our initial meeting. He had watched the NATO headquarters for several months with some disdain and told me that nothing would happen if I didn't make it happen. He was not alone; the previous year a senior British officer had reviewed the work of the NATO mission and reported to the Chiefs of Staff that it was "in crisis". I also read a colourful report from a Royal Marine, who was one of my predecessors, expressing his frustration at the indolence of the officers of some nations, who found many excuses to avoid work.

Fortunately, I had plenty of NATO experience commanding troops and running special operations in Sarajevo. I had also worked on the 'partnership for peace' programme in Poland, so I had some cultural understanding of the Warsaw Pact countries, which provided more than a third of the staff in the headquarters.

During the first week in Baghdad, I discovered that national political caveats encouraged a risk-averse attitude. However, there were plenty of strengths in the headquarters. Foremost amongst these was the depth of relationships which the mature NATO advisors had developed with senior Iraqi military and police officers working at the strategic level.

Not every member of the Alliance participated in the operation in Iraq. At the time of the invasion, the North Atlantic Council had been reluctant to be drawn into full spectrum operations. Subsequently, they provided communications and logistic support to the Polish-led multinational division in the central region. Then in August 2004, they agreed to scope an operation limited to "non-kinetic" effects. The Military Committee received the implementation report favourably and decided to establish a mission with 200 military officers organised to mentor and advise Iraqis at the strategic level. To ensure the lines of activity did not conflict with the coalition, they agreed that the leadership would be assigned to the American commander of Minsticky, Lieutenant General David Petraeus.

At the time, the United Kingdom was reviewing its force levels. We had been invited by the Iraqis to lead the reconstruction of the military academy at Ar Rustamiyah, which was built originally by the British Army in 1924 and had been a regional centre of excellence for officer training before it was looted and pillaged in 2003. It seemed sensible in developing this junior officer capability to place it alongside the other NATO lines of activity, and it quickly became the jewel in the crown of the operation.

Command relationships were not simple. The NATO operational chain reported through Naples to Shape. Separately, there was the United Kingdom chain of command where I worked for the Senior British Military Commander, who reported to London. He had a small headquarters in a beautiful villa on the banks of the River Tigris, named after General Maud, the British commander in World War I, who landed in Basrah in 1916 and retook Kut before capturing Baghdad and then dying from cholera.

Finally, there was the coalition headquarters commanded by David Petraeus, who ultimately controlled all military activity within Iraq. He held a daily battlefield update assessment, which was the focus for all the aspiring American officers to be seen and heard. The senior NATO officers also attended these meetings, but usually sat in silence.

This byzantine organisation appeared to be a bit of a swamp. However, the challenge of turning around the poor reputation of the NATO headquarters held some perverse fascination. There were some first-class people in the headquarters and the key to unlock the ambiguity was to use the good officers to supervise those who hid behind their national caveats and worried more about parking places than military output. I spoke to everyone in a group and then quietly talked to the individuals who I sensed were letting down the team, reminding them that our situation was more benign than the environment faced by the soldiers patrolling the provinces.

Perceptions are so important. A common theme in their feedback was that they did not understand the strategic context other than the need to fly their nation's flag in Baghdad. I agreed that it was important that we demonstrated NATO's full support for the independence, sovereignty, unity and territorial integrity of the Republic of Iraq. Then I explained how our work in the national command and control centres and professionalising the Iraqi security forces strengthened the central pillars of government and prevented the conditions which favour insurgents. Some didn't understand the important role that intelligence plays in defeating the enemy, so I did my best to convince them that by improving the awareness of our sister headquarters, we could improve the probability of strategic success.

I was fortunate, because the operations centre was led by a very experienced British lieutenant colonel who was a great support to me. There were also some excellent logistics officers, headed by the calm Estonian deputy chief of staff and a very resourceful American finance officer, who knew how to work the bureaucratic NATO processes to our benefit. He persuaded the Supreme Headquarters Allied Powers Europe, known for its cold war spy thriller acronym of Shape, to release extra funds for our increased programme of training assistance. My job was to develop the whole group into more than the sum of its parts, building relationships and connecting effectively with the many organisations that we touched.

* * *

After a fortnight in Baghdad, I went to have my hair cut in the Palace. There were three Iraqis working in the barber shop and waiting in the queue was quite an ordeal as I watched the American soldiers in front of me choose their style of cut. There were three choices: a flat top, flat sides or flat all over. I emerged looking like an extra in the film *Shaun of the Dead*, but did not feel out of place when I entered the dining facilities.

The NATO food was very good. A Bangladesh contractor provided lunch in our headquarters, when the electricity worked, which was on more days than I expected. They offered a wide choice and catered for almost every appetite, be it Muslim, vegetarian or just plain hungry.

In the evenings, I joined the coalition forces in the American cookhouse. There was a 10 o'clock dinner for those who needed to work late and could not make the early sitting. Surf and turf on Sunday night was always a highlight and it was easy to see how some people put on weight during their tour of duty. I have always disliked using running machines in air-conditioned halls, so to burn off the extra calories I often sweated around the grounds of the palace wearing body armour and occasionally swam in the open air pool, or joined the staff in a vigorous game of volleyball.

I invited three important Iraqi generals to dinner on my wedding anniversary. Away from the work environment, they were delightful company and I was surprised at some of the stories they told me about life under Saddam's regime. One of the officers commanded the National Defence College where we were running a master's degree course in international security. He told me about the time he had crash-landed his MiG aircraft outside Baghdad in the 1970s. He was eternally grateful to the British doctors in London who had treated the second degree burns he suffered all over his body and conducted the plastic surgery operation.

In return for this dinner, I was invited to a feast where I met many of the Iraqis who worked behind the scenes in the military headquarters. This provided an excellent foundation for the friendships which are so important when living and working in a Muslim country. I liked the Iraqis who I met, although there were clearly one or two who had shady pasts in the previous regime.

During May and June, an ocean of sand blew in from the desert and covered our vehicles and equipment. The Iraqis commented that it was unusual and blamed it on the lack of rain in the winter. When I patrolled the perimeter of our grounds in the balmy evenings, the pink haze often merged with the sounds and smells of the hinterland. Melodious imams sang in their mosques, cats screeched in the scrub and Black Hawk helicopters churned their engines overhead.

There was still much evidence of the shock and awe that had preceded the invasion. Crumpled government security buildings and gaping holes with peeled-back steel supports in sandstone palaces told of precision weapon strikes. Externally, the architecture and monuments were impressive, but the interiors were poor imitations of Soviet-style design with oversized thrones and opulent furnishing.

★ ★ ★

On 20th May, the Iraqi security forces began phase 1 of the plan to clear and hold Sadr City. This followed a peaceful demonstration by about five thousand people who expressed a desire for the government of Iraq to restore peace in the district. This deliberate operation to clear the area of improvised explosive devices and occupy each major road intersection was a great success, although many of the criminals and militia merely moved to neighbouring areas, in order to evade detention. The key to success was to follow up the security operation with a 30-day clean-up campaign to repair infrastructure and compensate anyone for the unintended damage to their property.

My main effort was to reinvigorate the national command and control centre by running an exercise programme, which had stalled after the assassination of the Joint Operations Centre Director, Brigadier N'brass. I attended the Deputy Cabinet Ministers' meeting in government and then joined my commander in an assignment with the studious National Security Advisor, Dr Mowaffak Al Rubaie, who agreed to an exercise on 4th June. We knew that we had to avoid the perception that these exercises would criticise senior Iraqis. That meant our staff had to conduct most of the initial work whilst teaching the Iraqis how eventually to do it for themselves.

I also had to write a script for the Friends of Iraq conference in Abu Dhabi. This was an important opportunity to encourage more NATO members to fill some of the gapped posts in the establishment and to provide training augmentation teams. We knew we would not be able to shift Mr Zapatero's Spanish Government position of no troops on the ground, but there were countries, such as Belgium, which expressed an interest in gaining access to the Iraqi Defence market and might be persuaded to provide some training in non-confrontational subjects such as air traffic control.

The national command and control exercise on 4th June was a huge success. There were a few shenanigans before the event when a coalition officer tried to steal the intellectual property of the NATO author of the main events list. However, after I briefed our consummate commander, Lieutenant General Jim Dubik, the American saboteurs withdrew.

The Iraqis performed better than expected with the new communications and information system. For the first time the Prime Minister's National Operations Centre shared real time information and worked together with the Ministry of Defence Joint Operations Centre and the Ministry of Interior National Command Centre to develop a common operational picture. As a result of this progress, they agreed to run a programme of six exercises focused on the election security with the control centres in the Provinces integrated into the training programme. This led directly to NATO's most significant achievement in Iraq, the success of the national elections in 2009.

Whilst the Iraqi security forces and the coalition continued their surge operations in Mosul, Basrah and

Baghdad, a new rotation of officers flew into the capital. Staff officers are often given the unfortunate sobriquet of "fire extinguishers", since they are believed by many front-line soldiers to be oxygen thieves. There were certainly some of those departing who responded so feebly to the rocket attacks that they could have snuffed out the fiercest inferno. However, the new contingent was much more enthusiastic and after a series of briefings set to work with a refreshing determination.

Part of the surge operation was to increase the number of Iraqi security forces from 380,000 to 560,000. One of our key outputs was the national police training programme which was controlled by 40 Italian Carabinieri. Their training base was in Camp Dublin, close to the international airport, where they graduated about 450 police every two months through an intensive course. Their instruction covered a wide range of subjects from basic forensic investigations to weapon handling and riot control drills. They commenced the programme in October 2007. This was after the Jones Commission had recommended the disbandment of the Iraqi National Police due to institutional corruption and militia infiltration.

The Carabinieri started using the best Iraqis from the first course as instructors and ran specialist training, such as a sharpshooters' course for 24 policemen using a Dragunov sniper rifle. Sensibly they used local interpreters to translate their lessons directly from Italian to Arabic, rather than attempting to teach the lessons in broken English. A young lieutenant told me that these Iraqis ran many risks when working for NATO. They were under a constant threat of kidnapping or assassination, but they continued to be reliable and helpful by improving the educational experience.

I knew the tough Carabinieri commander from my time in Sarajevo, where we had worked together on the special operations to hunt war criminals. He took me to meet the Head of the Iraqi National Police, Lieutenant General Hussein, whose face bore the marks of the torture he had suffered under Saddam Hussein's henchmen. The newly-promoted general was delighted with the work of the Italians. He explained that after the first battalion had graduated, they deployed to Basrah and performed extremely well in Prime Minister Nori Al-Maliki's successful mission to evict the Jaish Al Mahdi and restore order on an operation named Charge of the Knights.

As a result of this success, we were given the challenge by General Petraeus to double the throughput of training. There were many hurdles to overcome, with the key issue being the requirement to increase the number of instructors. The Italians were very concerned that they would fail. However, Prime Minister Al-Maliki was visiting the freshly re-elected Silvio Berlusconi in Rome that month, so we included the formal request to the Italian Government in his papers. Meanwhile, our new deputy commander, who had arrived from a job in the Italian Ministry of Defence, briefed the Prime Minister's staff informally, so the request did not come as a surprise. We were relieved when this political finesse worked and we could start building the accommodation for the second Iraqi battalion, which started training ahead of schedule in October.

★ ★ ★

I produced the six-monthly out of cycle review in June and

sent it to Shape via the Joint Force Command at Naples. With very little revision, it was forwarded to the North Atlantic Council. Soon afterwards the Secretary General, Jaap de Hoop Scheffer, wrote to Prime Minister Al-Maliki to inform him that the Alliance had agreed to expand the NATO Mission along the lines recommended in the report.

Al Qa'eda was still very active around Baghdad despite the Iraqi security force operations. On 17th June they exploded a bomb at a busy bus stop in the Shia neighbourhood of Hurriya during the early evening rush hour. The blast set fire to a dozen shops and razed a multi-story building to the ground. More than fifty people were killed and another 75 wounded in the deadliest event for months. This was a sombre reminder to us how fragile security remained.

One of the criticisms of NATO was that apart from the British contingent at Ar Rustamiyah and the Italian Carabinieri near the airport, we rarely deployed outside the green zone. Part of this was due to the national caveats, but there was also a problem with transportation. I held a flexible contract with the security firm Olive, which provided a company of outstanding Ghurkhas to protect our headquarters and the accommodation at Ar Rustamiyah. They also ran resupply convoys in their South African armoured vehicles, but these were only used for short journeys outside Baghdad. For longer expeditions, we were dependent on the coalition for air transport and helicopters.

Despite planning and co-ordinating months in advance, we were always the lowest priority passengers, so we could not rely on the helicopter if a more important task appeared at the last minute. However, after meeting my counterpart in the coalition command, we came to an agreement and I was able to send advisory teams from Denmark, Italy and Great Britain to An Nasariyah in the south, Zakho in the north, Qaulachalon near the Iranian border in the east and Taji in the west.

In no-fly conditions, there were three ways to travel outside the international zone. The first method was in the straitjacket of a heavily-protected convoy, either strapped into one of the Cougars or in an armoured land cruiser. The second approach was more exciting and involved blue flashing lights, dodging and weaving through traffic and driving on the horn, whilst paired with another vehicle. The third method was to accompany a friendly Iraqi in his car and try to blend into the background as if there was nothing unusual. I tried all three ways, and the plain clothes tactic worked best, if you could trust the Iraqi and you didn't mind waiting in the interminable traffic jams.

An intense rivalry existed between the government ministries, replicating what happens in most other states in the world. One of our hardest jobs was to bring together the staff in the security ministries, who were very suspicious of each other. In many meetings, one side hurled abuse and the other walked out. Their squabbling was comical, but we needed to be scrupulously fair when offering places at NATO colleges in Germany, Italy and Norway.

In drawing up our training requirement, I relied on a very bright British officer working in the NATO headquarters, who had produced the Royal Navy's strategy for Iraq. He developed a transparent process for allocating courses and training assistance teams, which I explained to the Iraqi generals. They nodded when I told them that places were limited, but still submitted a thousand requests for irrelevant courses because they wished to outdo the other ministry.

In the first week of July, I said farewell to Jim Dubik and we awarded him his NATO medal. His ability to see through the fog of war and anticipate the future, not just deal with what was in front of him, was exceptional. He was a measured and considerate commander who understood that in War, the most important capability is the people who make things happen, irrespective of the systems and doctrine. He was an inspiring leader and we were very fortunate that his successor, Frank Helmick, the leader of the attack in Mosul which killed Uday and Qusay Hussein, proved to be every bit as good, but in a completely different way.

On 14th July, we celebrated the fiftieth anniversary of the creation of the Republic of Iraq with simultaneous officer commissioning parades at four academies around the country. We hosted General David Petraeus at Ar Rustamiyah and there was much to do to satisfy his American security advisors that it was safe for his visit, so I flew down early in the morning to supervise the work.

The ebullient chief mentor, Lieutenant Colonel Mark Butler, was an old friend from the 1980s when we had served in neighbouring regiments in Germany. He ran an excellent team of Army and Royal Marine mentors who had achieved magnificent results in a dangerous environment close to Sadr City in East Baghdad. When he arrived at the academy, the Iraqi staff officers were short on confidence and suffered from a lack of training equipment and unreliable support. This was exacerbated by acute instructor under-manning. Mark took it upon himself to arrest the decline and provide leadership for a training battalion of over 300 officer cadets.

I was particularly impressed with the only warrant officer at this isolated base, Stephen McGuckien from the Royal Signals. He was the mentor for the junior intake and also acted as Regimental Sergeant Major for the camp, working tirelessly to improve the crisis situation. Between March and June over 180 rockets and shells were fired at the Academy. By then, he had become a trusted mentor to the Iraqi officers and soldiers and was frequently alongside the cadets and staff during the most acute bombardments. In order to reassure them, he trained as a combat life saver and established a procedure after every attack whereby he would personally clear the base and check for casualties.

On at least three occasions, Stephen was first on the scene to provide first aid to soldiers with serious chest and body injuries. On 29th May, he treated an Iraqi brigadier who sustained leg and head wounds and then co-ordinated his evacuation to an American medical facility. This initiative, at significant personal risk, served to instil courage in the staff and demonstrated the standard of leadership that we expected of Iraqi officers. Through unswerving and selfless commitment, his work raised the esteem held for British senior non-commissioned officers in a culture dominated by tribal power and position. I was delighted after my tour when he was awarded an MBE in the operational honours list and Mark received the NATO Meritorious Service Medal for his exceptional leadership.

The graduation ceremony of 230 officers was held in the huge gymnasium with the Minister of Defence, Abdul Qadir Mohammed Jassim, delivering a colourful address which was received enthusiastically by the cadets and audience. I was slightly worried when the families sitting behind us started throwing hundreds of sweets over our heads at the newly-commissioned officers, but it turned into a joyous celebration, which attracted widespread television and news coverage throughout Iraq.

The next day two suicide bombers blew up a crowd of recruits at the Al-Saad army base in Baquba, the capital of Diyala province 35 miles north east of Baghdad. One of the bombers was dressed in uniform and the other wore civilian clothing; they waited until the names were being called before setting off their bombs, which killed at least 35 and injured more than 50 people. Despite this horrific event, many young men continued to sign up for the Iraqi security forces and reject the threat of Al Qa'eda.

Occasionally, I had to clear the missiles and rockets which fell in our area around the cultural centre. However, there was no point in fretting about them. To my mind, the risk of being hit by a rocket was far less than the chance of a roadside bomb, and this proved the case on 24th August, when the International Maxx Pro Mine Resistant Ambush Protected vehicle carrying my commanding general was hit by a suicide vehicle bomber. The MRAP, which had only just been brought into service, was a charred mess, but the crew and passengers were unhurt apart from an Iraqi general and the interpreter, who both suffered cuts and bruises because neither of them had fastened their straps securely.

In August, it was the turn of the National Defence College to take the spotlight. The ceremony for eighteen students at the conclusion of the twelve month master's degree course was attended by Prime Minister Nori Al-Maliki. We were fortunate to welcome him because his Chief of Staff, Arkan Al Tarboshee, was graduating together with the President's Secretary and many other senior government officials.

This course had been a huge success thanks to the chief mentor, a jovial Italian Air Force colonel. Most of the other teaching staff hailed from the universities of Baghdad and An Nahrian, but some of the technical supervisors were assigned from the private sector. The great attractions for the students were the visits to Brussels and Rome to learn about NATO's political work.

There was also a graduation at the Defence Language Institute organised by the senior British mentor. Elementary English courses for ministry officials started in 2006, but we now prioritised "Train the Trainer" courses with a team brought over from England. There was a bit of tension with the Coalition when an overzealous officer told us to use American lesson plans. However, NATO has such a strongly-endorsed international system that we were able to resist this pressure and carry on, even though he pulled out some of the teaching resources in a fit of pique.

The Iraqi commander of the Institute was a student with me at the Royal Military Academy Sandhurst in 1979, so we had friendly meetings which tended to go on longer than might normally be expected as we always asked about each other's families. Unfortunately, his deputy was assassinated on his way into work later that year. His memorial service was one of the most poignant ceremonies I attended during my time in Iraq.

Before the start of Ramadan, we graduated another 424 Iraqi police and hosted a congressional delegation. The fasting month certainly affected the work schedule of the Iraqis, so we were able to catch up on other work and host a visit from Shape, which included the Deputy Supreme Commander, General Sir John McColl. I arranged a fruitful meeting for him with the National Security Advisor, Dr Al Rubaie to discuss what needed to be done to secure the future of NATO in Iraq.

The General was keen to see the Prime Minister's national operations centre where our mentoring team had run another exercise. An experienced Dutch Marine Colonel briefed him on our assessment process, which had been validated recently by a team from Allied Command Transformation. Afterwards, we flew to Ar Rustamiyah, where he met the British contingent and Iraqi cadets before inspecting the dilapidated buildings in the staff college on the other side of the camp.

On 16th September, I attended the ceremony at the Al-Faw Palace when the United States Secretary of Defence, Robert Gates, presided over the change of command between General Petraeus and General Raymond Odierno. This was a no-fly day due to the thick sand in the air, so there was absolute chaos when many armoured convoys brought hundreds of coalition officers into Camp Victory. The outgoing commander deserved his two-minute standing ovation for his tremendous achievements. Whenever I had to brief him, I was always impressed with his perception and the way he assiduously engaged with the key issues.

Four days later, I had to deliver a presentation to General Odierno about NATO's progress in 2008 and the new lines of activity. These included the initiatives to broaden our work into areas such as border security, counter-terrorism courses and paramedic training. However, he appeared to be focused more on enabling the Iraqis to take over responsibility and accelerating the international zone transition. This reflected the changed mood in Iraq that we had seen in the past few weeks, as it became clear that the government was not keen on extending the status of forces agreement. This uncertainty made it difficult to obtain NATO members' support for widening the operation, but at least I persuaded the Ministry of Defence in London to increase the United Kingdom's commitment to the mission.

On the whole, I did not have too many disciplinary problems in Iraq. However, the new Polish infantry platoon providing security at Ar Rustamiyah proved to be less effective than their virtuous predecessors from Hungary. On 22nd September, one of the warrant officers was discovered drunk and unconscious at the bottom of the stairs in their accommodation, bleeding from the nose. He was air-lifted to the United States hospital at Belad accompanied by his platoon commander.

Disciplinary procedures in NATO headquarters are always a matter for the senior national representative. I was on best terms with the senior Polish officer in the headquarters, who was the chief of the training equipment synchronisation cell. He had just managed to secure a donation of 60 T-72 tanks from Slovakia, so I allowed him the time and space to deal with the incident, in accordance with Polish custom.

Two days later, I attended a dinner at Maud House for Dr Liam Fox, the Shadow Secretary of State for Defence. We deliberately steered clear of discussing political issues in Basrah after the British Army's poor showing during the Charge of the Knights operation. He explained his ideas for defence if his party won the next general election, but he didn't mention that he would cut the British Army by 20,000 soldiers.

I often visited our Embassy to meet with the Defence Attaché, who organised the training of Iraqi cadets selected to attend the Royal Military Academy at Sandhurst. The Embassy was also the operations hub for the work to release the British hostage Peter Moore and his bodyguards, who had been kidnapped by the Jaish Al Mahdi in May 2007. Occasionally, I received relevant information from an Iraqi, which I passed immediately to a colleague responsible for the ongoing negotiations with the militias and insurgents.

The Night of Power and the Eid festivities concluded Ramadan, which had been remarkable for the low levels of violence. The subsequent rise in October was less than anticipated. Attacks were mainly in the north, but Al Qa'eda also began a sniper campaign of intimidation against civilians living in Baghdad. We received more indirect fire into the NATO compound and I had to clear two 122mm rockets from the scrub by our vehicle checkpoint. However by the end of the month, the number of weekly incidents dropped to the lowest level since the insurgency began, with only 33 recorded in the capital.

The success of our training programmes drew many international visitors to our headquarters. These included a dozen ambassadors from the NATO contributing nations, who enjoyed meeting General Odierno over lunch and being entertained with an impromptu address from the United States Ambassador, Ryan Crocker. We also hosted journalists from the *Wall Street Journal, Washington Post, National Review* and *Philadelphia Inquirer* at Camp Dublin. They started by asking many sceptical questions, but concluded the session with a much more positive outlook.

At the end of October, it was the turn of the joint campaign assessment team from Washington to visit. This large group was led by a squat general and included a couple of retired American ambassadors and some of the best national security strategists in the United States. We set them up in our conference room, where they conducted a round table discussion, which was slightly less formidable than the Minsticky inquisition that I had witnessed two days earlier.

Just before they arrived, the head of the Iraqi Training and Doctrine Centre explained his idea to expand the site at Ar Rustamiyah. His plans included building a centre of excellence for Iraqi Defence Education, together with a new language institute and a war college. I was very cautious about relocating the Defence Language Institute out of Baghdad. I believed that if it was moved so far out of town, it would not attract the cross-government support that it presently maintained and would simply become an Army tactical school, rather than a strategic asset.

At the beginning of 2008, my American general could authorise the finance for this sort of project. However throughout the year, the Iraqi government had antagonised Washington by not agreeing to several major equipment procurements and procrastinating over the status of forces agreement, so the purse strings were noticeably tighter in October.

As the security situation improved, life returned to a more civilised tempo and I joined the network of military attachés for their monthly meeting. Assembling at the Polish Ambassador's residence, we listened to a lecture about

Poland's activities to protect the cultural sites in post-war Iraq. They had initially been criticised for causing damage to Babylon and other archaeological sites, but then they made a huge effort to educate their soldiers and deploy civilian experts to work with UNESCO and protect the heritage sites.

The recovery of looted Iraqi treasure was a high priority for the United States. For example, in 2008 experts in New York identified a pair of stunning 3,000-year–old gold earrings from a royal Assyrian tomb in Nimrud for sale in a Christie's auction catalogue. These were heart-warmingly returned to Iraq, after the customs officers completed their investigations.

On 28th October, the Czech Embassy arranged a concert of music by Dvořák and Fibich, played by members of the Iraqi National Symphony Orchestra. This was held in the Ministry of Foreign Affairs, so it entailed a risky drive outside the international zone. The piano was played beautifully by a Czech lady, who had married an Iraqi, but had not left her apartment in Baghdad for three years. This was a slightly surreal occasion as the seated audience was outnumbered by the bodyguards standing in the aisles.

My successor, who had studied at Staff College with me, arrived a few days later. As he reached Baghdad, the weekly number of casualties fell to the lowest on record and Wasit became the 13th province out of 18 to make the transition to Iraqi control. All our established education programmes and training courses were full and we had just started a pilot course to train 42 senior non-commissioned officers from the armed forces.

In the space of six months, our transformed mission had become the focus for the future. The United Kingdom decided to pull out from Basrah and reinforce its NATO contingent, in order to maintain a long term security relationship with Iraq. The central programme for the United Kingdom focused on the Iraqi Army officer training at Ar Rustamiyah. In addition, my top Royal Navy officer journeyed to the strategically vital deep-water port at Umm Qasr and wrote the training programme for the Iraqi Navy, which continued to be supported by the United Kingdom after the withdrawal from Basrah.

When I departed from Baghdad, it was still not safe for Westerners to walk around the bazars unprotected, but there was a real sense of progress and the Iraqi government was exercising its sovereignty at every opportunity. Fortunately, no one under my command was killed or wounded, but we knew several Iraqis who died and the families of the British hostages who were still being held captive must have been suffering badly.

On my return to England, I joined a Middle East Peace Process working group through which I maintained contact with some of my Iraqi friends from Baghdad. We were all disappointed when the United States of America pulled out prematurely on 31st August 2010 because we knew the fledgling Iraqi security forces were still very fragile. With the departure of the Coalition, the NATO mission folded and departed before the job was completed.

Jim Dubik was right when he said that growing a professional officer corps is a decade-long process and the return on investment cannot really be measured in a year or two. Although the Iraqi security forces had the required numbers of equipment and people, they were reliant on the Americans for the vital supporting functions, including intelligence, command and control systems, logistics and effective training and education, based on sound doctrine.

It did not surprise me when Al Qa'eda in Iraq, renamed Islamic State under the Salafist leader Abu Bakr Al Baghdadi, made significant gains in 2013. There is no doubt in my mind that the current situation in Mesopotamia could have been avoided if we had maintained the same level of mentoring and training support that we had established in 2008.

CHAPTER 6

Benghazi 2011 – Operation Vocate

Lay the coin on my tongue and I will sing of what
the others never set eyes on.
Keith Douglas

The crump of mortar and artillery rounds crept closer as we spoke to the students and teachers at the engineering college in Bani Walid. Already, four locals had been killed and another twenty wounded in the fierce fighting around the military barracks that we should have been inspecting. We were very fortunate that the Head of Surgery, Professor Elhejaji, delayed our programme at the hospital by twenty minutes, otherwise we would have been trapped in the deadly attack.

Suddenly, there was an explosion fifty metres from where we stood and our Libyan hosts led us rapidly into the hard shelter. They looked uncomfortable, but I was quite relaxed about the situation. I didn't wish to abandon them in their hour of need, but I knew the political repercussions would be disastrous if any of my British Army team was injured. The Government had denied deploying British soldiers to Libya and had been embarrassed when it had been caught out early in the campaign. However, the bottom line was that I could offer neither close air support nor Tomahawk missiles to counter the assault by Gaddafi's forces, because NATO had ended its operations at the end of October. Reluctantly, I said farewell and drove north-east to Misratah, the nearest of my four British bases in Libya.

Bani Walid is a very important strategic gateway to the Sahara. I was conducting a reconciliation visit in my capacity as the Senior British Military Commander in Libya, having been appointed two days before Muammar Gaddafi was captured and killed. My command overlapped the combat operation to enforce the United Nations Security Council Resolutions and the post-conflict stabilisation operation, which started on 1st November 2011. The span of responsibility included four Army-led teams of military specialists located in three influential cities on the north coast, Benghazi, Misratah and Tripoli, or *Tarabalus*, as many locals named their capital city.

My mission began with two priorities set by the Chief of Defence Staff. The first was to hunt for the former regime leaders indicted by the international criminal court, and the second was to set up a multi-national, cross-ministry operations centre that would allow the newly-appointed government to work with the international community to reconstruct the country. This changed in November when Saif al-Islam was captured and the final indicted regime leader, Abdullah al-Senussi, the late dictator's brother-in-law and intelligence chief, escaped through Niger into Mali.

The sustained fighting which coincided with my visit to Bani Walid had been trailed for some time and fitted the pattern of deteriorating security reported to London in my weekly assessments. I had been invited by the head of the council to talk to the tribal elders, but it took a long time for the clearances to come through from the permanent joint headquarters in Northwood, so I was not able to visit until January 2012. My plan was to offer assistance across a range of stabilisation activities with visits to the hospital, schools, police headquarters and military barracks.

Although it is only a small town of about 85,000 people, Bani Walid lies at an intersection of important roads. The town was the last to be captured before Gaddafi was killed in Sirte and it suffered much damage when 7,000 triumphant *Thuwaar,* the "Guardians of the Revolution", concentrated there from the battlefields of Tripoli, Zawiyah and Misratah. The harm caused in the aftermath of victory alienated the local population, drawn mainly from the Warfalla tribe, which was very traditional in its customs and culture.

We met the head of the council, Mohamed Bashir, south of Tarhuna's famous vineyards, which used to provide some of Libya's best wine. He had been a pilot in the Libyan Air Force before leaving for America. Returning during the revolution, he was appointed head of the military council and then promoted after Embarak Saleh Fotami resigned on 2nd January 2012. Bashir escorted us to the engineering college, where we met eight members of his gloomy assembly. They claimed they were starting from a point below zero and welcomed any external support, but they argued amongst themselves when the chief of police, Colonel Rajab Mohammed, admitted his troops were being outgunned by the former Gaddafi loyalists attempting to retake the town.

Unfortunately, the new Town Council was not supported by the majority of inhabitants, who did not appreciate radical outsiders being imposed on them by the transitional government in Tripoli. After an attempt at reconciliation failed in December, they took up arms again in the New Year. The lack of an inclusive agreement meant that a much-needed financial grant of seven million dinars had been frozen, although it was difficult to prove whether the funds were paid or not.

Without money, there was limited progress in the education and health sectors. Twenty-four computers donated to a secondary school were stolen overnight. The run-down hospital was desperately short of equipment in the accident and emergency and intensive care departments. More importantly, there was no programme to integrate the militias into the Libyan Security Forces or to provide them with alternative employment.

The future of the *Thuwaar* was the most important security challenge in the immediate aftermath of the revolution. Many of the victors expected to profit from the revolution, but the traditionalists were unwilling to cede power. On Christmas Day, I spoke at a large demilitarisation conference in Tripoli, but several of the *Shabiyah* invited to the gathering, including the one covering Bani Walid, did not send local community representatives.

In January, the tension increased when a young man from Bani Walid, Attiya Al Kmehi, was killed by fighters from the Souq al Juma'a militia. His tribe called for revenge and soon afterwards they carried out a very successful retaliation. In the meantime the town elders selected an alternative leader of the council, but the self-elected incumbents were unwilling to cede power. In this sense, Bani Walid was a microcosm of the whole of Libya. Strong leadership was required to sort out the weak institutions, but this did not sit well with Western Powers' notions of democracy for which many revolutionaries had died.

* * *

British armed forces became involved in Libya when the Foreign and Commonwealth Office sent a formal request to the Ministry of Defence to evacuate more than 600 British nationals from across the country. Soon afterwards, I joined a renowned strategic working group led by a past British Ambassador looking at Libya's future. Although the French Foreign Minister claimed in March 2011 "the destruction of Gaddafi's military capacity is a matter of days or weeks, certainly not months", we were more cautious about predicting how the conflict would end. The main opposition was based in Benghazi, but the dictator had a very strong power base and had deliberately neutered any potential source of internal threat over many years, so we knew this proxy war would depend completely on external support.

Two early recommendations from our working group helped prevent a prolonged period as a failed state. The first suggestion was to confer the Transitional National Council with *de facto* governing status. Although there were questions about their support within Libya, they did produce a vision of a democratic Libya, which became a foundation to rally diverse opposition parties to a single cause. The second recommendation was to ensure that the future livelihoods and living conditions of ordinary Libyans were not damaged by the external military action. Of course it is impossible to prevent all collateral damage when using air power on the scale used in this campaign, but the Libyan Chief of the Air Force told me after the war that NATO's restraint was a key factor in winning the hearts and minds of the population.

The botched plan to land a team of MI6 and SAS soldiers by helicopter on 3rd March also had serious ramifications for my post-conflict stabilisation work. After the Foreign Secretary, William Hague, explained to Parliament what had happened and lifted the veil from Britain's intelligence agency, their movements in Libya were constrained. In effect, the Section in Tripoli became totally reliant on my military teams for real time information outside the capital.

One of the pivotal events of the war occurred on 19th March 2011, two days after the United Nations passed a resolution authorising the "No-Fly Zone" over Libya. The United States command in the Mediterranean identified a convoy of armoured vehicles heading north on the coast road into Benghazi. They rapidly planned a series of air strikes with British and American cruise missiles launched against the air defence systems and French aircraft tasked against the armour. There is no doubt that this convoy intended to wreak havoc in the city and that the air strikes saved the lives of many innocent civilians that day. I saw the burned out tanks destroyed by the French aircraft and spoke to rebel leaders, who admitted in hindsight that the revolution probably would have been crushed at that time without this foreign intervention.

A week later, NATO took over command of the operation from the United States of America, even though only eight members of the Alliance agreed to participate in the air strikes. However, an intense diplomatic effort widened the coalition participants to 33 countries, including many nations from the Arab League and African Union. For the United Kingdom, there was also a very important contact group with three other countries: Qatar, the United Arab Emirates and France.

Unfortunately, the early success in Benghazi led to overconfidence in the Western capitals. Government officials underestimated the resilience of the forces controlled by Gaddafi's sons and overestimated the military capabilities of the opposition. In May, our politicians became very nervous at the military setbacks when Gaddafi recaptured Brega in the east and Zawiyah in the west. They also railed against certain NATO Allies for their continued lack of military support. After another meeting in London, my working group presented three scenarios for Libya's future: a negotiated end that allowed the dictator to exit safely from the country; a collapse of the regime under popular and economic pressure; and a separation of the country between the east and west. None of these were desirable, but the lack of a clear military mission and the reluctance to deploy troops on the ground hindered progress. And the humanitarian community were beginning to raise their concerns from the touchline.

As the flow of migrants across the Mediterranean increased, more refugees were killed as overloaded craft sank on their way to Italy. In response to the criticisms, the Prime Minister announced the deployment of Apache Attack

Helicopters from the Army on board HMS *Ocean* to add to the range of United Kingdom capabilities at the disposal of the NATO Commander. Our combat forces included a Trafalgar Class submarine, HMS *Triumph* and a Type 42 destroyer, HMS *Liverpool*, as well as the Tornado and Typhoon aircraft flying precision attack missions around Libya.

Despite the huge international force, Gaddafi was holding out successfully. At the beginning of June the tally of NATO strike sorties totalled 3,584. Political credibility was at stake and so unsurprisingly the Secretary General, Anders Fogh Rasmussen, announced an extension of 90 days of military operations whilst the United Kingdom deployed the enhanced 2,000lb Paveway III to escalate their air strikes against the regime's underground bunkers.

I met the Parliamentary Under Secretary of State in early June and he claimed that those who described the situation as a stalemate had missed the point. The welcome shift in the position of Russia, Germany and China meant that Gaddafi was increasingly isolated and his regime would not recover. However, I was aware that in hardening our stance, we would create more problems for the transition once the regime collapsed and that there were many unanswered questions about the capability and reliability of the groups we were supporting.

The media played their usual game by highlighting the divisions and tensions in the plans. They made mischief out of the First Sea Lord's complaints about the government's planned cuts to the armed forces and in particular the decision to scrap Harrier jump jets. They reported the French for breaching the United Nations resolutions by supplying arms to the rebels. And they raised the spectre of a humanitarian crisis with no clear road map and the possibility of food shortages, poisoned water, power cuts, disease and public disorder.

A military friend who had worked with me on humanitarian relief projects and commanded a civil-military unit travelled to Libya to assess the challenges in July. He pronounced temporary hardships, but no crisis. He described the front line as fluid with large tracts of disputed land frequently changing hands; battles were not that intense because Libyans did not really wish to fight each other. He suggested that the post-conflict division of the country would be neither like Iraq nor Afghanistan and the families of the martyrs, who gave their lives to the revolution, would hold the loudest voices. Finally, he confirmed that the Libyan people remained suspicious of international involvement because they knew they were sitting on 187 billion dollars of assets as one of the richest countries in North Africa with some of the largest oil and gas reserves in the World.

On 26th July, the Chairman of the United States Joint Chiefs of Staff, Admiral Mike Mullen, acknowledged that the military component of the international mission in Libya was stalled. Gaddafi held the eastern revolutionaries from strong defensive positions around the Brega oil terminal and he contained the rebels in the port of Misratah with mercenaries from Chad. These soldiers of fortune lived in Tawurga, a new town built by Gaddafi especially for them, twenty miles down the coast. Tripoli remained as his centre of gravity with vital supply routes open to Tunisia. The committed support for the regime in Tripoli was estimated as 70%, but shrinking rapidly as the extensive secret police network loosened its grip on the oppressed population.

Soon afterwards, our working group met to discuss the challenges of transition. We had a major concern about the fractured opposition in Benghazi following the murder of General Abdul Fattah Younes, a prominent member of the Obeidi tribe. The revolution's cohesive strength was based around a common desire to be rid of Gaddafi. The work of turning the rag-tag and ill-disciplined militias, with divergent political agendas, into an effective fighting force was a Herculean task, but Younes was one of the few leaders who had the experience to do this.

After absorbing more media criticism, the breakthrough came in the middle of August. It was the Zintan Brigade which made the difference. They secured the vital terrain of Jebel Nafusa and then stormed the last working oil refinery at Zawiyah before tightening the noose around Tripoli by approaching from the south and west. The head of the Zintan forces was Usama Juwayli. He was assisted by British soldiers who accompanied him throughout the advance on Tripoli, advising him on tactical options and marking the targets for the NATO aircraft when they attacked Gaddafi's stubborn defenders.

In London, we reached ahead of ourselves when a newspaper published Lord Owen's summary of the campaign and his optimistic conclusion that the Libya operation had proven that a constrained form of humanitarian intervention could still work. Meanwhile, Gaddafi clung to power and NATO prepared for another extension and considered how to sustain the campaign by changing personnel and broadening the air offensive.

By the end of August, most of Tripoli was in the hands of the rebels and the National Transitional Council had begun arriving in the capital city amidst continued violence and chaos. The focus of the main fighting had shifted to the heart of Gaddafi's tribal support area around Sirte. Many people believed the dictator had escaped through the Fezzan in the south-west, whilst his son remained in Bani Walid marshalling defences. A number of Tuareg tribal leaders crossed into Niger and reported confusion everywhere as the regime fled to the neighbouring countries of Algeria, Niger and Chad.

The most important judgement call for Britain took place when Tripoli fell on 28th August. We always believed the key to military victory was not the eastern front at Ajdabiya but the western axis of Misratah, the Jebel Nafusa and the internal resistance in Tripoli. So the British Mission flew to Misratah, leaving a small team behind in Benghazi, and drove at dawn through a series of anxious checkpoints into a sleepy capital to establish a new office in the Radisson hotel. Two weeks later they organised the visit of the Prime Minister, David Cameron, who arrived with Nicolas Sarkozy to offer support to the new rulers of the country.

In turn, the National Transitional Council attempted valiantly to restore order and establish a democratic process with all the associated governance architecture. They wanted to change Libya for the better and there were no doubts about their aspirations, but it became clear very quickly that the baseline they inherited was very low. They needed help, but they did not know how to frame their requests to the international community and there were many distractions to divert them from the hard work of reconstruction.

The primary diversion was the continued presence of Gaddafi in the country. His final stronghold was in his home town of Sirte, where he moved from hideout to hideout in an ever-shrinking pocket held by a dwindling group of 150 loyalist fighters. He swung from rage to despair over his loss of power and finally he made his fatal dash for freedom towards the end of October. It was an ignominious ending, which he could have avoided by handing over power six months earlier. After his body was left on public display in Misratah for four days, he was buried secretly with his son Mutassim and former defence minister, Abu Bakr Younis.

★ ★ ★

A week before Gaddafi's death, the Foreign Secretary reopened our embassy in Tripoli and a request came around the British Army seeking a volunteer to take the United Kingdom lead in advising the Libyan Ministry of Defence. The day after discussing this with my personnel centre in Glasgow, I received an email from the permanent joint headquarters informing me that I had a week's notice to deploy. I was told very firmly that there was no budget for the land operation because the Government did not acknowledge the presence of any British troops on the ground. Fortunately, I had retained my desert clothing from Baghdad, and since I had been involved in the campaign from the outset, I felt prepared and ready to travel immediately.

I spent a day listening to the latest staff briefings in the Cabinet Office and other ministries in London. One officer informed me about the Friends of Libya gathering in Doha, opened by the Heir Apparent of Qatar. Apparently, the entire conference gathered in the top-floor restaurant at the apex of the pyramid-shaped hotel and had to use a single, snail-paced elevator which only took eight at a squeeze. The first eight piled in and then took an age to reach the ground floor, before the lift returned to the top. Meanwhile, the remainder waited in the narrow corridor in shifty-eyed silence, shuffling their feet as the delegations competed to return to the auditorium on time. They clearly needed the mellow tones of *The Girl from Ipanema* in the background to relieve the tension.

I was very concerned about the lack of recognition for the United Kingdom Land Forces in Libya, which added to the risks I inherited as Commander. The most dangerous consequence was the absence of any formal pre-deployment training for my soldiers. I created a cultural awareness package which they learned in Tripoli, but it was unfair on them not to be trained properly before they arrived in theatre. Annoyingly there was also no personal equipment issued, so individual soldiers had to purchase their own kit without any authorisation for their out-of-pocket expenses. Other frustrations included having no scheme of rest and recuperation and the fact that we were denied the Operational Service Medal for our efforts.

The ad hoc nature of the operation could be viewed either as an enormous burden or an exciting opportunity. The risks associated with any activity have to be assessed from all angles; fortunately, I had a very good idea of the art of the possible from my previous independent command appointments. I had also been a member of a Middle East Peace Process advisory group for the past three years and the six-monthly meetings prepared me for some of the cultural aspects of working in a Muslim country.

There was a fundamental problem in our planning, caused by the Libyans' reluctance to sign a status of forces agreement with any of their international partners. We tried the personal contacts I had established with the National Transitional Council through the Chatham House working group, but these came to nought. After watering down the agreement to an exchange of letters, similar to many bilateral arrangements around the World, David Cameron telephoned his counterpart on 5th November and asked Abdel Rahim al-Kib to sign the document. Our Prime Minister received an undertaking from the new Libyan leader that he would take care of this issue but in the end, we received an unsatisfactory response signed by a low-level staff officer, which when translated, left my military teams in a state of legal limbo.

Ultimately, the senior leadership in the National Transitional Council were very wary of allowing any foreign troops the freedom to conduct military activities in their country. They wished to exercise their new-found sovereign authority at every opportunity, but their reluctance to deal with the international community according to established ways and means had serious consequences in terms of the stabilisation of the country.

These problems were not just witnessed in the Defence and Security sector. I heard similar stories from colleagues in the British Embassy about re-establishing business contracts with industry and when dealing with the ministries of health and education. The United Nations Mission, which held the lead for security sector reform and demining, also reported the same frustrations during our frequent meetings. After 42 years of Gaddafi's rule, Libya was just not able to engage effectively with the international community.

I insisted that all the military teams should learn about Libyan history and culture, and my reasoning was straightforward. Success on modern operations is achieved almost always through the results of actions on the ground, because the resolution of conflict involves people and where they live. I expected my teams working alongside the Libyan security sector to establish and build strong relationships and to interpret nuanced information, not merely collect data. They had to develop the ability to understand the culture in order to influence decisions at all the military levels: strategic, operational and tactical.

The vast majority of the seven million people in Libya are traditional Sunni Muslims. Although there is a small Christian population, there isn't the large-scale religious divide found in Iraq or Bosnia. Community divisions are based on historical tribal enmities and regional rivalries. For example, the origins of the fighting which flared in the south-east around Kufra and prevented my planned visit in February were decades old. The nomadic Toubou tribe, which controlled the desert routes extending north from Chad, resented the restrictions and taxes imposed by the Zawiya tribe, which controlled access to medical facilities, government institutions and markets in the town.

It was vital that my troops understood the historic causes of violence and treated rival groups fairly. Several international partners gained reputations for partiality and as a result, they were marginalised at the strategic level. The safe alternative was to do nothing but talk. This was tempting, but to my mind it abrogated our implied responsibilities, so the trick was to remain engaged and active. Fortunately, the British Ambassador, a consummate

Arabist, supported me fully when I explained the alternative choices of calculated military operations.

★ ★ ★

Libya has experienced regular periods of foreign control since the Greeks and Romans built their majestic sites, exemplified by the Palace of Zeus and Leptis Magna on the fertile north coast of Africa. Through all the comings and goings, the Berber tribes have been the one ethnic constant, so their *al-Masigh* pennant was flown frequently alongside the new flag of Libya during the victory celebrations. It was important to understand the background to their fierce independence. In the last century, this was built on the 1920s resistance movement against the Italian fascist regime's brutal campaign to suppress the population, with heroic leaders including Omar Mukhtar and Mohammed Fekini, who fought in the west until his exile in 1930.

The United Kingdom shared very strong bonds with Libyans because they freed them from Italian rule. Early in the Second World War, a small force of two divisions commanded by General Richard O'Connor defeated ten Italian divisions and captured Tobruk. Ironically, he had fought with the Italians in the First World War and received the Medaglia d'Argento for capturing the island of Grave di Papadopli, so when he became a prisoner of war in Florence, he was assisted in his escape by the Italian Resistance.

The British Army finally liberated the whole of Libya in 1943 with a series of famous battles immortalised by the brilliant war poet Keith Douglas in his poignant memoir, *Alamein to Zem Zem*. The portrayals of the grim fighting and his Crusader tank being hit by a German shell bring the desert war to life in a unique way. I drove past the battlefield near Sirte where his regiment was decimated, but I did not wander away from the main road because Rommel's minefields, where Douglas suffered multiple injuries, have still not been cleared completely.

After the war, the United Kingdom assisted Libya to become an independent kingdom following a United Nations Resolution. We helped the country form its new government with 60 tribal leaders from the three autonomous regions or *Muhafazat*, Tripolitania in the north-west, Cyrenaica in the east and the Fezzan in the south-west. We also helped build its navy and army in the 1950s with important bases retained in Tobruk and in Benghazi.

Libyans are polite and well-mannered and practise their religion in a pragmatic way. Women are free to dress in Western-style clothing and wear make-up; they often wear colourful hijabs and Sophia Loren-style sunglasses. Drinking alcohol is banned throughout the country, but it is not a taboo subject. Night life in the town revolves around the community, with people sharing *shishas* in the many cafés or shopping in the late night markets. At weekends, families picnic together and enjoy the wonderful coastline where 90% of the population live.

The communities I met were sociable, respectful and appeared content with their newly-won freedom. Rogue activity was often explained away as bored youths, or *shabab*, showing off, but there was also an undoubted power struggle happening in our midst. Every night in Tripoli and the other major towns there were explosions and shootings as local turf wars were played out. We made an effort to avoid these confrontations, but occasionally we were drawn into the violence. We worked out ways to deal with any incidents without causing embarrassment to the Government.

Away from the coastline, life was harsher. The traditional town councils were made up of tribal elders presiding over day-to-day activities. Fewer women were seen on the streets than in the capital city and employment was based on family connections. The working day started late and after a mid-afternoon break, or *istiraha*, it continued into the night. On several occasions, I was called by a senior Libyan for a meeting after 9pm, and generally these were more successful and decisive than those held in the morning.

There was an element of fatalism in all aspects of life in Libya. It was really important to understand their belief that everything is dependent on God's will. This could be frustrating for Western minds, especially as it manifested itself into a scant regard for road safety.

Although the infrastructure is good in Libya, traffic jams are commonplace because drivers ignore the Highway Code, particularly inconvenient red traffic lights. Libyans appear intent on clogging up their roads as often as possible. They drive on kerbs and hard shoulders, cross central reservations and turn three lanes into seven if they believe they can save a minute on their journey. Pedestrians are no better and walk straight into traffic expecting it to slow down and allow them to cross the motorway on foot. I was worried about the associated risks with driving in Libya until I stumbled on the solution, which is simply to behave like a Libyan and enjoy it!

Arabic is the major language spoken throughout the country. The dialect varies from the more Gulf region sounds around Tobruk and Benghazi to the African tongue around Tripoli. When I spoke at formal gatherings, I tried communicating both with a short Arabic speech and with a simultaneous translator. Although the Libyan listeners were very polite and welcomed a few words of introduction, there was no doubt they appreciated my use of an interpreter much more than my *gauche* efforts with their language.

Gaddafi stopped the schools from teaching English in the 1980s after the United States bombed Tripoli, so there is a whole generation which is less well-educated than their parents. I decided early on that the reintroduction of English language training to military officers was a vital step on the road of recovery for Libya and we managed to set up the first course at the naval academy in Jansoor before the end of my tour.

* * *

My deployment reminded me of my first operational tour of duty in 1981. After a painful hepatitis inoculation and a day waiting at Brize Norton, I flew in a C-130 at night via Malta to Tripoli, wearing the uniform insisted upon by the Royal Air Force. I had learned enough to avoid the Elsan bucket at the back of the aircraft, but unfortunately, I had to contend with the tin urinal at the front used regularly by the Royal Air Force Regiment guard force.

Bleary-eyed after a broken night of sleep, we landed at Mitiga Air Base and I was met on the runway by a British Army warrant officer, H, who immediately told me to change out of my desert uniform to avoid being arrested by the local militia. I stripped under the wing of the aircraft, pulled on a pair of jeans and loaded my rucksack into the back of the Land Cruiser. There was an acute sensitivity about the unannounced arrival of British soldiers, which stemmed from the Special Air Service mission which had been deported after landing by helicopter near Benghazi in March. However, H had established good relationships with the soldiers that controlled Mitiga and so we were allowed to drive straight out of the airfield, bypassing immigration control.

Soon after I arrived in Tripoli, news came in that Saif al-Islam had been captured in Jebel Nafusa. He had made the mistake of hiring a Zintani militiaman, Yousef al-Hotami, to drive him at night to the south-western border with Algeria, without realising he was being taken to a place where a revolutionary *kateeba* was waiting. He was arrested and held in a local prison, pending a decision about jurisdiction.

A delegation from the International Committee of the Red Cross confirmed that he was not being ill-treated in custody, but I decided to visit Zintan as soon as possible to check the situation for myself. There were two important military leaders who could authorise a journey to the Jebel Nafusa and the first was the commander of Tripoli International Airport, Moqtar al-Aktar, who I went to meet soon after my arrival.

I was introduced to him by a British lieutenant colonel who had been working in Libya for three months. Moqtar wore the traditional black headdress of the Zintan warriors. I was impressed with the way he dealt with people. In the space of an hour, he gave a sensible account of himself to a pushy Western journalist, he issued instructions for the security of the airport, he arbitrated between a local dispute involving grazing rights and he traded war stories with me over a cup of mint tea.

Having achieved the necessary permissions, the second person I had to meet before embarking on the patrol was the head of the Zintan Military Council, Usama Juwayli, who was now the Minister of Defence. Fortunately, I had a personal letter to hand to him from our Secretary of State, Philip Hammond and this provided me with the opportunity to introduce myself.

Juwayli was one of 65 ministers appointed in November to the interim government. The list of names showed that the old executive office had been replaced with strong consensus candidates. Ostensibly, it had appeared the Qataris were behind some of these decisions. However, at three different meetings in my first week I heard that their attempts to influence ministerial selections would fail.

This proved to be correct when the new government appointments were announced within the 30-day deadline imposed by the Constitutional Declaration. It was clear the National Transition Council was dividing the spoils fairly between the victors because the new interior minister, Fawzi Abd al-Ali, was a revolutionary brigade commander from Misratah and one of the leading figures in the Supreme Security Committee. Libyan military and police establishments were secular and very nervous about Islamist agendas, so it was sensible to ensure that neither of the key security ministries were led by supporters of the February 17 Martyrs' Brigade or other Islamist groupings.

As a former tank commander, Juwayli had a good relationship with the established military leaders, and as a father of a martyr, he also commanded the respect and trust of the *Thuwaar*. I need not have worried about meeting him, as I received a very warm welcome in his office. He took the Secretary of State's letter and sat down with me for an hour, talking about the war and the vast challenges of his new appointment. He was extremely grateful to Britain for the help we had given him during the final assault on Tripoli and asked me to pass on his best wishes to the team that had assisted him, which had returned to the United Kingdom. He immediately agreed to my proposal and generously offered to provide a guide for the day.

I was joined on the visit by the British police advisor and a representative from the Department for International Development, who had recently completed an arduous tour in Sudan. Before we departed from our base in Tripoli, I checked all our equipment; we had enough personal weapons to get ourselves out of a hole if we were trapped and enough provisions to last a few days in the desert. I issued all the soldiers with a set of information requirements covering security, politics, economy and the pattern of life. Our Special Forces escort briefed us on the routes and actions in case of an emergency and then we slipped quietly out of the capital before the cockerels began crowing on a cool November morning.

To British soldiers, the Jebel conjures images of harsh and rugged terrain testing infantry soldiers to the extreme. As we approached the road leading up the severe slope, we passed a number of abandoned military camps and war-torn factories covered in graffiti declaring "Zintan won the War!"

We skirted around Yfran, passing a checkpoint manned by local militia. I was impressed with the discipline of the soldiers; their weapons were clean and they appeared energetic and effective. The young commander smiled at us; not the cynical smile of corrupt authority, but the cheerful smile of worthwhile employment in an exciting new venture. This guard was a worthy testament to the British mentoring team which had trained and advised the Zintan Brigade.

On cresting the escarpment, I was surprised at the size of the rambling towns astride the main road. The land was fertile, with the red soil contrasting with the lush crops. There was little obvious damage to many of the villages, but the infrastructure in Zintan was in poor condition.

We drove into the military compound where we were due to meet our host. At first I thought it was a derelict building, because there was a disassembled anti-aircraft gun on the ground and the accommodation block looked in dire need of refurbishment. But then a soldier emerged and greeted us warmly.

We met Colonel Mohammed, the local military commander and Colonel Juma from the Western Military Council, together with their deputies. Mohammed wore an old combat uniform which reminded me of the Honduran Army of 1985, whereas Juma wore a new uniform provided by a Gulf state. Mohammed spoke little English; Juma spoke English well. Both wore stubble, unlike the Chief of Police, Colonel Abdul Karim al-Borgha, who joined us with two intelligence officers. They all looked me in the eyes, which was unusual in Libya. It was immediately clear that they represented an independent community, one drawn from ancient nomadic tribes who were proud of their warrior heritage.

Mohammed's meeting room was cold and furnished with tattered chairs and carpets. He described the organisation of his *kateeba* and the division of security responsibilities between the police and militia in the town. We asked when the police would take full control and about the plans for providing alternative employment for the militia, but they were pessimistic about the central government's ability to deliver anything soon. He was the first of many Libyan officers who told me that the army needed everything from uniforms and vehicles to basic military training. We were grateful for their candid replies and accompanied them on a tour of the town, ending at the police station in front of the prison. There we were taken to a large room to meet the young team of attorneys working on the legal cases, including Saif al-Islam. They claimed he had been moved from Zintan, but were unwilling to reveal his exact location.

After an hour discussing local problems, we were introduced to six archetypal tribal elders. Some were wrapped in ample white *jerbs* as preparation for the cold mountain nights, whilst others wore colourful braided waistcoats and Turkish pantaloons. They were about to meet with other members of the reconciliation council to deal with minor disagreements, such as livestock ownership and waterhole rights. It was extraordinary to think that these colourful characters controlled an area about as large as Scotland.

We bade farewell to our hosts and I decided to return on a different route. Heading west out of town, we passed a Toyota pickup truck with a multiple launched rocket system loaded on the back. In Robejan, we stopped at a smartly-maintained parachute training camp, where the duty officer was most welcoming.

After an hour on the road, we came across a new town

next to Jadu. This was deserted apart from a heavily-guarded building with an empty office of the International Committee of the Red Cross. If Saif was not in the Zintan prison, this was the most likely location to find him, but no one would speak with us and so after checking the layout of the buildings and the grid references using our global positioning system, we headed north to the coast and drove back to Tripoli as darkness descended.

Two days later, I was invited to attend the chaotic ceremony marking the first integration of a local rebel force into the new Libyan Army. We travelled west on a packed road to Zawiyah, passing a company of six wheeled personnel carriers with powerful cannons parked by the side of the road. We picked up a blue-light escort two miles before our destination and drove on the wrong side of the road at breakneck speed behind the Libyan military police car.

We had to walk the final half mile through throngs of cheering Libyans and were helped onto the VIP platform by our escort, Salahedin Ali. He was a thirty-year-old officer in the Libyan Army who had started the revolution at a university in Malaysia. He had returned to fight with the rebels in the Western Military Council in Zawiyah and Bani Walid before moving back to Tripoli where his family lived.

He introduced me to the local commander, Colonel Sadek Fhelbom and to the senior general in the National Transitional Council, Omar Hareeri. I felt slightly isolated as I appeared to be the only non-Muslim guest, but then I saw the head of the United Nations Mission sitting a couple of rows behind.

The ceremony took the form of a parade and a march past the dais, followed by speeches and an afternoon feast.

To one side, there was an equipment display and it was interesting to see a freshly painted T-72 tank driven around recklessly with no regard for the safety of the people clinging to the sides. The Libyan Army still held a large variety of modern weapons in their armoury. We had observed a very rare Russian anti-tank guided weapons system, Khrizantema, which our technical experts were keen to inspect, but the formal opportunities to do this were reducing as the new Libyan authority exerted control wherever and whenever it could.

I was surprised to see several of Gaddafi's female bodyguards and a couple of *doppelgängers* standing in the crowd, but they seemed to be celebrating as much as anyone and were clearly accepted by the officials in charge of the event. The highlight of the morning was the performance of a local man who had been imprisoned by the Regime for his irreverent humour. Wearing mock uniform, he was handed the microphone after a dozen officials had drily pledged their allegiance to the new government and praised the victorious soldiers on parade. By then, the crowd had closed in on the VIP stand and in a good-humoured way called for me to make a speech. My stumbling words were received enthusiastically and it was noticeable that they not only recognised the British Prime Minister's name, but cheered him loudly when I reminded them about his role in freeing Libya from the tyrant.

Then, to much acclaim, Shawar al-Zawiri took the stage. For about ten minutes, we listened as he chanted the same rhyme to the crowd, which responded in an increasingly hypnotised and frenzied manner. I had seen this several times before in Iraq and it often preceded a tipping point when a

Map of Libya. I divided the country into seven areas of security interest. All had unique characteristics, whilst sharing common themes. I was forever amazed how Libyans were connected closely to each other and heard the mantra "we are all cousins" wherever I went.

Jadu, gateway to the Jebel Nafusa; the local Zintan Council acknowledge
NATO's help in the revolution.

Zintan, December 2011, where Colonel Gaddafi's son Saif was imprisoned;
the Elders who looked after an area larger than Wales.

Zawiyah, 17th December 2011. I addressed a boisterous crowd at the ceremony to integrate the Zawiyah militia into the Libyan Army.

My de-mining team defusing an unexploded NATO bomb in Tripoli.

Bani Walid, gateway to the Sahara on 23rd January 2012; the day the transitional government lost its authority in Libya.

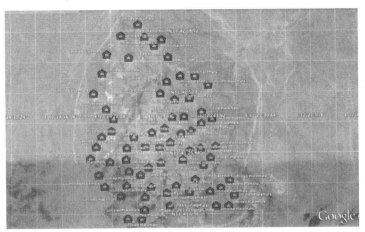

The layout of an ammunition compound in the Sahara hit by NATO missiles; the bunkers are marked with red locators.

A destroyed bunker in the desert showing the kickout, including the remnants of several rockets.

Hunting for surface to air missiles.

A bunker which survived.

Inside the bunker that survived.

The missile that failed to explode, which we disarmed.

Tobruk, 14th February 2012; one of the last working
Mig-21 aircraft in Libya.

Misratah – scene of the worst fighting (and atrocities)
during the revolution.

Disposing of some remnants of war distributed around Misratah airport.

Desecrated graves at the Commonwealth War Cemetery in Benghazi.

peaceful crowd turned into a violent mob. Fortunately for us, the officials restored control, but it reminded me how menacing these situations could turn in an instant. This was emphasised as we departed when a serious-looking bearded man warned me that Libya did not want any foreign troops on its soil. I was pleased at that moment that I had followed H's advice and worn civilian clothes.

I met dozens of Libyan revolutionaries in the first month. Many were men of peace, driven to violence by the political situation. Some had scores to settle; others were out-and-out criminals who benefited from a chaotic and weak political system. Most wished to return to their families and civilian work after the end of the war, but there was a small core intent on a violent path.

The problem for countries where political violence is seen to be successful is that the threshold for peace is very low. In stable countries, where governance is well-established, political disagreements are settled in the debating chamber. However, in countries such as Libya in 2011, where the genie has been let out of the bottle, it becomes too easy to reach for the gun to settle disputes. Fortunately, there was no religious figure promoting violence. Grand Mufti Sheikh Sadik al-Ghariani was a moderate traditionalist, who encouraged the fighters to return to their homes.

In December, there was a positive sign from the National Transitional Council with the sight of a Libyan plan to offer the *Thuwaar* four options. These were either to work in the Ministry of Interior, using the French model after World War II; to join the military and work at oil installations and on the border; to attend education courses at universities and colleges, or to apply for a grant to set up a small business.

However, when we looked into the ministries we discovered that there were no civil servants capable of turning this sensible idea into a practical, co-ordinated programme. More importantly, there was no database of the soldiers eligible to take up the offers.

There was an expectation following the international conference in Paris that the United Nations would lead the stabilisation work and the security sector reform programme for three years. However, the United Nations Mission was primarily a political organisation and although they produced a framework, their organisation lacked experienced mentors and the practical people much needed by the new Libyan government.

The United Nations disappeared on leave over the festive period, so I was the only Western representative at the international conference to support national institutions held in Tripoli on Christmas Day. I made a short speech offering the support of the United Kingdom, which was well-received. After the plenary session, I met Abdul-Hakim Bel Haj, who spoke about reconciliation, and congratulated him for his wise words and measured address, calling for a peaceful transition.

This was one of a few conversations that a British government official held with Bel Haj before we were banned by London from engaging in substantive discussions. Unfortunately, clear evidence had emerged that the United Kingdom had been involved in his abduction and rendition with his pregnant wife from China to Libya in 2004. He had been imprisoned and tortured for six years by Gaddafi's henchmen in the infamous Abu Salim prison and was attempting to sue our government for damages.

It was a bad judgement call from London not to allow us to make peace with him immediately. He was backed financially by the Qataris and clearly he was now a rising star in the Libyan leadership, having successfully commanded the Tripoli Brigade during the revolution and established control of a large part of the capital city, including Mitiga Air Base.

★ ★ ★

I missed the November meeting of the Chatham House working group which discussed the challenges after liberation, but I understood that there were two schools of thought about the quandary of public sector reform. The first approach advised external actors to step back to avoid damaging the domestic legitimacy of the transitional government. However, those with a deeper understanding were concerned that a *laissez faire* approach would merely lead to the failure of democracy and to a second civil war, resulting in the emergence of another strong leader, as happened in Russia, Spain and many other countries.

To my mind, it was important for us to be there for the long term and hold a strategically-balanced position in terms of time and space. There was no doubt that some countries got it wrong in their attempts to influence the political settlement. However, it was a greater crime to do nothing and in this sense, I was extremely disappointed that neither the United Nations nor the European Union stepped up to the plate in the ways Libya needed in the immediate aftermath of the revolution.

Libya is the 17th largest country in the world and dwarfs Iraq and Afghanistan. Soon after arriving in Tripoli, I produced a campaign plan based on my analysis of the terrain, in which I divided the country into seven areas of strategic interest. Each of these had unique security challenges as well as the common problems of militia integration and border security.

After examining Zintan, Zawiyah and the western towns on the coast road to Tunisia, my next priority was Misratah, a large port and steel town on the Gulf of Sidra. The question that exercised me at this time was what we could do for the Misratah population, given that they had suffered most during the revolution?

Fortunately, we had a technical agreement signed by the Libyan Ministry of Defence, which authorised our work to create an inventory of all weapons and ammunition storage areas. By mid-November we had catalogued more than four thousand missiles, mostly SA-7, but some SA-24s. Working with US teams, we had visited several of the desert bunker complexes which had been attacked by NATO. However, the British work was now drawing to a close and we were looking for another worthwhile task.

When an air-to-ground missile such as a Storm Shadow hits a bunker full of ammunition, not all the ordnance is destroyed. There is a huge amount of what is known as "kick out", which spreads the tools of death over a large area. In Libya, the remnants are seen as commodities to be collected and sold on the black market by locals. However, the people who do this don't understand the consequences and so there are many injuries, amputations and deaths caused by individuals picking up unstable ordnance, mines or rockets.

After a sobering visit to Shormelkhail, a complex lying 120 kilometres south of Sirte, the British team leader put together a proposal. He suggested that he could make a start clearing the sites at the Misratah airfield and he arranged for me to discuss the safety aspects associated with this highly dangerous work with the local Security Council. I was uncertain how we would be received because there was still a lot of fighting in Misratah with gun battles and large explosions keeping the team alert every night.

The local council had established a museum of the revolution on the main high street of the town. This was the scene of the fiercest fighting and where Prime Ministers Cameron and Sarkozy made their famous victory speeches. Inside, the building, they hung a photograph of each of the 1,200 martyrs who had died in the battles and another 1,000 photographs representing those who had "disappeared". There was also a section reserved for the Army officers executed after they had dared to challenge Gaddafi in the 1980s.

This museum became a collection point for all sorts of remnants of war. Every day people brought unexploded bombs and unstable ammunition which the caretakers lined up outside the building. Many were damaged, and our first priority was to remove anything which might "cook off" without warning.

My meeting with the town council went well, and we won the confidence of the leaders who authorised the operations at the museum and air base. They provided us with a team of young assistants led by Colonel Turjman to work on the safety tasks. The airport was about two miles out of town on the top of a hill. Gaddafi's troops had used this high ground to shoot tank shells into apartment blocks in the centre of town. After NATO destroyed all the armoured vehicles and hit the ammunition bunkers it became a *Mad Max* scene of devastation with burned-out tanks and unexploded bombs distributed across the area.

Our progress was slow due to the risks all around the site. The work had to be done in a methodical and meticulous manner, but sadly, the young Libyan assistants kept cutting corners and on a day when we were not supervising them, one was unfortunately killed. As a result, they agreed to organise some training, which reduced the amount of time we could spend on the demolitions and rendering safe procedures.

There were also regular interruptions as the fighting continued between rival militias. In February, a battle broke out at the Dafniyah checkpoint on the main road between Tripoli and Misratah. Several stray rounds hit a container storing a large quantity of ammunition, which exploded, scattering rockets, missiles, mines and other munitions in the vicinity of a school and a fuel park.

The United Nations held the lead for the de-mining and assigned a Danish organisation to clear the area, but tragically, an Estonian contractor was killed at the site the following day. Such was the level of regard for my team working at the air base that I was called and asked for help. In essence, we were up against an unknown enemy, the Type 84 anti-tank sub-munitions from a Chinese 120mm rocket. We were particularly nervous about these weapon systems because they were known to have multiple means of detonation, including magnetic influence, anti-disturbance and seismic sensors. There was also an automatic timed self-destruct system once it had armed, and it was this which had killed the Estonian.

After making a plan and assessing the risks, one of my warrant officers, Q, deployed to the site and found twelve rockets intact and a similar amount expelled, leaving many sub-munitions in a highly dangerous state. He identified five mines as urgent priorities. He could have blown these in place, but this would have caused devastation to the school, so he removed the fuses in a very dangerous operation and during the next fortnight, he cleared the remainder of the site until life returned to normal for the locals.

Q had already rendered safe a huge number of NATO blinds, including a French 2,000lb bomb, a British Mark 20 1,000lb bomb and an American Tomahawk warhead. He also travelled deep into the desert to recover a British Storm Shadow missile which had failed to explode. This long-range, air-to-surface stealthy weapon weighs 2,866lbs and costs almost a million pounds, so it was important to bring it back to the United Kingdom so the technicians could work out why it had failed to detonate. Together with his outstanding work at the air base and the museum in town, he made a fantastic contribution to making Libya safer, so I was delighted when he was awarded the Queen's Gallantry Medal in the operational honours list for his conspicuous courage.

The fifth key area of strategic interest was the area on the north-east coast from Benghazi to the Egyptian border, including Jebel Akhtar, or the Green Mountains. Within this area, there were four important cities: brash Benghazi, aristocratic Bayda, surly Derna and gallant Tobruk. Early in the conflict, the military officers in these cities, who were members of influential tribes such as the Obeidi and Brassa, defected from the regime and declared their support for the revolution.

The new Chief of the Libyan Air Force, General Saq'r, had commanded the military rebels at Tobruk and invited me to inspect the air base with a view to contracting British business to rebuild the dilapidated infrastructure. His message was clear: Libya did not wish to return to its former partnership with Russia and needed urgent help to rebuild their forces. Tobruk is the closest city to the troublesome border with Egypt and holds a place dear to the heart of any British soldier, so I did not hesitate in accepting his invitation. To assist me to scope the work, I organised a technical team of Royal Air Force officers to travel over from England for a week in early February.

Blustery rain fell on the Falcon Fifty as we taxied across the Mitaga runway before the two-hour flight across the Gulf of Sidra. Our escort was Colonel Rafa, who had commanded one of the Tobruk fighter squadrons in 2008 and then all the eastern air operations before he was promoted to the Air Staff. When we arrived at the General Abdul Nasser Airbase, he was welcomed as a returning hero.

After an acrobatic flypast by the base commander in his Mig-21, we were taken to the operations centre. The tattered map on the wall appeared to have been there since it had been put up almost fifty years before our visit. The local pilots deferred to Rafa during the briefing about their operational missions and flight paths. We toured the maintenance hangars and the looted stores. They were short of specialist tools and consumables, including ejector seat cartridges, which meant there were only three working aircraft at the base. We were showered with requests for support as we saw at first-hand how Gaddafi had neglected the armed forces in favour of his son's elite troops.

Following this enlightening visit, we drove to the cemetery commemorating 850 commonwealth service men killed in the Siege of Tobruk, where we laid a wreath and paused for reflection. I was reminded of Eric Newby's compelling account of his time with the Special Boat Service on motor torpedo boats, loaded with high octane fuel, operating in the harbour and firing their twin Oerlikon guns at the German Stukas as they dive-bombed the supply port. He would not have been any better off if he had stayed with his regiment, the Black Watch, as they lost 24 officers and 456 men killed or wounded breaking out of Tobruk on 20th November 1941.

Further west, we found the second Commonwealth cemetery at Knightsbridge below the escarpment where one of the old caravan routes, *Trigh Capuzzo*, ran for more than a hundred miles. The bell of HMS *Liverpool* hung on the porch, a poignant association with the 2011 operation in which the Type 42 HMS *Liverpool* performed so successfully. We entered the well-maintained grounds and the sun's reflection on the compacted white clay and limestone soil made us squint. The custodian, with his father and son, had looked after the cemetery for sixty years and they were delighted to be recognised for their loyal and dedicated work.

After our reverent visits to the immaculately cared-for cemeteries, we met the town council in a sparsely-occupied hotel. They reported that about 500 illegal immigrants were crossing daily from Egypt and they explained how they were caring for these people and dealing with the deteriorating security situation on the border. I met several officials who told me their father or uncle had fought with the British during the siege and there appeared to be a real depth of affection for Great Britain. My driver was the manager of the Tobruk football club which had recently beaten Zuwarah 4-0. He cheerfully told me that life had more or less returned to normal in the town. Utilities were operating at about 75%, employment was evident in the oil refinery, port and workshops, the university had restarted its courses and several construction sites were busy.

As we drove from one location to another, we witnessed a peculiar Libyan phenomenon with our convoy. When we departed from the air base, five vehicles drove in an orderly manner into town, but after each stop two or three security cars joined the *cortège*. By the time we were due to return, we had tripled in size and the drivers of all these vehicles then decided to race each other at full speed back to the airbase. It was the sort of exuberant behaviour we had come to expect and it was with some relief that we boarded the Falcon aircraft for our return flight to Tripoli.

★ ★ ★

The sixth area I needed to assess was Kufra, an ancient oasis linking the caravan routes between Chad, Sudan and Egypt. Its sweet water flows 1,000 miles from the equatorial rain belt before it wells up and irrigates palm-groves and gardens of millet. The area is symbolic to many Libyans whose families had fled there during the brutal Italian counter-insurgency of the 1920s. It was the final town to be captured by Graziani's fascists in 1931 after they executed the heroic leader, Omar Mukhtar. The end of the resistance led thousands of destitute Libyans to settle in Egypt around Alexandria, before they joined the Libyan Arab Force in World War II.

Kufra was captured by the Free French with the aid of the Long Range Desert Group in March 1941. Its airfield became a Royal Air Force base for 216 Bomber Squadron and provided vital logistic support for the disparate raiding parties interfering with Rommel's lines of communication. These included a daring plan for five independent but simultaneous attacks in the north-east of Libya on 13th September 1942.

The Long Range Desert Group was scheduled to attack Benina airfield and Barce; the Sudan Defence Force was to attack Jalu and the Special Air Service, under David Stirling, was to surprise Benghazi with 200 men and release thousands of prisoners of war. However, the most fanciful idea was John Haseldon's scheme to drive into Tobruk with eighty commandos, relying for ammunition and supplies on what he would find in the town. He planned to capture the coastal batteries and link with Royal Navy ships and Motor Torpedo Boats to seize and hold the port.

With the exception of the Barce raid, all these schemes failed. Unfortunately, loose tongues wagged in the bars and night clubs of Cairo and the bedtime revelations were converted into military intelligence and passed to the enemy command in Cyrenaica. The Royal Navy lost two destroyers and several patrol boats and the Army lost many adventurous young men when they were ambushed by well-prepared troops. As a result, Lieutenant Colonel Shan Hackett was pulled into General Headquarters Middle East at Alexandria, in order to tighten control of all the disparate raiding parties in North Africa.

Seventy years on, I had to evaluate Kufra as part of my work with the Libyan ministry of defence to develop their border security plans. A representative from the interior ministry had briefed me that the detention centres for illegal immigrants there were "sub-human". It was also a key location for our oil and gas industry, and neighbouring Jalu was one of the pick-up locations for the non-combatant evacuation operation Britain conducted in February 2011. We had to update these plans and establish relationships with the local forces.

I had already developed a concept of operations and sent this to London in January for clearance. I had also researched the previous violence and clashes in the area, which stemmed from three sources. There were national tensions between Libya and Chad dating back to Gaddafi's war in the disputed Tibesti Mountains; there were ethnic tensions between Arabs and Africans; and most relevantly, there was a history of tribal clashes between the Tebou and Zawiya tribes. The former had joined the revolution early in the campaign and now expected to receive the spoils of victory with greater control in the town, but instead the Zawiyans were taxing them heavily and denying many of them the rights of citizenship.

Once the clearances came through from London, I sent down my specialist reconnaissance team in their vehicles and flew to Benghazi to negotiate with local commanders for a *khabir*. A *khabir* is a local guide or sponsor to whom a stranger is entrusted and holds responsibility for their life. The relationship is easily entered into, but once undertaken is binding unto death. I received offers from several tribal leaders, who invited me to travel via Jebal Akhtar, but first I had to rendezvous with my team at our operations base, commanded by a young major in the Intelligence Corps.

The reconnaissance party had travelled to the overnight stop at Jalu, where they met a British contact providing security for the oil installations. He warned them that the situation in Kufra had deteriorated and there was a security operation around the town which might prevent our visit. Listening to their report, it was mighty tempting to proceed with the plan and to drive down the next day. However, the reality of the situation was that they had driven 300 miles and been prevented from entering the town at a cordon where seven military vehicles blocked their progress. If we hadn't experienced our close shave at Bani Walid, I probably would have pressed on, but in the end I decided to postpone the operation until the situation improved.

More importantly, my team in the eastern part of Libya was there to keep track of the growing Islamic influences in the area from Benghazi to Derna on the coast and the Green Mountains to the south. They understood that in a closed community such as Libya, rumour and intrigue are the very breath of life, so they adopted local customs, smoking *shisha* at night and drinking hot sweet tea during the day. As a result, they were well-tuned to the latest gossip and told me that change was in the air because the Islamic movement was gaining traction.

We had built extremely strong relationships with the military opposition in Benghazi during the revolution. The *Thuwaar* ranged from secular units which had defected from the regime, including 1st Infantry Brigade, to local militias with romantic names such as the 17th February Martyrs'

Brigade and the Gathering of Revolutionary Companies. However, many of the influential leaders were forgotten after the war. General Haftar, the leader of the Cyrenica Military Command, expected to be made the Chief of the Armed Forces. However, the National Transition Council believed that he and the six other nominations were not "one nation" Libyans, so they appointed an officer who was acceptable both to the east and the west of the country, Major General Yousef Manqush, who fought in the revolution until he was captured in Brega in April.

Haftar was not the only leader in Benghazi who felt snubbed by the National Transitional Council. However, I was more concerned about the growing number of disaffected young men joining violent extremist organisations than the slighted egos of the former elite. The change in mood of the population was epitomised by the flags flown at the regular protest demonstrations in Martyr Square. In the immediate aftermath, anyone producing a black flag would be told to put it away and to cheer for the new Libyan colours. Three months later there were more black flags than Libyan flags, as further recruits were attracted to the Islamic movement.

At the end of February I was suddenly called by my team, who reported that about 150 gravestones in the Commonwealth Cemetery had been smashed with sledgehammers and damaged by a group of young men. Allegedly, this was in retaliation for the recent burning of holy books by American soldiers in Afghanistan, which had attracted widespread condemnation around the World.

I telephoned the Head of the Commonwealth War Graves Commission in Tripoli and together we made a plan to repair all the gravestones. I advised him not to visit the cemetery until we had received an apology from the government. The British Ambassador immediately spoke with the Libyan Prime Minister, but regrettably it took some time to extract a suitable pronouncement from the Head of State, which we ensured was published widely in the country. In the meantime, I flew across to Benghazi to inspect the damage for myself and to lay a wreath at the vandalised monument in the cemetery.

This cemetery was full of poignant stories. There was a large section devoted to Muslims from Asia and Africa as well as many of the irregular forces which worked behind enemy lines. The most fascinating headstone was that of the 24-year-old Geoffrey Keyes, awarded the Victoria Cross in November 1941 when he was killed during the ill-fated raid on General Rommel's quarters. Interestingly, the details on the grave do not correspond with contemporary memoirs, but that just shows how chaotic operations behind enemy lines were in the early days of Britain's Special Forces.

I believed it was really important to nurture our hard-won confidences in Benghazi. My team had successfully mapped the emergence and development of parallel security structures, and discovered the truth behind many of the frequent outbreaks of fighting. However, in March, the decision was taken in London for budgetary reasons to close down our military operations in the east after almost twelve months' work. The intention was to replace the team with a temporary contractor to monitor the situation , but this failed before it even started due to the security deterioration.

The withdrawal of the military team was a calamitous

error. I certainly believe we could have prevented the death of the United States Ambassador, Christopher Stevens, on 12th September if we had maintained our permanent presence in Benghazi. This could have been achieved with a better understanding of the local conditions and more effective protection from our friendly militia.

I organised an exciting expedition smuggling all the accumulated British weapons around the Gulf of Sidra. On our return route we avoided setting a pattern by making a quick diversion south. We checked the Great Man-Made River, which runs underground in pipes for 1,750 miles from its source in the Sahara to the thirsty population on the northern coast.

In this semi-desert, we saw hundreds of dromedaries with single humps browsing on *agram* and *hillah*, which is something between a bush and a small tree. There didn't appear to be anyone looking after these Arabian camels, or the small areas planted with wheat and barley and fenced with rusty old barbed wire retrieved from the Second World War minefields. However, we did eventually greet a friendly Bedouin family by their tented camp, busy in their nomadic pastoral life on the edge of the Sahara.

A few miles further on, we passed a Toyota pick-up truck with two camels sunbathing in the back. We laughed at the sight, but did not begrudge their indulgence. In Libya, every bit of the camel is useful. Their hair is woven into blankets, their hides are turned into sandals, their hump contains lard and their dung is burned as fuel. They cost next to nothing to maintain, can live for fifty years and carry loads up to 1,000lbs. They are incredibly hardy, supporting themselves on a diet of dry twigs and detecting water up to a mile away. It is no wonder that the Bedouin love them so much.

* * *

Apart from the obvious perils of working in isolated locations and driving on Libyan roads, I grouped the strategic security risks into ten categories. Much was made of former Regime loyalists attempting to regain lost ground through violence, but apart from Bani Walid, most of them lay low, or fled the country. Border security in the ungoverned and porous Sahel worried the transitional government throughout my six months in Libya. Organised criminal networks benefited from the weak governance in the aftermath of the revolution. Remnants of war, including mines and Man-Portable Air Defence Systems or Manpads, continually occupied me. Tribal clashes flared sporadically in all the *Muhafazat*. Ownership of resources such as water, oil and the nuclear material at Sabha provided local militias with a reason to fight. Human rights abuses caused Médecins Sans Frontières to pull out of the Misratah jails, where they claimed they were keeping prisoners alive so the guards could continue to torture them. Islamic violence against women was reported at education establishments and on the Tripoli beaches, where girls were beaten for wearing swimsuits.

There was also an international terrorism menace which worried the United States of America. They were particularly concerned about the sightings of Mokhtar Belmokhtar in Tripoli. He was the leader of Al Qa'eda in the Islamic Maghreb, or AQIM, an international terrorist organisation spawned from the Algerian militancy, which made little secret of its intention to expand operations in the Sahel region.

Seven countries close to the Sahel, including Libya, had met in 2010 to consolidate military efforts to counter AQIM. However, Mali had released four suspects in order to secure the freedom of two hostages abducted in the border region. In the aftermath of the revolution, Belmokhtar was known to be buying weapons in Tripoli, including Manpads, and shipping them to his bases in Mali.

The commander of United States African Command presented a compelling case for action to the Libyan leaders, but it fell on deaf ears. After much nagging, the government eventually allowed over-flight rights to American surveillance aircraft, but they absolutely refused permission for American soldiers to operate on the ground. The Libyans naively believed they would never be affected by terrorism and simply didn't understand the uncompromising American position "you are either with us or against us".

AQIM was also one of the top four priorities for our National Security Council. I hosted the SAS Commanding Officer who was considering the best regional hub for United Kingdom special operations. In many ways, Libya offered the prime location, but political uncertainty about its future was a negative factor in the analysis.

The risk of being taken hostage was all too evident. One night in March, I was awoken by a call on our secure communications system and asked by an officer in London to provide authority for a military flight over Libya that morning. This was for the Special Boat Service team on their way to attempt the rescue of Chris McManus, a 28-year-old engineering contractor from Greater Manchester, who had been held in the north-west of Nigeria by a splinter group of Boko Haram since May 2011. Sadly, he and his Italian fellow captive, Franco Lamolinara, were both killed in the operation.

The tenth security risk was the most relevant to the smooth transition of Libya to a stable, democratic country. I was very worried about the number of disaffected young men joining violent extremist organisations. In the First National Survey after the war conducted by Oxford researchers in December 2011, 16% said they were ready to use violence for political ends. This represented 630,000 potential fighters, which when viewed against the 280,000 who took up arms against Gaddafi, was a considerable increase. I was reminded of an article in the *International Herald Tribune* from 2004 about the demographics of discord. The genie was out of the bottle in Libya and the interim government was beginning to understand that it had to act fast to sort out the security problems. The majority of the population put stability as their top policy priority, but six months after the fall of Tripoli there was still no effective disarmament, demobilisation and reintegration programme run by the government.

General Manqush realised the scale of the problem and invited all the international partners to a graduation ceremony for a thousand soldiers. I was surprised to see representatives from the countries which had supported Gaddafi's regime, but the following week the General narrowed us down to a small coterie of advisors and asked for our help in the professionalisation of the Libyan armed forces.

The United Kingdom offered a host of strategic training courses for the four services (Air Defence was separated from the Air Force) using university partners and military instructors. I interviewed dozens of Libyan officers to select the most suitable to attend British courses. On the advice of Manqush we ensured that officers from both the east and the west benefited equally and I accompanied the first two chosen to attend a strategic course at the United Kingdom Defence Academy, which was just as well because immigration control at Heathrow was unprepared for Libyan military officers.

We established a position for a de-mining advisor to work with the Libyan Mine Action Centre and build on the solid progress made by my military team in Misratah. We placed a Royal Navy technical advisor in the Chief of the Naval Staff's headquarters and a civilian strategic advisor in the Minister of Defence's outer office. However, the most important work was to produce the first draft of a Libyan Defence White Paper, which we completed in April through a series of workshops with the Head of their Staff College.

There were some major hurdles which had to be overcome in this endeavour. We quickly settled on a mission for the armed forces to "defend the homeland, constitution and people", but the hard parts were the red lines. For example, what role did Libyans envisage for their Army in the constitution; did they wish to be like Pakistan or Turkey with a political role to take over if the government fails or did they wish it to be a non-political organisation? And what about the role of the Head of State; did they wish to have a civilian as the Commander in Chief like the President of the United States of America? I was delighted that my interpreter was awarded a Queen's commendation in the operational honours list for his valuable work on this vital project.

There were also key structural challenges, as we discovered during the discussions about border security. The *Harras Wattani* had been formed under a separate ministerial organisation led by the devout Sadiqi Mabruk from Derna. However, to my mind, a single military chain of command was an essential requisite for success, but unpicking the complex and interwoven defence and security arrangements created by the National Transitional Council needed strong leadership and this was not forthcoming.

In the meantime, the security situation in Tripoli remained fragile. We worked close to a boundary between two rival militias which regularly fought street battles outside the British Embassy. During the visit of the Permanent Under-Secretary of State on 16th January, my car was hit by a bullet and a migrant worker was shot dead in front of the restaurant where we were eating lunch. I played this down because I did not want London to curtail our freedom of movement and hand over the "influence space" to malevolent forces.

One of the militia groups was led by Faraj Swehli, part of a dominant family in Misratah, who had taken vacant possession of the former barracks of Gaddafi's female bodyguard on the coast road. One evening, Swehli and his cronies picked up two British citizens who were working for the Iranian state-owned *Press TV*. Foolishly, they were taking photographs of a government building which had been destroyed by NATO in September.

The two men were in their thirties and during their interrogation one of them arrogantly antagonised Swehli. As a result, they were detained in the militia compound for what turned out to be almost a month. The British Ambassador worked through official channels, but the Minister of Interior appeared powerless to do anything. This was not really a military problem, but I was closely involved in all the decisions and more importantly, my team was alone in holding the confidences of the *Thuwaar*, so we were called in to help.

During the weeks that followed, we regularly visited the recalcitrant captives and took them some basic supplies. In the absence of the vice consul, I asked my warrant officer H to befriend the guards in the compound and investigate the layout of the buildings. Then I brought in one of my specialist teams to develop a plan of rescue, if necessary using force. They were very nervous about the possible consequences of mounting such an operation, but I needed a strong hand for my strategy to work.

The key to their release was not in Tripoli, but Misratah. Fortunately, we had earned much credit there due to our work disposing of their remnants of war. I informed the military council that I held them responsible for this intolerable situation and if the two British citizens were detained illegally for more than a month I would stop all the de-mining work at the airbase and call in the Special Air Service to forcibly release the two journalists.

The carrot and stick approach worked a treat and soon afterwards, we were suddenly called by Swehli as he released the journalists into our custody. The next morning, we whisked them out of the country and I was relieved that I did not have to use force to extract them. For his calm approach under severe provocation and threats from the Swehlis over this sustained period, H was rightly awarded an MBE in the operational honours list.

* * *

My seventh area of strategic interest was the Fezzan region in the south-west. After the Second World War, this area came under French influence as it bordered with the Gallic colonies of the Sahel. The regional capital in Sebha controlled the ancient caravan routes in the same way Kufra controlled the south-east.

Gaddafi stored his nuclear yellow cake, or uranium concentrate powder, in Sebha. After the war, we were very concerned about its control and at the very first meeting I attended in Tripoli, we highlighted the dangers of it falling into the hands of a rogue state with enrichment facilities and weapon-making capabilities. We suggested to the reluctant minister that Libya should sell it to one of the licensed international handlers.

The control of chemical, biological, radioactive and nuclear materials was one of the few areas where the United Nations worked effectively. Their role was to support and co-ordinate the inspections and activities of the organisation for the prohibition of chemical weapons and the international atomic energy agency. During my time in the country, good progress was made in the destruction of chemical stocks and the Libyan Nuclear Energy Establishment was willing to take the right action with the yellow cake in terms of its tight security and ultimate disposal.

Before examining Sebha, I decided to travel to Ghadamis, an oasis town of 12,000 people on the tri-border apex between Tunisia, Algeria and Libya. This astonishing world heritage site lies on the ancient north-south trading route between the salt flats in Mali and the Libyan coast. The last caravans had long ago replaced their camels with pick-up trucks, but it still remained one of the most important staging posts for illegal contraband from equatorial Africa and continued to be a source of tension and insecurity after the revolution.

All the families that lived there had been moved into new buildings by Gaddafi in the 1980s. However, they still returned to their old bleached, lime-washed houses and covered alleyways in the summer because they offered cool shelter from the baking temperatures. Each house was laid out in a similar vertical way, with stores on the ground floor, family living areas upstairs and the roof terraces reserved only for women.

Three communities lived in Ghadamis: members of the original seven Berber tribes, the largest and most influential of which is the Tasco; descendants of slaves; and the nomadic Tuareg, who own the desert and the valleys. Their symbiotic relationship is ordered according to history. During the revolution, the Tuareg were characterised by many as Gaddafi's enforcers, but when I investigated further, I discovered that individuals from all sides crossed allegiances and took his blood money. Whatever the rights and wrongs, there remained a fundamental divide between the communities, which prevented the return of British oil and gas companies which had worked in the area before the war. I needed to see if there was something I could do to resolve this problem and return the situation to normality.

I developed a plan and passed it back to London for operational clearances. In the meantime I sent one of my specialist teams on a reconnaissance, giving them specific limits of exploitation. They returned with auspicious tales and a formal invitation from the local council with the promise of a *khabir* to guide us around the local area.

Fortunately, one of our locally employed interpreters had been held in Abu Salim prison with a Tasco tribal leader, so he was immediately accepted by the Ghadamsee. I also took with me an Embassy representative from the Department for Business Innovation and Skills and a development expert, so we could have a meaningful discussion with the local council about their economic woes.

After a ten-hour drive through the desert, we arrived at night and met the local council for two hours in their chambers. They fully understood the complex relationship between security and economic development and were very keen to demonstrate to me that they had a measure of the key risks and threats they faced. Even in the darkness, I could see that the distinctive buildings and wide avenues made this town quite unique.

The next morning, the local military commander led us on a border patrol, while the Embassy staff visited the airport and school. On the way, we were shown the remains of a camp used during the revolution by Gaddafi's fighters. The *dénouement* had ended in a battle which left fifteen dead, eight Tuareg and seven locals. Then we were driving south, sometimes straying across into Algeria and I realised how easy it was for determined smugglers to enter the country without apprehension. Suddenly an Air Force Mirage plane flew overhead to offer a further escort. I asked how long their patrols normally lasted and was slightly surprised to be told three days.

They drove me across the desert to an ancient battlefield on the Algerian border at Ras al-Ghoul, marking the limit of Arab exploitation in the eighth century, where they were defeated by the Berber tribes. I found it extraordinary that only 40 years after the death of Mohammed, the Arabs had extended their empire across the whole of what is now Libya. They were also very proud of their square-minaret *atiq* mosque to rival the oldest recorded in Libya at Awjila near Jalu.

It was an impressive, if one-sided, performance. To balance the discussion, I asked our hosts if we could meet with the Head of the Tuareg community, Sheikh Musaa Amaa. Grudgingly, they agreed, but we had to wait until the end of the day and we were almost giving up hope when the elegant Sheikh glided into our hotel with a small entourage dressed in their ceremonial robes. They were all over two metres tall with hawkish eyes, and mouths covered in veils. The seeds of strategic success are formed on such occasions and all my senses were alert to pick up the nuances of language, appearance and movement.

The venerable Sheikh was splendid company. We talked for over an hour about the hardships of living in the desert and he told me about the burning of their houses and cars and the killing of their animals in reprisal for what happened during the revolution. He was looking for justice, but didn't labour the point. He explained that the Tuareg focus is now on a new town which they wish to build fifty kilometres west of Ghadamis. However, their plans see this on the main supply route from Dirj, astride the oil and electricity lines which run north-south for hundreds of miles. This would effectively give them strategic control of the region, so the local council will never support it.

It was clear that neither side would abandon their "brothers" and reconciliation between the Ghadamsee and Tuareg would take time and judicious mediation. However, both sides realised that they had to put aside their dispute in order to attract the return of tourists and the oil industry, the lifeblood of their economy. On reflection, I believed it was fundamentally safe for tourists and they had a very well-organised airport and a secure town where no weapons were allowed to be carried. Unfortunately, I could not persuade the Foreign Office to lift their travel advice and so another window of opportunity was lost to British business.

* * *

Soon after this expedition, my capable successor arrived in Tripoli. I knew that for the next six months, my work would be carried on because we had served together successfully in Baghdad. The small team he inherited was well prepared for the challenges ahead, starting with the promised elections before Ramadan.

From a personal viewpoint, this was a hugely fulfilling operation. In many ways, the Libya experience was unique and yet it also pointed to the shape of Britain's future military operations in the age of austerity with the onus on small specialist teams operating in isolated locations. As a low-cost proxy war without the waste of the blood expended in Afghanistan and Iraq, it was preferred by both politicians and finance ministries. On 8th February, the House of Commons Defence Committee reported that it was "a successful operation, but HM Forces will face new difficulties if given another Libya-size operation".

It is often said that the nature of war doesn't change and that there are similarities between all past conflicts. I certainly agree with the commentators who likened the military intervention in Libya to the Kosovo War in 1999. A handful of Western governments intervened in a sovereign state using a doctrine and a United Nations resolution that was not universally agreed. It is no wonder that the abstract concept of humanitarian intervention remains controversial and that the same protagonists that defeated Gaddafi were subsequently unable to convince the world that the case to intervene in Syria was incontrovertible.

There is no doubt that the United Kingdom's armed forces saved thousands of civilian lives in Libya in 2011. The Royal Navy and Royal Air Force personnel performed magnificently well and were rightly lauded when they returned home. However, this was not the same for the Army officers and soldiers with me who were denied a medal for their efforts, despite working under constant and severe personal risks throughout their tours of duty. I understood why the government was not keen to publicise the work of the land element, but I believe it was mean-spirited to remove recognition from our team because the attacks on British and American targets in 2012 vividly demonstrated the threat. All the troops operating in Libya deserved an operational service medal as much as any soldier serving in Camp Bastion, which I passed through later that year when I visited my regiment in Lashkar Ghar.

This was not the only mistake the government made. The nervousness of many officials in Whitehall about becoming fixed in Libya whilst Afghanistan was still running hot led to many missed opportunities. On 22 February, we produced in Libya a pretty good effort at a United Kingdom cross-government strategy which was agreed at desk level in London. Unfortunately six weeks later the document which was passed to me was no longer a strategy, but a list of pet projects loosely strung together with a slightly incoherent logic. The focus had changed from conditions to process, with an opaque approach and important issues stripped out. It certainly was not a comprehensive campaign plan for partnering an important ally in North Africa and so I was not surprised when the security situation deteriorated after I departed.

Contrary to some media reports, I felt very well supported in Tripoli by Number 10 in London. However, that political backing did not translate to substantive care from the permanent joint headquarters in Northwood. Simple things like the removal of medal recognition and the lack of mail deliveries were bitter blows to the morale of my soldiers. The fact that there was no official budget for the operation, so we all had to pay for our own equipment, was shameful, but the worst aspect was that not one senior military officer visited the British troops under my command. My situation appeared to be straight out of a "Mission Impossible" film, as I was encouraged to "carry on until caught".

On returning to Brize Norton from Libya, there was no military transport for the onward journey home because the operation had no budget. A kindly corporal from Chilwell driving a minibus full of Afghan reinforcements to Nottingham agreed to take me to the A 34 trunk road at Oxford. I called my wife to pick me up and waited inside a fast food outlet on the Botley Road, still wearing my full combat uniform and carrying my bulletproof vest and helmet. A middle-aged lady came up to me to say thank you for serving the country. It was a fine welcome home, in contrast to the "Go To Hell" placards that had met the Royal Anglian soldiers in Luton on their return from Afghanistan.

Bibliography and further reading

Chapter 1

Pile, Stephen, *The Book of Heroic Failures*, Futura 1979

Brady, Colin, Three Soldiers Killed in IRA Ambush, *Daily Telegraph* 26 March 1982

Weekes, William, Warning on "loose" talk about IRA, *Daily Telegraph* 26 March 1982

Hamill, Desmond, *Pig in the Middle: The Army in Northern Ireland 1969-1984*, Methuen 1985

Dewer, Mike, *The British Army in Northern Ireland*, Arms & Armour Press 1985

Van der Bijl, Nick, *Operation Banner: The British Army in Northern Ireland 1969-2007*, Pen & Sword 2009

Wharton, Ken, *An Agony Continued: The British Army in Northern Ireland 1980-83*, Helion and Company 2015

Chapter 2

Clausewitz, *Vom Krieg*, 1832

Runciman, Steven, *A History of the Crusades*, Cambridge University Press 1951-1954

Liddell Hart, Basil, *The Soviet Army*, Weidenfeld & Nicolson 1956

The Treaty of Alliance between the Kingdom of Greece, the Republic of Turkey and the Republic of Cyprus signed at Nicosia on 16th August 1960

Cyprus Bulletin Issued by the Public Information Office, Republic of Cyprus, Nicosia, 17th October 1973

Hackett, General Sir John, *The Third World War August 1985*, Sidgwick & Jackson 1978

MacDonald Fraser, George, *Flashman at the Charge*, Barrie & Jenkins 1973

Northern Army Group, Public Information Booklet May 1987

The White Lancer and The Vedette 1978–1992, including Gulf Supplement

Keegan, John, Iraqis 'Facing battle tactics never tried in real warfare', *Daily Telegraph* 15 September 1990

De La Billiere, General Sir Peter, *Storm Command, A Personal Account of the Gulf War*, Harper Collins 1992

Cordingley, Major General Patrick, *In the Eye of the Storm: Commanding the Desert Rats in the Gulf War*, Hodder & Stoughton 1996

Ker-Lindsay, James, *The Cyprus Problem: what Everyone Needs to Know*, Oxford University Press 2011

Chapter 3

West, Rebecca, *Black Lamb and Grey Falcon*, Macmillan & Co 1942

Maclean, Fitzroy, *Eastern Approaches*, Jonathan Cape 1949 (Pan Books 1956)

Cuddon, JA, *The Companion Guide to Jugoslavia*, 1968 (Collins 1984)

Stewart, Bob, *Broken Lives*, Harper Collins 1993

The Rat: The Break-up of Yugoslavia, 4th Edition June 1994

Owen, David, *Balkan Odyssey*, Gollanz 1995

The Yugoslav Tragedy, *Prospect Magazine* 1995

Riley, J, White Dragon, *The Royal Welch Fusiliers*, Wrexham 1995

Whitaker, DJ, *United Nations in Action*, UCL Press 1995

Bishop, Patrick, Lancers get ready to face worst from Serbs, *Daily Telegraph* 3 June 1995

McGrory, Daniel, Saviours of the Children, *Daily Express* 5 June 1995

McIlroy, AJ, Soldier who lost leg in Bosnia seeks damages, *Daily Telegraph* 4 February 1996

Glenny, Misha, *The Fall of Yugoslavia*, Penguin 1996

Bellamy, Christopher, *Knights in White Armour*, Hutchinson 1996

Rose, General Sir Michael, *Fighting For Peace*, Harvill Press 1998

Kent-Payne, Vaughn, *Bosnia Warriors: Living on the Front Line*, Robert Hale 1998

Ripley, Tim, *Operation Deliberate Force*, CDISS Lancaster University 1999

Simms, Brendan, *Unfinest Hour: Britain and the Destruction of Bosnia*, Allen Lane 2001

Stankovic, Milos, *Trusted Mole*, Harper Collins 2001

Allin, Dana, NATO's *Balkan Interventions*, Adelphi Paper 347, Oxford University Press 2002

Barry, Brigadier Ben, *A Cold War: Front Line Operations in Bosnia 1995-1996*, Spellmount Publishing 2008

Bell, Martin, *In Harm's Way: Bosnia, A War Reporter's Story*, Icon Books 2012

Chapter 4

Foreign Secretary's statement to the House of Commons on Operation Veritas Campaign Objectives, 16 October 2001

CIA Memos declassified and released through the final Report of the National Commission on Terrorist Attacks Upon the United States 26 July 2004

House of Commons Defence Select Committee Reports on Operation Veritas and SDR New Chapter

United Nations Resolutions in response to 9/11

Downing Street guide to corridors of power, *Daily Telegraph* 2001

Defence Corporate Communications Unclassified Digest on Operation Veritas

Inside the Command Post in the Hunt for the World's Most Wanted Man, Unclassified Newhouse News Group 8 March 2002

Measures to Eliminate International Terrorism, United Nations General Assembly A/RES/49/60 9 December 1994

Maslow, A, *A Theory of Human Motivation, Psychology Review 1943*

Newby, Eric, *A Short Walk in the Hindu Kush*, Secker & Warburg Ltd 1958

Glubb, General Sir John Bagot, *The Great Arab Conquests*, Hodder & Stoughton 1963

Howard, Michael, *The Causes of War and other Essays*, Temple Smith 1983

Kaplan, Robert, *Soldiers of God: With the Mujahidin in Afghanistan,* Houghton Mifflin 1990

Hopkirk, Peter, *The Great Game,* Oxford University Press 1990

Bin Laden, Usama, Declaration of War against the Americans Occupying the Land of the Two Holy Places, Fatwa 1996

Hoffman, Bruce, *Inside Terrorism,* Columbia University Press 1998

Newman, Nick, *Asymmetric Threats to British Military Intervention Operations,* RUSI Whitehall Paper 49 1998

Krulak, General Charles, The Strategic Corporal: Leadership in the Three Block War, *Marines Magazine* January 1999

Rashid, Ahmed, Taliban: *Militant Islam, Oil and Fundamentalism in Central Asia,* Yale University Press 2000

United Nations Millennium Declaration New York 6-8 September 2000

Bassiouni, M Cherif, International Terrorism: Multinational Conventions (1937-2001), Transatlantic Publishers Inc, New York 2001

McKenzie, Kenneth, *The Revenge of the Melians: Asymmetric Threats,* 2001

Future Issues for Defence Conference, Shrivenham, 26 February 2001

Global Forum for Law Enforcement and National Security, June 2001

Studer, Meinrad, The ICRC and Civil-Military Relations in Armed Conflict, *International Review of the Red Cross,* Volume 83 No 842 June 2001

Inderfurth, Karl, The Muslim World Ought to Lecture the Taleban, *New York Times* 30 August 2001

Responsibility for the Terrorist Atrocities in the United States, 11 September 2001 – unclassified update by Her Majesty's Government

Ahmad Shah Massoud Obituary, *Daily Telegraph* 17 September 2001

Building Damage in Lower Manhattan, *Construction News* 20 September 2001

Will London Win Through? *The Sunday Times* 23rd September 2001

Department for International Development Afghanistan Crisis Situation Report No 4, dated 25 September 2001

US Homeland Defence Unclassified Situation Report, 26 September 2001

Hodgson, Jessica, A Gentleman's Agreement, *The Guardian* 1 October 2001

Unclassified Immediate Signal on 8 October 2001 from Secretary of State to All Personnel, announcing the first phase of the military response to the attacks on the United States on 11 September

This War could take years, Britain at risk of terror reprisals, warns Blair, *Daily Telegraph* 9 October 2001

Ignatius, David, An Intelligence Coalition at War in the Shadows, *International Herald Tribune* 15 October 2001

Operation Enduring Freedom and the Conflict in Afghanistan: An Update, House of Commons Research Paper 01/81 31 October 2001

Symposio Argentina por la Paz Internacional: Alternativas y Oportunidades, 7/8 November 2001

Maddox, Bronwen, NATO is Nowhere and Russia Loves It, *The Times* 8 November 2001

US Commander a Good Soldier in a Difficult Battle, *International Herald Tribune 10*, November 2001

Informal Meeting on Afghanistan, Watson Institute of International Studies and US Army Peacekeeping Institute, 14 November 2001

Terrorism, Assassination and International Justice, International Security Information Service Briefing No 80, November 2001

United States Joint Centre for Lessons Learned Unclassified Quarterly Bulletin on Homeland Security Volume IV Issue 1, December 2001

Agreement on Provisional Arrangements in Afghanistan, UN Talks on Afghanistan in Bonn, December 2001

France-Russia-UK Symposium Report, Wilton Park December 2001

JDCC Joint Military/Civilian Workshop Report, December 2001

Afghan Women's Summit for Democracy, The Brussels Proclamation 2001

British Agencies Afghanistan Group Monthly Reviews

Harding, Thomas, Marines sent to Kabul with Faulty Rifle, *Daily Telegraph* 24 December 2001

Combating New Security Threats, *Defence Review*, Winter 2001

Cordesman, Anthony, *The Lessons of Afghanistan, War fighting, Intelligence and Force Transformation*, Center for Strategic and International Studies 2002

Rayment, Sean, Marines' Chief Under Fire for Afghan Farce, *The Sunday Telegraph,* 19 May 2002

September 11th: Has Anything Changed? *Forced Migration Review*, June 2002

McColl, Major General John, Return to the Northwest Frontier, *Defence Review* Summer 2002

Living with the Megapower: Implications of the War on Terrorism, Consultation at the Royal Institute of International Affairs July 2002

Hearts and Minds Workshop Report, Oxford, 25 July 2002

Security Monitor Volume 1 Issue 1, Royal United Services Institute July 2002

The "War on Terrorism": 12 month Audit and Future Strategy Options, Oxford Research Group September 2002

Morality in Asymmetric War and Intervention Operations, Conference at the Royal United Services Institute September 2002

Quillen, Chris, Posse Comitatus and Nuclear Terrorism, *Parameters* 2002

Bobbitt, Philip, *The Shield of Achilles*, Allen Lane 2002

Strategic Trends (Unclassified), Joint Doctrine & Concepts Centre March 2003

Davis, Anthony, Afghan Security Deteriorates as Taliban Regroup, *Jane's Intelligence Review* May 2003

Play to Win: The Commission on Post-Conflict Reconstruction, Center for Strategic and International Studies January 2003

Straw, Jack, We Should Have Hit AQ Sooner, *Daily Telegraph* 20 March 2004

Pakistan Lost Bin Laden Trail, BBC News, 15 March 2005

Hoon, Geoff, *Reflection from over the Park*, 27 May 2005

Lane, Roger and Sky, Emma, The Role of Provincial Reconstruction Teams in Stabilization, *Royal United Services Institute Journal* June 2006

Terror Suspects Vanish in Spider's Web, *Daily Telegraph* 8 June 2006

Horgan, John, *The Psychology of Terrorism*, Routledge 2006

Wilkinson, Paul, *Terrorism versus Democracy: The Liberal State Response (Second Edition)*, Routledge 2006

Ranstorp, Magnus, *Mapping Terrorism: State of the Art, Gaps and Future Direction*, Routledge 2007

The Epistemology of Terrorism, Reading University December 2009

Terrorism and War: The Changing Relationship, St Andrews January 2010

Kershaw, Sarah, Inside the Mind of a Terrorist, *New York Times* 2010

Jackson, Richard, An analysis of EU counterterrorism discourse post September 11, *Cambridge Review of International Affairs* 2010

Towle, Philip, *Going to War: British Debates from Wilberforce to Blair*, Palgrave

Fisher, David and Wicker, Brian, *Just War on Terror?* Ashgate 2010

Zaeef, Abdul Salam, *My Life with the Taliban,* Hurst & Co 2010

Terrorism and Political Violence, Volume 23 Number 1, Routledge 2011

The killing of Bin Laden is no matter of regret, *Daily Telegraph* 6 May 2011

Targeting Terror, *Jane's Defence Weekly,* 11 May 2011

Dunne, Tim, 9/11 and the Terrorism Industry, *International Affairs* 2011

Ten Years After 9/11: The Next Stage, Chatham House July 2011

Freedman, Lawrence, *9/11 Ten Years On,* British Academy September 2011

Ripley, Tim, *Operation Enduring Freedom,* Pen & Sword 2012

Chapter 5

Lawrence, TE, *Seven Pillars of Wisdom,* World Books 1935

Bray, NNE, *A Paladin of Arabia,* John Heritage 1936

Glubb, General Sir John, *Britain and the Arabs,* Hodder & Stoughton 1959

Emck, TH, When Should an Officer Disobey Orders? *British Army Review* 1995

Fuller, Graham and Leasor, Ian, *Persian Gulf Myths,* Foreign Affairs 1997

Moore, Jonathan, *Hard Choices: Moral Dilemmas in Humanitarian Intervention,* Rowman & Littlefield 1998

Gulf Security: Opportunities and challenges for the new generation: Royal United Services Institute 2000

Perle, Richard, *Next Stop Iraq,* Foreign Policy Research Institute 30 November 2001

Pullinger, Stephen, Military Action against Iraq: the Nuclear Option, International Security Information Service Policy Paper April 2002

Moseley, Alexander and Norman, Richard, *Human Rights and Military Intervention,* Ashgate 2002

Living with the Megapower: Implications of the War on Terrorism, The Royal Institute of International Affairs July 2002–June 2003

Iraq: Consequences of a War, Oxford Research Group October 2002

Programme for 1st Armoured Division Study Day in Germany 21 October 2002

Nationbuilding: Peacebuilding and Transitional Administrations: Policy seminar in the Foreign and Colonial Office, 19 December 2002

Muslims of Europe International Conference organized by Al Khoei Foundation and the Forum Against Islamophobia and Racism, London January 2003

Chapman, Hamed, Blair Warned of Muslim backlash against Iraq War, *Muslim News* 24 January 2003

The Stability of Iraq: The Role of the Kurds, Past Present and Future, Royal United Services Institute 27 January 2003

Iraq: The Regional Fallout, The Royal Institute of International Affairs, February 2003

General Guidance for Interaction between United Nations Personnel and Military Actors in the context of the Crisis in Iraq, New York, 21 March 2003

Johnson, Boris, In Search of Saddam, *The Spectator* May 2003

Operations in Iraq: First Reflections, Produced by Director General Corporate Communications, July 2003

Operations in Iraq: Lessons for the Future, Produced by Director General Corporate Communications December 2003

The Vedette 2004 – 2008

A New Security Paradigm, The Cambridge Security Seminar Report, University of Cambridge 2004

Iraq: A Job for NATO? *Royal United Services Institute Newsbrief*, March 2004

Nye, J, Soft Power: The Means to Success in World Politics, *Public Affairs* 2004

Synott, Hilary, *State-building in Southern Iraq*, The International Institute of Strategic Studies 2005

Mackinlay, John, *Defeating Complex Insurgency: Beyond Iraq and Afghanistan*, Royal United Services Institute 2005

White, Andrew, *Iraq: Searching for Hope*, Continuum 2005

Salacinski, Krzysztof, Poland's Activities in the Field of Protection of Cultural Properties in Post-War Iraq, Ministry of Culture of the Republic of Poland 2005

Ryder, Bryan, TE Lawrence, Reader's Report 1929, University of Reading 2007

Trip, C, *A History of Iraq*, Cambridge University Press 2007

Defence Equipment and Support News Issue 5, August 2007

Urgent Operational Requirements Coherence Study (Unclassified), Defence Equipment and Support, 3 September 2007

Dodge, Toby, *The Failure of Nation Building and a History Denied*, Columbia University Press 2008

Britain can't fight two wars at same time: Sir Jock Stirrup, Agence France Press, London 25 June 2008

The Scholar of Iraq, *Sunday Times Magazine* 29 June 2008

Arms Control and Security Improvements in the Middle East Conference, Izmir February 2009

The Changing Character of War, International Conference as part of the Oxford Leverhulme Programme, March 2009

Hollis, Rosemary, *Britain and the Middle East in the 9/11 Era*, Chatham House Wiley-Blackwell 2010

Schneller, Rachel, Iraq and the American Pullout, *The World Today*, Chatham House August 2010

The British Institute for the study of Iraq, Newsletter May 2010

Muslim Networks and Movements in Western Europe, Pew Forum on Religion and Public Life September 2010

Chapter 6

United Nations Security Council Resolutions 1970, 1973, 2009, 2011, 2016, 2017, 2022, 2040 (26 February 2011–12 March 2012)

Douglas, Keith, *Alamein to Zem Zem*, Faber and Faber 1992, (Editions Poetry 1946)

Peniakoff, Vladimir, *Popski's Private Army*, Pan 1957, (Jonathan Cape 1950)

Montgomery of Alamein, Field Marshal Viscount, *A History of Warfare*, Collins 1968

Newby, Eric, *On the Shores of the Mediterranean*, Picador 1985, (Harvill Press 1984),

Vanderwalle, D, *Libya Since Independence*, Cornell University Press 1998

Cincotta, Richard P and Engelman, Robert, Conflict thrives where young men are many, *International Herald Tribune* 2 March 2004

Ammour, Laurence, An Assessment of Crime Related Risks in the Sahel, NATO Defence College Research Paper November 2009

Joint Doctrine Publication 3-40 Security and Stabilisation, The Military Contribution

Del Boca, Angelo, *Mohamed Fekini and the Fight to Free Libya*, Palgrave 2011

Libya's Future, Middle East and North Africa Programme Roundtable Summary, The Royal Institute of International Affairs, March 2011

Wintour, Patrick, William Hague approved botched Libya mission, PM's office says, *The Guardian* 7 March 2011

Harding, Thomas and Gilligan, Andrew, RAF launches new precision strikes against Gaddafi forces, *Daily Telegraph* 11 May 2011

Libya's Future: Toward Transition, Roundtable Discussion, The Royal Institute of International Affairs

Gelfand, Lauren, NATO extends operations in Libya for 90 days, *Jane's Defence Weekly* 8 June 2011

Gelfand, Lauren, UK, US acknowledge stalemate in Libya, *Jane's Defence Weekly* 3 August 2011

McElroy, Damien, Bloody battle for Libya's last working oil refinery, *Daily Telegraph* 18 August 2011

Libya: Policy Options for the Transition, The Royal Institute of International Affairs 18 August 2011

Owen, Lord, We have proved in Libya that intervention can still work, *Daily Telegraph* 24 August 2011

Accidental Heroes, Britain, France and the Libya Operation, An Interim RUSI Campaign Report, September 2011

Gelfand, Lauren, Sirte battle will end Libya conflict, interim leaders say, *Jane's Defence Weekly* 12 October 2011

Embracing Victory, *Jane's Defence Weekly* 26 October 2011

UN Security Council concern over Libya Arms Stockpile, BBC News 1 November 2011

Ripley, Tim UK Apache, Storm Shadow strikes during Libyan operations detailed, *Jane's Defence Weekly* 2 November 2011

Tigner, Brooks, Gadaffi is gone, but what next for NATO? *Jane's Defence Weekly* 2 November 2011

Spencer, Richard and Sherlock, Ruth, Tribesman who gave up a million to help capture Saif Gaddafi, *Daily Telegraph* 23 November 2011

Ellamy Lessons Identified – Influence Operations, Royal United Services Institute 25 November 2011

Libya to UN: Give us our Money, *The Tripoli Post* 10 December 2011

Lacher, Wolfram, Families, Tribes and Cities in the Libyan Revolution, *Middle East Policy Council Journal*

Libya Trapped in Chaos, *Hurriyet Daily News* 26 January 2012

Mangoush: Kufra is Quiet, Under Control, *The Tripoli Post* 25 February 2012

Libya: Militia Should Transfer Journalists to State, *Human Rights Watch* 27 February 2012

Bingham, John and Spencer, Richard, Families' Shock as Libyans Smash British War Graves, *Daily Telegraph* 5 March 2012

Rhinelander, Marcus, Distrust in Ghadames as Tuareg dream of a new city, *Libya Herald* 7 April 2011

Security and Post-Conflict Stabilisation in Libya, Royal United Services Institute 12 November 2012

Abdul-Hakim Bel Haj torture case against UK rejected, BBC News 20 December 2013

Wars In Peace: British Military Operations Since 1991, edited by Adrian L Johnson, RUSI 2014.